The View from Pluto

*A light-hearted, rollicking cruise
along Queensland's Barrier Reef coast*

by

STUART BUCHANAN

CORAL COAST PUBLICATIONS

To Vicko — Best wishes from:

Stuart Buchanan

14/11/2006
BUSTARD HEAD
LIGHTHOUSE.
& YACHT "PLUTO"

By the same author:

THE LIGHTHOUSE KEEPERS

LIGHTHOUSE OF TRAGEDY
The Story of Bustard Head Lighthouse

Front cover illustration and cartoons by Paul Lennon

First published 2002 by Coral Coast Publications,
P.O. Box 90, Samford, Queensland 4520, Australia.
Telephone/Fax (07) 3289 1827

National Library of Australia Card Number and
ISBN 0 9586433 1 8

Typeset by Sun Photoset Pty Ltd., Brisbane.
Printed by Harding Colour, Brisbane.
Wholly produced in Australia.

CONTENTS

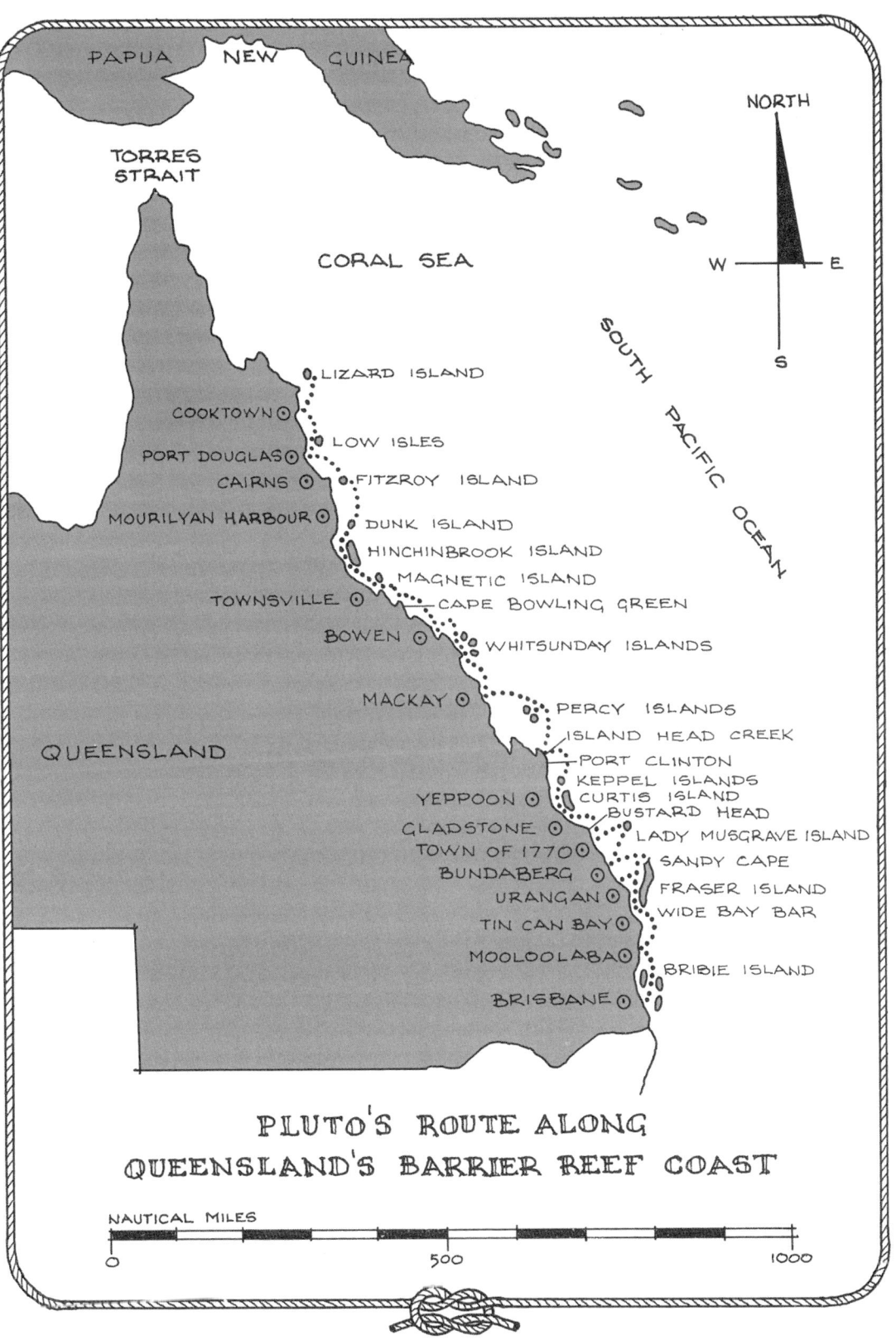

PAPUA NEW GUINEA

TORRES STRAIT

CORAL SEA

NORTH

W E

S

SOUTH PACIFIC OCEAN

LIZARD ISLAND
COOKTOWN
PORT DOUGLAS
CAIRNS
MOURILYAN HARBOUR
LOW ISLES
FITZROY ISLAND
DUNK ISLAND
HINCHINBROOK ISLAND
MAGNETIC ISLAND
TOWNSVILLE
CAPE BOWLING GREEN
BOWEN
WHITSUNDAY ISLANDS
MACKAY
PERCY ISLANDS
ISLAND HEAD CREEK
PORT CLINTON
KEPPEL ISLANDS
YEPPOON
CURTIS ISLAND
BUSTARD HEAD
GLADSTONE
LADY MUSGRAVE ISLAND
TOWN OF 1770
SANDY CAPE
BUNDABERG
FRASER ISLAND
URANGAN
WIDE BAY BAR
TIN CAN BAY
MOOLOOLABA
BRIBIE ISLAND
BRISBANE

QUEENSLAND

PLUTO'S ROUTE ALONG QUEENSLAND'S BARRIER REEF COAST

NAUTICAL MILES

0   500   1000

For Shirley

who encouraged me to buy Pluto, *despite her dislike of boats.*

Chapter 1

MY SHIP COMES IN

The first indication that *Solace* was sinking came about an hour after we left the marina. The breeze was fresh and the small yacht was moving along briskly. At the skipper's invitation I had gone below to have a look at the layout of the saloon.

"Hey, Bruce!" I called out. "Do you know the carpet's wet down here?"

I took over at the tiller, while Bruce went below.

"I think it's only from that shower of rain they had up here last night," he eventually replied. "The front hatch must have been left open."

I wasn't convinced. It seemed a hell of a lot of wetness for a shower of rain. At least, I thought, we're only about 500 metres from shore — it isn't too far to swim.

Solace had been recommended to me by a yacht broker in Brisbane who had arranged for the owner Bruce to drive me up the coast to the sleepy fishing village of Tin Can Bay where the boat was moored. Bruce was a nice bloke, and the conversation had flowed easily during the three-hour drive. He told me that *Solace* had been taken out of the water earlier in the week for some repairs. This worked out well, as it gave me the opportunity to inspect the hull before we went for a test sail. Within thirty minutes of arriving at Tin Can Bay, *Solace* was back in the water and we were motoring out of the marina.

Seven miles down Tin Can Bay Inlet, I went below again to check if we had taken any more water on board. The water was now well above my ankles and tasted salty.

"Bruce, I think we've got a bit of a problem down here."

Again, I took over at the tiller while Bruce went below.

"I can't see any obvious place where the water's coming in, Stuart," Bruce said after a while. "I think it must be leaking through the stern gland."

"Have you got a bilge pump?" I asked.

"Yes, an electric one. I'll switch it on."

There was a lengthy silence before Bruce spoke again:

"The bilge pump won't work. I don't know what's wrong with it."

"Have you got a manual pump?" I asked.

"No. Only the electric one."

"I think we should head back Bruce. If the water gets any higher we'll have to bucket it out."

"I don't think I've got a bucket on board."

"Got any tea cups?"

Bruce laughed, but quickly headed *Solace* back to the marina. The water was almost up to my knees by the time we arrived there.

After hurriedly arranging for *Solace* to be lifted out of the water, Bruce returned to the yacht.

"Well, Stuart," he said enthusiastically, "despite the leak, what do you think of her?"

I looked at Bruce's hopeful face as he stood there with the water lapping around his legs and I had to admire his optimism. However, with or without the leak, *Solace* wasn't the yacht for me, just like so many other yachts I had looked at during the last few months.

For twenty years I had had a dream — to sail my own yacht along Queensland's Barrier Reef coast. I wouldn't say that salt water flowed in my veins, but in my early teens I had discovered that 'mucking about with boats' was good fun. Many of my weekends and holidays were spent with friends building small boats and sailing them on a nearby creek. Then, secondary school, interest in the opposite sex, college and a job in architecture, drove boating from my mind.

Ultimate boredom is probably too strong a description of my eight years in architecture, but it's certainly close. There were highlights of course, but the constraints of four office walls and the prospect of an uneventful future always prevailed. However, one event made those eight years all worthwhile — I met Shirley. Eighteen months after our marriage, we decided to leave our city jobs, buy a Land Rover and caravan, and set off to see Australia.

This decision was influenced by books we had read about people who left secure suburban existences to explore more adventurous ways of life. On the cover of one of those books — *Cruising The Coral Coast* — author Alan Lucas had noted:

> *"Cruising the Coral Coast is written not only for the boatman, but for anyone whose spirit of adventure draws him towards the tropical wonderland of the Queensland coast with its fringing reef and sunwashed islands and coral cays . . ."*

Yes! Yes! That's us! That's us! We're not boatmen. But by God, we've got the spirit of adventure! With rose-coloured glasses we headed off to the "tropical wonderland".

Months later, while in Cairns, we had the opportunity to apply for a position as lighthouse keepers on Booby Island in Torres Strait. Aha! Here was our chance to live on a "sunwashed island". Our application was successful, and we took off on our next "adventure". But the "adventure" turned into a lifestyle which we grew to love dearly. For the next nine years we revelled in the beauty and isolation of the lightstations of the Great Barrier Reef.

In the mid 1970s we were stationed at Bustard Head lighthouse, 30 miles south-east of Gladstone. On the western side of the headland lay Pancake Creek, one of the best cruising yacht anchorages on the Queensland coast. Many of the yachties visited the station and had a meal with us, and in return invited us out to their yachts. At the time, I was completely content with our lifestyle, but little by little I realised my interest in boats was returning. I liked the feel of being on a yacht, its motion at anchor, the sound of the wind as it hummed past the rigging, the gurgling of the water as the tide ebbed and flooded past the hull, the robust stainless steel fittings, winches, sheets, cleats and a hundred other utilitarian bits and pieces.

Shirley and I were visiting a yacht one afternoon when the owner suggested we go out for a sail. I was delighted. As the vessel cleared the mouth of Pancake Creek, the skipper hoisted the sails and cut the motor. The breeze freshened and I stood in awe as the huge white sails ballooned out high above us. Winch ratchets whirred as the sheets were pulled on; the yacht heeled over and picked up speed, slicing, dipping and rising silently through the deep-blue water. The yacht had come alive; ten tonnes of vessel pushed gracefully along by the wind alone. At that point I became irredeemably addicted to yachting, and knew that sometime in the future I would want a yacht of our own.

Unfortunately, I knew that Shirley didn't share my enthusiasm for boats. For years, Shirley had travelled hundreds of miles on various stores boats to isolated island lightstations, often when sea conditions were atrocious. But she had to do it, as it was the only way to reach those places. Shirley did not hide the fact that she disliked boats, and often said: "I love the sea, but I want to be beside it, definitely not on it." I knew that buying a yacht was going to be a big problem.

In the meantime I subjected every yachtie who visited Bustard Head to vigorous interrogation: "How much would a yacht like yours cost?", "How can you afford to cruise for months without having to work?", "What sort of motor's in your yacht?", "Do you have refrigeration?", "What do you think is the best type of anchor?". It was a wonder they didn't tell me to mind my own business. In between times I studied navigation and seamanship from dozens of books. Shirley appeared to accept it all with resigned tolerance.

Our stint in paradise ended in 1982. A government policy to automate the manned lighthouses of Australia was well underway. The future of lighthouse keeping was doomed. We made our decision and resigned.

We devoted ourselves to a business venture, and for six years did little else but work seven days a week. Our aim was that by the end of 1988 we could retire from full-time work.

During those years I was invited to crew on a friend's racing yacht, contesting the Sydney to Mooloolaba and Brisbane to Gladstone yacht races. I wasn't keen on racing, my real interest lay in cruising, but I realised that with every race I was gaining valuable experience.

As planned, we leased out our business and left Brisbane to tour Australia by campervan. Every time I saw a marina in the distance, I'd head for it, dragging an unenthusiastic Shirley along every pontoon, while I gazed intently at yacht after yacht. Each month I could hardly wait for the new edition of the 'Book of Dreams' (*Trade A Boat* magazine) to arrive on the newsagents' stands. I think Shirley suspected it wasn't going to be too long before the subject of buying a yacht arose.

This was delayed a few years by the decision to write a book about our life in the lighthouse service. I finished writing the manuscript in 1993 and while waiting for the book to be published I casually mentioned to Shirley that I would like to buy a yacht and cruise the Queensland coast.

"I've been waiting for this to happen for years," Shirley replied wryly, "so I've had plenty of time to decide what *I* want to do. There is no way I'm going to sail for months each year on a yacht — I'd hate it. And I'm not the only woman who thinks that way. At Bustard Head, while you were engrossed in talking to the men about their boats, the women were pouring their hearts out to me."

"What do you mean?" I asked.

"Well, a lot of women told me they weren't enjoying cruising up the coast. Some had been seasick and others were so frightened after sailing through bad weather and rough seas, they dreaded each time they had to leave port. They just wanted the trip to end."

"Oh, I don't know. I've met some women who say they love the cruising lifestyle."

"Sure, but they're a minority — and I'm not one of them."

We were both silent for a while, and then Shirley continued:

"But as I said before, I have a suggestion. We're only in our early fifties, not exactly old yet, so if you're certain you want to try cruising, you should do it now while you're still fit. Why don't you buy a yacht you can handle by yourself? I can meet you at places of my choice and sail with you for a couple of weeks. That way I'm not subjecting myself to being miserable, and I'm not spoiling your enjoyment."

"You mean sail single-handed?"

"Well why not? A lot of people do these days."

The more I thought about it, the more the idea began to make sense. Sailing single-handed wouldn't be bad at all. Much better than having someone on board who really didn't want to be there. And I'd still be seeing Shirley every so often.

With renewed enthusiasm it was back to the 'Book of Dreams'.

But many months later, which included my experience with *Solace*, I hadn't found a yacht that was right for me. We had looked at countless boats. I say "we", because Shirley usually accompanied me not just for the outing, but to see what I was going to spend 'our' money on. Shirley must have been a yacht broker's nightmare. She declined every broker's invitation to go on board, and often, if it was a particularly ugly vessel, she'd just walk away, while I went through the cursory motions of looking at the boat and telling the broker I wasn't interested.

The main problem wasn't finding the right yacht, but finding the right yacht for the money we were prepared to spend. Because of the decision to sail single-handed, I wasn't looking for anything luxurious, just something well-found and of pleasant design set up for coastal cruising.

Then one day in the 'Book of Dreams' I saw a 9 metre Kan Walker designed Herreshoff 28 fibreglass ketch named *Pluto*. Who the hell would call a boat *Pluto*? I said to myself. The asking price was almost double what we had agreed to spend, so I didn't consider it; but as I had always admired this particular design, we decided to drive up to Mooloolaba to look at it anyway.

Pluto was just what I wanted. The ketch was Australian registered, well maintained and had a two-cylinder Yanmar diesel, Fleming wind vane and autopilot. There were no frills, not even an icebox, though the yacht had sailed extensively between Adelaide, Tasmania and Lizard Island. And *Pluto* felt right.

I found it difficult to hide my disappointment as I explained to the broker that the price was much higher than we wanted to pay. I looked around for Shirley, but she was nowhere in sight. I assumed she had gone back to the car. Suddenly I saw her head appear through *Pluto*'s companionway hatch. Good grief! I thought, she must have accepted the broker's offer to go on board. I left the broker and walked over to Shirley.

"Are you feeling all right?" I asked facetiously.

"This is the boat, Stu," she said quietly, ignoring my remark, "I like *Pluto*."

"But what about the price?" I reminded her.

"I don't mind, if you don't," she replied, running her hand slowly along the smooth varnished teak trim of the companionway.

I couldn't believe my ears. But I certainly wasn't going to argue. That settled it. I could hardly contain my jubilation as we negotiated a slightly lower final price. Then, after slipping, survey and test sail, *Pluto* was ours.

I spent the first two years sailing *Pluto* on Moreton Bay, working out how to handle the boat by myself in varying weather conditions. I had a built-in icebox added and installed a more powerful solar panel. The inconvenience of running the motor to keep a refrigerator going didn't appeal. A block of ice lasted nine days in the icebox, and that suited me perfectly.

During the same period my book *The Lighthouse Keepers* was published, so in between getting to know *Pluto* there was time to publicise the book.

In June the following year I was ready to leave on my maiden voyage north. As the day of departure grew closer, I developed doubts about leaving Shirley. I knew that in the months ahead we would be apart for weeks, more so than at any other time of our twenty-five years together. I felt guilty about leaving her behind, while I took off to enjoy myself sailing up the coast. Shirley, on the other hand, seemed more than happy at the prospect of flying up and down the coast to meet me, and was already absorbed in pinpointing on the charts the places that most appealed to her.

The taxi I had booked to take me to the marina arrived early. I gave Shirley a hurried farewell hug.

"Take care, I'll see you soon," she said.

"Bye, honey, I love you."

I had planned for an early start to get the assistance of the outgoing tide. At 2.30 a.m. I started the motor, untied the mooring lines and reversed out of the berth. As I stood at the tiller in the cold morning darkness, waves of self-doubt, apprehension and nervousness flooded my mind. Was this trip a mistake? Should I be leaving Shirley? Did I have enough experience to sail single-handed along the Barrier Reef coast? Then, as the sails filled and *Pluto*'s bow rose to meet the first incoming swell, a surge of exhilaration swept away all my doubts. For better or worse, my dream of twenty years was about to become reality.

Chapter 2

THE BLIND LEADING THE BLIND

It couldn't have happened at a more inopportune time. The heavens opened and the rain bucketed down, quickly reducing visibility to a few hundred metres. *Pluto* was just rounding the shallowest part of the channel off Skirmish Point at the south-eastern end of Bribie Island. The chimney at the Redcliffe Hospital, some 7 miles away, which I was using as a stern mark, had disappeared from sight; so had the white-capped breakers formed by a sandbank on the starboard side. Relying solely on the compass and depth sounder, I steered blindly around the point, hoping that *Pluto* was not heading into danger.

The previous evening the Bureau of Meteorology had predicted a 15 knot south-easterly, just right for the first leg of the trip to Mooloolaba. They had also predicted a shower of rain — not showers, just *a* shower. Shortly before the downpour began, the wind had changed to a 25 knot northerly, which was now right on the nose. I started the motor, attached the autopilot to the tiller and grappled my way along the deck to drop the noisily flapping headsail. The bow plunged violently up and down, waves and spray crashed over me as I clung to the safety lines and at the same time tried to secure the sail. As I returned wringing wet to the cockpit, there was a metallic crash, then *Pluto* veered wildly to port. I saw the arm of the autopilot, attached by its power cable, rolling around the cockpit slamming from side to side. I lunged at the tiller and brought *Pluto* back on course. At first I thought the autopilot had just jumped out of its socket in the cockpit seat, but then discovered that the pin which held the autopilot in the seat had broken away from the main arm.

I hove to and tried to figure out how to repair the break, all the while hoping that the tide and wind weren't carrying *Pluto* towards the still-hidden sandbank. A proper repair would require an electric drill and a vice, neither of which I had on board; but I managed a temporary repair using a length of light-gauge wire. The saloon carpet was strewn with tools I had emptied out of the tool-bag in my haste to find some wire, and the chart table was

8

drenched with rainwater that had been driven in through the companionway hatch.

Just as I was becoming really concerned about the situation, the rain eased and the visibility improved. I gave a sigh of relief when I saw *Pluto* was still well clear of the sandbank. Within thirty minutes the wind veered to the north-east and I was able to sail close-hauled along Bribie Island.

"So," I said out loud, "this is what cruising's all about — and I've only been at it five bloody hours."

By midday, my clothes had dried, order had been restored in the saloon, and patches of blue sky and sunshine began to appear through the clouds. The wind was blowing a steady 15 knots from the south-east, pushing *Pluto* quickly past Caloundra towards Mooloolaba.

I moored *Pluto* at a canal pontoon belonging to friends who had invited me to stay a few days. Phil and Betty Shanahan were congenial hosts, and after the rush of preparing to leave Brisbane, the time spent with them gave me the chance to unwind and relax. Each day I went surfing with Phil, and in the late afternoon we sat on the patio talking and enjoying a few drinks. I repaired the autopilot in Phil's workshop, and after a test run I was once again ready to head north.

The night was glorious. There wasn't a cloud in the sky, and the full moon lit the crests of the small waves to form a silver, shimmering pathway to the horizon. A light land breeze from the south-west pushed *Pluto* gently along at 4 knots. It was also freezing. Even dressed in thermal underwear, woollen shirt and trousers, shoes, wet-weather gear, balaclava and gloves, the cold night air seemed to penetrate the lot. I shivered and went below to make another cup of coffee.

It was 2.00 a.m., seven hours since leaving Mooloolaba. I checked the chart and estimated that *Pluto* would arrive at the Wide Bay Bar around 7.00 a.m. as planned. I was apprehensive about the bar crossing. Many boats and lives had been lost there over the years. The bar itself, the southern entrance to the Great Sandy Strait, lies 3 miles offshore from Fraser Island with a maximum depth of 4 metres at low tide. The ocean swells roll in, building in size as the water shallows. Breakers, steep enough to broach and capsize a boat, can form with little warning. The chart showed a flashing white directional light, positioned on Hook Point at the southern end of Fraser Island, to guide vessels over the bar. I had been advised to make my approach on a flood tide during early morning, with the advantage of having the tide and sun behind me.

Dawn arrived as *Pluto* rounded Double Island Point. In the distance, further out to sea, I saw two yachts. They appeared to be heading in the direction of the bar. Then ahead of me and to port, two other yachts came from behind Double Island Point headland. I assumed they must have anchored there overnight. They too appeared to be heading for the bar.

Through the binoculars I saw they were much larger yachts than *Pluto*, and all carried radar. And probably GPS as well, I thought. I didn't have GPS, but instead obtained my position by dead reckoning, the traditional method calculated by plotting a course on a chart.

As the sun rose above the horizon, I noticed a bank of fog extending off-shore along the mainland and Fraser Island. By the time *Pluto* was within 2 miles of where I thought the bar should be, I couldn't see any land at all. If the four yachts ahead of me *were* intending to cross the bar, according to my reckoning they were at least a mile too far north and heading for white water. But how could four yachts with radar and probably GPS all be wrong? Beginning to doubt my present course, I went below and checked and rechecked my calculations on the chart. I couldn't find anything wrong. When I returned to the cockpit, the four yachts appeared to be still heading in the same direction as before and had drawn even further away from *Pluto*. What should I do? Rely on my own inexperienced judgement, or follow the other yachts? If I followed them, how could I ever have faith in any decision I made on navigation?

I decided I had to trust my calculations. I dropped the main, and sailed under jib alone. As we approached where I thought the bar should be, I started the motor, closed the companionway hatch and put on my safety harness. I went forward to the pulpit and knelt down on the bowsprit, my eyes glued to the binoculars hoping that through the fog I'd see the welcoming flash of the directional light. To port and starboard I saw white water and felt the swell increasing as the water shallowed. Then, dead ahead I saw a dull flash of white light. Unsure whether my eyes were playing tricks, I waited. Another flash! Then another! I stood up and shouted at the top of my voice:

"You bloody beauty!"

I looked northward towards the other yachts. Almost instantaneously I saw the leading yacht's mast tilt drunkenly. It came upright, then went over again, its spreaders almost touching the white water that seemed to be sur-rounding it. As though a cat had been thrown amongst the pigeons, the three other yachts immediately scattered and headed back out to sea. I returned to the tiller and steered *Pluto* through the steep swells towards the light. The first yacht was being buffeted around in the breakers, but still appeared to be afloat. I changed course on the next set of leads, which were now plainly visible on the mainland. The first yacht was running parallel to the coast, still in white water and still being thrown around. I slowed speed in case I could be of assistance. The three other yachts had run south and were fol-lowing my course over the bar. The first yacht caught up to me in the calm waters of the passage between Fraser Island and the mainland. Named *Free-style 11*, I noticed she was carrying a GPS antenna. The four crew appeared shaken, their eyes wide and staring. Only the helmsman, who I presumed was the skipper, had an embarrassed ear to ear grin.

"Everything OK?!" I shouted.

"Yes — seems to be!" the skipper shouted back. "Everything happened so quickly. We've got a fair bit of water below, but I think it came in through the companionway hatch!"

"How come you were so far north? — You've got GPS, haven't you?"

"Yeah, we must have entered the wrong waypoints."

And with that, the skipper waved, pushed the throttle forward, and *Freestyle 11* surged quickly ahead of *Pluto*.

I anchored in the protected waters of Pelican Bay and fried some sausages for breakfast. A veteran yachting friend of mine had told me it was a tradition on his yacht for the crew to have a rum after each crossing of the Wide Bay Bar. It was a tradition I decided to inaugurate on *Pluto*. Rum and sausages at nine o'clock in the morning wasn't my normal fare, but I found it delicious, and soon afterwards collapsed into my bunk for a solid eight hours' sleep.

A strong wind warning from the south-west, issued over the VHF radio next morning, decided me to leave Pelican Bay and find shelter further up Tin Can Inlet. A study of the chart showed a small creek leading into a place called Carlo, 4 miles from where *Pluto* was presently anchored. The water depths didn't look encouraging, but if I could make my way in, the shelter would be good.

Cautiously, with sometimes less than half a metre beneath the keel, I followed the well-marked channel, found a deep hole and dropped anchor. The only sign of habitation ashore was a building perched over the waterfront. With a minaret topped by a flagpole at one end, and a canopy of white sails reaching for the sky at the other, it looked almost surreal in such otherwise pristine surroundings. In front of the complex, a cruiser and two yachts lay tied to a pontoon.

Later in the day I launched the rubber duckie and went ashore. A man, dressed in paint-splattered T-shirt and shorts, was fixing a sign to the building that read "Sandy Strait Yacht Charters".

"G'day," he said to me as I passed, "that's a nice little yacht you've got out there. It's an H28 isn't it?"

"Yes, that's right," I replied.

"Not too many yachts come in here. It's a bit shallow, but you'll be right where you're anchored. Anyhow, my name's Glenn."

"Stuart," I replied, shaking hands.

"Are you sailing single-handed?" Glenn asked.

"Yes, my wife's not too keen on sailing."

"I haven't met many women who are," Glenn laughed. "And sometimes that can cause a lot of trouble."

"What sort of trouble?" I asked.

"Take a friend of mine for example — he built a yacht while he was living in Perth. Then he decided he wanted to sail the boat round the world and persuaded his wife to go with him. Two days after leaving Perth they hit some really rough weather. Next morning she gave him the ultimatum: 'It's either me or the boat'. He chose the yacht, dropped her off in Adelaide and kept on sailing."

"Did she ever go back to him?"

"No, they eventually divorced."

"What about you Glenn, have you been bitten by the yachting bug?"

"Oh yeah," Glenn replied, "I was Assistant Manager of a mining company in Kalgoorlie, W.A., when the bug bit me. I thought there had to be something better to do than the town's main pastimes of gambling and drinking, so I built a 14 metre yacht, trucked it to Sydney and sailed the east coast for two years."

"Have you still got the yacht?" I asked.

"No, I've put down roots here now," Glenn said. "I own Sandy Strait Yacht Charters and also manufacture a shoal draft yacht I designed called the Mangrove Jack. This building is my latest venture — it'll be finished within a month. Apart from the charter base, it'll have a restaurant, a Skippers' Bar and showers for boaties."

"It looks great Glenn, it's a pity I'm a month early."

The strong south-westerly blew in as predicted, and lasted for three days. *Pluto* seemed securely anchored, so each day I went ashore and walked the few kilometres to Rainbow Beach where I swam in the surf and explored the adjoining national park.

The wind was still blowing quite strongly when I left Carlo and headed *Pluto* further up Tin Can Inlet to the Tin Can Bay Marina. I had no sooner tied up when a bloke came over to me.

"Did you come over the bar this morning?" he asked.

"No, I've been down at Carlo for a few days. I crossed the bar about four days ago."

"How was it?"

"OK, except for a bit of fog."

"It can get pretty hairy out there sometimes, you know," the bloke said. "A few years ago my mate sailed up from Sydney single-handed. When he got to the bar it was blowing 35 to 40 knots from the south-east and the waves were huge. He was advised by the Coast Guard not to cross. He hove to for three days, but conditions didn't improve. By the fourth day he'd had a gutful of just sitting there being knocked around in the swell. So he drank a bottle of rum, rolled himself a joint a foot long and an inch thick, smoked it, and then crossed the bar. It gave him such a buzz, he went back out and did it twice more."

I started to laugh, but the bloke wasn't smiling, so I assumed it wasn't a joke after all and just shook my head in mock amazement.

"Boy, did we knock off a few bottles of rum celebrating that bar crossing," the bloke added.

I changed the subject.

"Do you know if the local hotel serves meals tonight?" I asked.

"You mean The Sleepy Lagoon?"

"That's right."

"I wouldn't go up there if I were you, mate. A few months ago I was up there, just sitting at the bar having a quiet drink and minding my own business, when all of a sudden seven blokes appeared from nowhere, dragged me outside and punched the shit out of me. I woke up an hour later back at the marina with an ambulance officer bending over me, patching up my wounds."

I thanked him for his warning as he wandered away.

After a welcome hot shower, I decided to risk a visit to The Sleepy Lagoon. It was a pleasant stroll through the tree-lined streets from the marina to the hotel. Apart from two old blokes who appeared permanently attached to the bar and were gazing silently and fixedly upwards watching a television set that was suspended from the ceiling, there was little action. I bought a beer and ordered a meal, then sat at the bar poised to take instant flight should I see a flicker of movement behind me. But nothing happened. The beer was cold and the meal was reasonable. I even made it back to *Pluto* without being set upon. Pretty uneventful stuff. But then, what else could be expected from someone whose idea of a wild celebration after successfully crossing the bar is having one nip of rum and two fried sausages.

". . . he drank a bottle of rum, rolled himself a joint a foot long and an inch thick, smoked it, and then crossed the bar. It gave him such a buzz, he went back out and did it twice more."

Chapter 3

ON THE STRAIT AND NARROW

Although it had only been ten days since I left Brisbane, I could hardly wait to see Shirley again. For some inexplicable reason it seemed as though I had been away for years on another planet. The bus bringing Shirley to Tin Can Bay was running late, so, to wile away the time, I went over in my mind the places we could sail to in the Great Sandy Strait. I wanted Shirley to really enjoy this trip, as it might convince her to spend more time on *Pluto* further up the coast. At last, the bus rumbled round the corner and stopped. And then there she was, with the familiar welcoming smile I had grown so accustomed to over the past twenty-five years.

During lunch on board *Pluto*, we discussed what had happened since last seeing each other. Afterwards, we strolled along the waterfront to watch the wild dolphins that gather each day at the boat ramp, being handfed by some of the locals. The freshening afternoon breeze made the branches of the large overhanging trees sway back and forth as silver gulls wheeled and dived over the water in search of their evening meal. I deeply inhaled the clean salty air and couldn't have wished for anything more.

Rather than face the excitement of The Sleepy Lagoon, we dined that evening at the marina restaurant. The atmosphere, the food, and the company were excellent. It complemented an already perfect day.

Early next morning we left the marina and headed for the Great Sandy Strait between Fraser Island and the mainland. It was an exhilarating sail. With the main winged out to port and the genoa poled out to starboard, the fresh south-easterly breeze astern of us pushed *Pluto* along at maximum boat speed. With no swell in the Strait, it was an armchair ride. Even Shirley appeared to be enjoying it. We anchored at Garry's anchorage, close to a small sandy beach, and spent a few days exploring the maze of Fraser Island's old forestry tracks that wound across ridges and over freshwater creeks.

Assisted by the flood tide, we moved further along the twisting, but well-marked channel of the Strait. Although quite shallow, the Great Sandy Strait was first used by coastal traders in the 1860s. Vessels from the south would cross the Wide Bay Bar and negotiate the Strait to reach the port of Maryborough to load wool, timber and gold. This route was 120 miles shorter than going round Breaksea Spit at the northern end of Fraser Island. In those days the Strait was well beaconed and buoyed, as was the 20 mile stretch of the Mary River, which led from the Strait to the port of Maryborough. Even so, Sailing Directions of the time advised mariners unfamiliar with the area "to procure the assistance of one of the natives from Fraser's Island, some of whom are very intelligent and have a good knowledge of the river; they will readily come aboard and are very useful".

No longer able "to procure the assistance of one of the natives" we nonetheless successfully steered *Pluto* through the trickiest and shallowest part of the Strait and dropped anchor at South White Cliffs. *Pluto* was the only yacht at anchor, and as the afternoon closed in, the wind decreased until the water was like a sheet of glass. As the sun dropped towards the horizon, the surface of the Strait became a kaleidoscope of colour. The only sounds were the occasional plop of a fish and the gasp of a turtle surfacing for air, causing a series of radiating ripples to enhance the already brilliant reflections. Shirley and I sat in the cockpit sipping a rum and marvelling at the beauty that surrounded us.

"You've got to admit, Shirl," I said, "this is bloody fantastic."

"Yes, I agree, it's great."

By nine o'clock that evening the wind was howling past the rigging at 35 knots and *Pluto* was straining at anchor like a wild hound on a leash.

"Yes, Stu, as you said — 'bloody fantastic'," Shirley commented.

The gale, along with heavy rain, continued for three days. But as there was no swell to roll the boat from side to side, it was very cosy on *Pluto* — dry, warm and protected from the elements. It was too rough to go ashore in the rubber duckie, but surprisingly, Shirley didn't seem to mind being confined to the yacht and was enjoying the whole experience as much as me.

"This isn't too bad," she said. "But if there was any sort of swell I would've swum ashore days ago."

The gale was followed by typically delightful Queensland winter weather — warm sunshine, bright blue haze-free sky and a light breeze. It certainly was from one extreme to the other; but this was what I was beginning to relish about cruising — the contrasts. A few days of bad weather seemed to heighten my appreciation of the good weather when it arrived. Just as the first hot shower after living at sea like a semi-slob for a few days was much more enjoyable than having a shower every night at home.

We sailed further up the Strait and anchored off Kingfisher Bay Resort on Fraser Island. The resort blended in so well with the environment, it was almost invisible from seaward. We motored ashore in the tender and walked along the beach towards a boat hire shack, where a suntanned man was repairing a small catamaran.

"G'day," I said. "We're off a yacht. Is it all right if we have a look at the resort?"

"Yeah, sure," he replied. "The day visitor centre is just up a little further— it's called The Sand Bar. You can have a drink and a meal there, and there're also hot showers and a swimming pool. Up behind the main resort building there's a general store and a bakery."

"Thanks very much," I answered, pleasantly surprised that so much was available to yachties.

The timber-decked Sand Bar overlooked a large free-form swimming pool, nestled amongst mature native trees and shrubs. We had cold beer and sandwiches for lunch as we sat looking across the pool with the Great Sandy Strait glistening in the background. Afterwards, we explored the rest of the resort. The award winning complex was certainly impressive. The main building had a soaring roof structure braced by stainless steel rigging and massive turnbuckles, seemingly designed by an architect with an interest in sailing.

"It's a pity *Pluto* isn't 100 metres long," I said to Shirley. "Those turnbuckles would've been just the right size."

We made the most of the perfect weather while it continued. Each day we went ashore and walked the tracks that led from the resort into the bush and the island's freshwater lakes. Returning to the resort in the late afternoon we showered, had a few drinks then dinner before returning to *Pluto*.

A nearby headland provided a bird's-eye view across the Strait to Woody Island and the mainland town of Urangan. Through the binoculars I could see the decommissioned lighthouse on Woody Island, established in 1867 and one of Queensland's earliest lighthouses.

"How about we sail over to Woody Island tomorrow and have a look at the lighthouse? It'll be quite OK anchored there in these conditions," I said to Shirley.

"Yes, that'll be good," Shirley replied. "I've read quite a lot about the lighthouse, so I'd like to have a look at it."

Next morning we anchored off a small shed beneath the lighthouse and motored ashore in the tender. When the light was demanned in 1959 it was converted to acetylene power. Rather than carry the dozen or so heavy acetylene cylinders up the steep hill to the lighthouse each year, the cylinders were connected together and stored in the shed beside the beach. An underground pipe fed the acetylene from the shed to the light.

We set off up a steep foot-track through the bush, which I assumed led to the lighthouse. Every so often we came across small inspection boxes for the underground pipe.

"I think we're on the right track," I said.

We soon arrived at the stony ridge where the lighthouse stood. Little more than 10 metres in height, it was sheeted with weatherboards and of pleasant proportions, but in very rundown condition.

"Some idiot has kicked the door in by the look of it," I said. "We might as well have a look inside."

We climbed the staircase to the lantern room, now bare of its lighting apparatus, and crawled out through the tiny door to the balcony. The view was magnificent.

"It's like being back in the lighthouse service," Shirley said.

"Weren't there two lighthouses on the island?" I asked.

"That's right," Shirley replied. "They were both built in 1867. This was the main light, and the lead light was 2 miles away at the northern end of the island. At first there was one family stationed on the island at the lead light, and each afternoon and morning the lightkeeper had to do a 4 mile round trip to light and extinguish this light. When local Aborigines began threatening the lightkeeper's wife and children while he was away, it was decided to station another family here at the main light."

We couldn't find any evidence of the lightkeeper's cottage, but followed what we thought was the old road leading to the northern end of the island. But after a kilometre or so the road petered out and became thick scrub. We decided to return to *Pluto*.

We motored into Urangan Harbour next day and tied up at the Sandy Strait Marina. Shirley had booked a flight from here to Brisbane.

"Are you sure you don't want to change your mind and stay on *Pluto* a while longer?" I asked hopefully.

"No, I've really enjoyed myself, Stu, but I've had enough for a while."

I accompanied Shirley in the taxi to the airport next day. We said our farewells and Shirley boarded the plane. I waited beside the runway fence until the plane had safely taken off and disappeared from sight. The sense of loneliness was overwhelming, a loneliness accentuated even more when I returned to an empty *Pluto*.

I spent the next day at the marina, washing clothes and reprovisioning the yacht before setting off for Wathumba Creek on Fraser Island. Although it was possible to enter the creek at high tide, I didn't like the look of the entrance, so I anchored outside its mouth. There was quite a sea running, which made it a very rolly and uncomfortable overnight stay. I was still missing Shirley, but on the other hand I was glad she wasn't on board to experience these conditions.

Even before first light next morning I was sailing across Platypus Bay for the 30 mile trip to Sandy Cape lightstation on the northern end of Fraser Island. The anchorage below the lighthouse was renowned for being swell affected, but I wanted to visit the station to see Dudley Fulton, a friend of mine who had been Head Lightkeeper of Sandy Cape for the past nine years. I dropped anchor at midday and called Dudley on the seaphone.

"G'day, Dudley, it's Stuart here. I'm anchored just below the lighthouse."

"G'day, Stu! How are you? I'll come down and pick you up in the four-wheel drive."

"Don't worry Dudley, I'll walk up. It'll be good to see the place again and at the same time stretch the old sea legs."

"Are you sure?"

"Yep."

"OK, see you in about thirty minutes."

I made my way up from the beach along a steep timber corduroy track that wound its way through thick forest, where the silence was broken by tiny colourful wrens chirping sweetly as they flitted from tree to tree. Compared to the powerful sound of the wind and sea, I found the gentle hush of the bush quite disconcerting. After about twenty minutes I reached a small grassy plateau where the freshly painted lighthouse and two lightkeepers' cottages were built.

"Anyone home?!" I called out through the back door of the Head Light-keeper's cottage.

"Come in! Come in!" Dudley called out before appearing at the door.

"Good to see you again!" we both said simultaneously as we shook hands.

Come on into the kitchen," Dudley said, "I've got some lunch ready."

"Isn't Sue here?" I asked.

"No, Sue's still in Brisbane, she's coming up next week. As a matter of fact, I only got back from leave early this morning. And as soon as I got back, Aubrey went on leave. So I'm the only one on the station."

"I'm lucky to have caught you," I said. "I didn't want to ring you on sea-phone any earlier in case the wind changed to a northerly and I couldn't anchor here."

"I think it will be your last chance to see me here," Dudley replied, "because I'm being made redundant in a few months."

"Well, I suppose we've all known it was going to happen, Dudley. So that will make you Queensland's last lightkeeper?"

"That's right. It's sad, isn't it?"

"You know, Dudley, it doesn't seem all that long ago that Shirley and I were at Bustard Head as lightkeepers inviting yachties in to lunch. We never thought it would change. And now *I'm* a yachtie being given lunch by the last remaining Head Lightkeeper in Queensland. It just proves you can't be certain about anything."

Later that afternoon, Dudley drove me back to the beach.

"Where are you heading next?" he asked.

"Lady Musgrave Island," I replied. "But if that northerly comes in tomorrow as predicted, I'll head in to the Burnett River and wait for a south-easter.

It was quite a comfortable night anchored off Sandy Cape, but about 4.00 a.m. the swell came in with a vengeance, and by first light the wind had changed to a northerly. I weighed anchor and headed for the Burnett River, 40 miles away. The wind freshened during the morning pushing the port gunwale to water level and moving *Pluto* along at a blistering pace.

Pluto's arrival at the mouth of the Burnett River was earlier than expected, so with the assistance of the flood tide I decided to sail 8 miles upriver to the town of Bundaberg. The river, although quite shallow in places, was well beaconed. It snaked its way through cane fields, past sugar refineries, and the famous Bundaberg Rum Distillery, the smell of which reminded me that the sun was well and truly over the yardarm. I moored *Pluto* almost in the heart of Bundaberg at the aptly named Mid Town Marina.

I paid my mooring fees at the marina office and received an armful of literature regarding the scenic and culinary wonders to be experienced in Bundaberg. I read some of the pamphlets while sipping a rum on *Pluto*. They emphasised the fine cuisine and friendly service offered by the town's many hotels and restaurants, so much so I succumbed to going out for a meal rather than cooking on board.

After shaving, showering and donning a clean set of clothes, I headed uptown, almost licking my lips in anticipation of the fine fare that lay ahead. Yes! A succulent rack of lamb and roast vegetables would go down well, or perhaps a large seafood platter with prawn cutlets and garden fresh salad. The main street appeared unusually quiet for a town as large as Bundaberg. I knew it was the Sunday night of a long weekend; even so, not one shop I had passed so far was open. And to my disappointment, when I eventually arrived at the restaurant I had selected from the pamphlets, it was in darkness. A search of both sides of the main street proved fruitless — every restaurant and hotel was shut.

I was about to give up and return to *Pluto*, when I passed a security guard coming out of a shopping arcade.

"Good evening," I said, "I don't suppose you know of a restaurant or hotel where I can get a meal tonight?"

"Gee, I dunno mate, it's pretty quiet in town on a long weekend. But hang on, I passed the Grand Hotel a while ago — I think *it* was open. You might get a meal there."

I followed his directions to the Grand Hotel. At first I thought the place was closed, then I saw some dull lights and a door leading into the public bar. Mmm, I thought, perhaps there's a lounge or restaurant somewhere inside. I swung open the door and stepped into the bar to be bombarded by an ear-shattering blast of heavy metal rock music and a cloud of cigarette smoke so thick I could only just make out some shapes standing beside the bar. I ventured closer and saw about a dozen denim and leather clad, long-haired, bearded and heavily tattooed bikies, accompanied by about a dozen equally heavily tattooed blonde bikies' molls. Disillusioned, but not beaten, I followed a corridor that led into a large shabby room. The visibility improved slightly and I saw a reasonably clean-cut man in a white shirt and dark trousers. He didn't look too friendly.

"Excuse me," I said, "do you work here?"

"Yeah pal, I'm the manager," he snapped and kept on walking.

"Is the hotel serving meals tonight?" I asked, following along behind him.

"Nuh."

"Oh. Do you know any place in Bundaberg that *is* serving meals tonight?"

"Nuh."

With ears ringing I walked back out to the main street and gulped a deep breath of semi-fresh air. I gave up and returned to *Pluto* to cook a meagre meal and read some more pamphlets about the gastronomical delights of Bundaberg.

Chapter 4

LADY OF THE REEF

First impressions can sometimes be very wrong, and this was the case in Bundaberg. With the exception of 'mine host' at the Grand Hotel, I found it a very friendly town. As the marina was so close to the main street, hardly a day passed that I didn't wander up to browse through a bookshop or have a counter lunch at a pub. Of course it was mandatory for any yachtie worth his salt to visit the Bundaberg Rum Distillery for a tour through the factory, and to gaze in awe at the giant oak vats containing many millions of dollars worth of maturing rum. Unfortunately, despite the fact that for years I had been such a staunch supporter of the company, I received only one small free sample.

It was in Bundaberg that I first discovered the camaraderie that exists between cruising yachties. Male and female alike greeted each other with a "Hello" or a nod of the head and a smile when passing on the marina. And it was very easy to stop and start chatting about yachts, places, or the weather. At the same time, most yachties seemed to have the natural ability of knowing when someone wanted to be left alone. Most afternoons a few of us would meet on one boat or another for a sundowner. It was tradition to bring your own drinks and nibbles. Future sailing plans and past experiences were discussed; whether it was about the continuation of a world voyage, or a few months cruising along the Barrier Reef, the conversation was always lively and entertaining. There appeared to be few social barriers between yachties; it didn't seem to matter if your yacht was worth hundreds of thousands of dollars or just a few thousand dollars.

Yachties come in a variety of shapes and sizes, but there must be something about them that stands out from the local residents. At a Bundaberg supermarket, the girl on the checkout asked out of the blue: "Do you want this delivered to the marina?" Perhaps it was the weather-beaten face look, or the somewhat crumpled clothes look, or maybe it was just the numerous cartons of UHT milk in the order that made her assume I was off a yacht.

However, there were two blokes at the Mid Town Marina who stood out from the locals *and* the yachties. They were in their mid-twenties and had porcelain white skin; both were over 180 centimetres tall, and were heavily but flabbily built with extremely rounded shoulders. They wore outlandish punk rocker type clothes and black Doc Marten boots. What really stood out though was their short spiky hair — dyed bright green on one bloke, and bright purple on the other. They passed me a number of times while I was on *Pluto*, but never made eye contact or gave any form of greeting. The yacht they climbed onto had one other person on board — a 'normal' yachtie who I assumed was the skipper; he was always accompanied by a scruffy, miserable looking dog with long, matted hair. The skipper stopped to talk to me one day. He told me that his two crew were "pommy backpackers" who he had taken on board to help crew the yacht and share the expense of sailing north.

A couple of days later I saw the backpackers loaded down with their backpacks leaving the marina.

"Has your crew abandoned ship?" I asked the skipper when I saw him later in the day.

"Yeah," he replied. "I came back to the yacht a bit pissed last night, and this morning they told me they didn't appreciate my behaviour and were leaving. I'm just off to the backpackers' hostel now to see if I can get another lot."

Next day I saw three very attractive girls in their early twenties lumping their backpacks along the marina followed by the skipper and his scruffy dog.

"You've done all right this time by the look of things," I said.

"They're all pommies and they haven't done any sailing before, but they sure are better to look at than those other two dudes."

The thought of having three backpackers on *Pluto*, no matter how attractive, who I had known for no more than five minutes, was horrendous. I could not imagine being thrown together for days on end in a space no bigger than a small bathroom, to cook, eat, sleep and perform all the bodily functions. What if someone had an irritating laugh, an annoying nervous habit, chronic flatulence, bad body odour, or worse still, was a drug addict? Maybe I was becoming a grumpy old man, but I needed my own space.

After about a week in Bundaberg, the wind swung from the north to the south-east, just what I needed to take *Pluto* the 45 miles out to Lady Musgrave Island on the edge of the Barrier Reef. I headed downstream on the ebb tide and dropped anchor a short distance from the river mouth. The chart showed that Lady Musgrave Island is actually a cay of about 20 hectares lying at the western end of a huge lagoon nearly 5 kilometres long and 3 kilometres wide, surrounded by a coral reef. A narrow opening on the northern side of the reef leads into the protection of the lagoon, which is strewn with coral bommies. A sailing guide states: "Once inside the lagoon move cautiously amongst the coral heads, assuming but not implicitly believing that all dark brown coloured patches carry at least 3 metres at low water springs, whilst those of a yellow colouring are very shoal and expose at low tide". I planned to leave the Burnett River at 10 p.m. to arrive at Lady Musgrave about 11 a.m. the following day on a flood tide. That time of day, providing the sky wasn't overcast, would give me maximum visibility of water depth in the lagoon, and the flood tide would give me a chance to quickly refloat *Pluto* should I go aground on a bommie.

I managed a couple of hours sleep before leaving the river. At about mid-night, the fresh south-easterly breeze eased and *Pluto*'s speed dropped to 2 knots. Unwillingly, I started the Yanmar diesel and motored for an hour; then the breeze picked up again and I turned off the motor. And so it went on for the remainder of the trip — alternately sailing and motoring.

Although I had allowed for the influences of tide and current in my course, it was reassuring to see the flash of Lady Musgrave lighthouse dead ahead just before dawn. As I approached the island the dense emerald green foliage that covered the cay seemed suspended over the blinding white beach, which was fringed by a line of white surf from the reef — a scene straight out of a tourist catalogue. But I put the island's attractiveness tem-porarily aside as I dropped sail, started the motor and headed for the reef entrance. The flood tide was racing through the narrow opening, pushing the yacht's bow constantly off course. Continually compensating with the tiller to steer as straight as possible through the centre of the entrance, I could plainly see jagged coral menacingly close to each side of *Pluto*. Safely through the entrance I immediately steered *Pluto* to starboard to avoid a large bommie marked with an isolated danger beacon. Then the water turned crystal-clear, and the coral bommies became easily visible against the white sandy bottom. With more confidence I weaved *Pluto* between the bommies and dropped anchor close to the cay.

Although tired from the overnight sail, my mind was well and truly alert from the experience of entering the lagoon. I made some lunch and sat in the cockpit absorbing the atmosphere and beauty of the island. There was a sparkling freshness and clarity about the lagoon. The water seemed clearer than crystal-clear; every grain of sand, plainly visible 8 metres below *Pluto*, seemed whiter than white; the blue of the sky and the green of the cay appeared to be almost bursting with vibrancy and life. Eventually tiredness won, forcing me below to collapse into my bunk.

Feeling refreshed next morning, I motored ashore in the tender to explore the island. A national park information board described how the cay had developed over thousands of years from just a few grains of pulverised coral and guano to the rich forest it is today. I strolled along a narrow pathway through a dense stand of pisonia trees; their massive, twisted and gnarled trunks supported a tangle of branches where thousands of noddies had vied for space to build their flimsy nests. Buff-banded rails, foraging in the leaf mulch, moved away into the shadows of this strange forest as I passed. It was hard to believe I wasn't lost in the middle of some primeval jungle and not on a coral island on the edge of the Barrier Reef.

On the eastern side of the cay I came to a small camping area, occupied by a group of about twenty divers from the University of New England. They told me that visiting Lady Musgrave Island was an annual event for them. They had been dropped off by charter boat from Gladstone and were staying ten days. The logistics of catering for such a visit were staggering — drums of fresh water, food, cooking equipment, tents, fuel, diving gear including air compressors, all carried from the waterline to the campsite.

Apart from four other yachts anchored in the lagoon, there were two daily visitors from Bundaberg — a six-seater tourist seaplane and the fast tourist catamaran *Lady Musgrave*. The catamaran arrived in the lagoon around 11 a.m. with sometimes up to one hundred people on board, who snorkelled the reef and went ashore on the cay. Although the tourist numbers made little impact on such a large island, each day I usually returned to *Pluto* about midday for some lunch, before going ashore again after the *Lady Musgrave*'s departure about 3 p.m.

For four days the weather remained perfect, ideal for snorkelling over the coral, seeing turtles, giant manta rays and a myriad of fish moving gracefully through the underwater paradise. Then early one evening the south-east trade wind blew in at 30 knots accompanied by squalls and heavy rain. It was good holding ground in the lagoon, so I wasn't overly concerned about dragging anchor. But I realised that, being inside the lagoon, if the anchor did drag while I was asleep, *Pluto* would most likely end up being smashed against the reef. I knew it had happened to other boats during such blows. Each time I awoke throughout the night I checked *Pluto*'s position with the lighthouse on the island and the anchor lights on the other yachts.

I awoke at first light. It was a miserable day. Completely overcast, raining and blowing 20 to 25 knots. I was just about to begin making breakfast when I heard the sound of an outboard motor within close range. I looked through the porthole and saw a dinghy with three people in wetsuits heading towards *Pluto*. As they drew closer I recognised the men from the University of New England diving camp.

"Anyone aboard *Pluto*!" one of them shouted.

I put on my wet-weather jacket, removed the companionway hatch boards and climbed out into the cockpit.

"Have you got a VHF radio on board!" the same man shouted.

"Yes. Why?" I replied.

"Our dive boat's disappeared. It must have broken away from its mooring sometime during the night."

"What type of boat is it?" I asked.

"It's a 6 metre long runabout with a 90 horsepower outboard. It's got a lot of diving gear on board too. We were wondering if you could call Bundaberg Volunteer Marine Rescue on your radio and ask them to put a general message over the air so that any boat in the area can keep a lookout for it."

"Yes, sure," I replied. "Come aboard."

I passed the details on to Bundaberg, who then broadcast the message to all boats. Although the divers didn't have VHF radio, they did have a 27 MHz radio on the island, so I arranged a two-hourly sked with Bundaberg, the results of which I would relay to the divers on 27 MHz.

"Who owns the boat?" I asked one of the divers.

"The University's diving club," he replied. "That's another thing, we'd better contact the Uni regarding the insurance."

It was back on the air to Bundaberg, who generously offered to make the necessary phone calls.

For the rest of the day I stood by the radio, in case the runabout was found by another boat. Bundaberg Volunteer Marine Rescue couldn't have been more helpful. They contacted the seaplane pilot, who offered to do a search of the area where the boat could have drifted. But without success. Hope of finding the boat lessened when the divers discovered that the bommie around which the anchor chain was wrapped had also disappeared. This meant that the runabout would be low in the water from the additional weight of the bommie, and with the rough seas of the previous night, could easily have foundered.

Next morning the weather once again turned perfect, and although Bundaberg continued to transmit the missing boat message every so often, I ceased the radio watch and went ashore. While walking around the beach, I saw the pilot of the seaplane having lunch with four of his passengers. I introduced myself and we began talking about the missing dive boat.

"I'd better be going," the pilot said after a while. "I'm picking up two passengers from the *Lady Musgrave* and taking them for a flight over Musgrave and Fairfax Islands."

"Two passengers?" I said.

"That's right."

"That means there's a spare seat?"

"That's right. Do you want to join us?"

"I'd love to. How much?"

"$25"

"You're on. But I'll have to go back to the yacht and get some money."

"OK," the pilot said. "Just bring your dinghy over to the plane and tie it to the mooring."

The Cessna spluttered into life as we drifted away from the mooring. The pilot headed into the wind and then gave the motor full throttle. At first the plane ploughed laboriously through the water. It slowly picked up speed, engine roaring and water exploding from its floats; then it rose slightly, skipping from crest to crest of the small waves, before lifting and banking over the lagoon.

To see the Barrier Reef while snorkelling is magnificent. To see it from the air is sublime. As the plane gained height, the whole lagoon became visible. The weather side of the reef was fringed by foaming stark white breakers, a direct contrast to the royal blue sea from which the breakers formed. Inside the lagoon, every coral bommie was blatantly visible through the turquoise blue calmness. The vessels lying at anchor were like toy boats in a giant's bathtub. As we circled the island, the black, delta-winged shape of the huge manta rays I had snorkelled over during the past few days appeared to hover motionlessly just outside the reef edge.

The pilot circled the lagoon twice, before veering towards Fairfax Island a couple of miles to the north. Although much smaller than Lady Musgrave, it had a central lagoon with a long, narrow cay. We headed back towards Lady Musgrave, spiralling down to land on the lagoon.

"That was great," I said to the pilot. "The best $25 worth I've had for a long time."

The following midday when the angle of the sun provided the best water visibility, I motored *Pluto* out of the lagoon and sailed across to anchor in the lee of Fairfax Island. My next destination was 45 miles away — a nine-hour sail to Round Hill Creek beside the Town of Seventeen Seventy. The bar at the mouth of Round Hill Creek was only passable for *Pluto* from mid tide upwards, which was late afternoon the following day. Rather than attempt leaving Lady Musgrave in the early morning when the water visibility was at its worst, I had decided to spend the night at Fairfax Island, from where I could leave about 7 a.m. for an unobstructed sail.

Next morning, as the fresh south-easterly breeze pushed *Pluto* along at a comfortable 5 knots, I sat at the tiller contemplating my visit to the Town of Seventeen Seventy. Shirley and I had been invited there by Des and Betty Mergard, proprietors of 1770 Environmental Tours. Des and Betty ran day trips with their amphibian LARC *Sir Joseph Banks* from Seventeen Seventy along the beach to Bustard Head lighthouse, where Shirley and I had spent five years as lightkeepers. Betty had telephoned me earlier in the year to ask if they could retail my book *The Lighthouse Keepers* in their shop, as some of the story was relevant to Bustard Head. Then later on, when Betty discovered I was sailing up the coast on *Pluto*, she suggested we have a belated book launch, or "Lighthouse Party" as she called it, at their marina complex.

Shirley and I had driven in to Seventeen Seventy some years ago. We found it a quiet little settlement, not really a place that I thought would generate much interest in a book launch. Perhaps half-a-dozen people would attend, with the late addition of one old man and his dog who happened to be passing by and called in to see what all the fuss was about. A quick cup of tea and a sandwich and we'd all be home by seven-thirty. However, Betty had been pretty persistent, telephoning a number of times to make sure we would be there on the day.

After safely crossing the Round Hill Creek bar, I headed *Pluto* along the shallow winding channel towards the small marina that lay well upstream. A group of men were standing on the pontoon. Their clothes and weather-beaten looks gave the impression they were professional seamen from way back.

"You can tie up here," one of them shouted, indicating a clear but very tight space between two other vessels.

There's little more embarrassing for the skipper of a yacht than to make a mess of berthing while an audience looks on. It reeks of inexperience and poor seamanship. And the greater the audience, the greater the embarrassment, and usually the greater the cock-up. The tide was screaming in, making any manoeuvre more difficult.

"I'm only going to get one go at this," I said quietly to myself.

I swung the tiller quickly over to starboard, until *Pluto*'s bow was head to the tide, then with a flick of the tiller and a burst of throttle manoeuvred into the space perfectly. I jumped nimbly onto the pontoon, and quickly tied on an aft spring and a bow line, as if this was just an everyday occurrence. Nothing to it my good men. But I was relieved they couldn't see the panic behind my apparent expert single-handed seamanship.

The man who had called out to me introduced himself as Des Mergard.

"Come up to the house and meet Betty," he said. "We'll just have time for a cup of tea before you have to move *Pluto*. We're expecting a spanner crab boat to come in soon for refuelling. But there's a mooring over in the basin where you can stay for the rest of the time you're here. When you come ashore, just tie up your tender at the back of the marina."

Oh no! I thought. Move *Pluto* so soon after that last performance! I couldn't be lucky twice.

Des and Betty's house was on the waterfront, overlooking the marina and the creek. Beside the house was the office, shop and workshop of their business. Over a cup of tea, Betty told me that Shirley had phoned confirming that she would be arriving with two friends the following day. They had rented a house a little way along the road.

"That's good, Betty," I said, "an extra two will bump up the numbers for the book launch. By the way, how many do you think will be attending?"

Betty laughed and shrugged.

"Oh, over a hundred I think," she said.

I laughed too, assuming she was joking.

Then Betty continued:

"The Mayor just rang to say he and his wife will be here for sure."

I started to wonder if Betty *was* joking.

Without too much drama I moved *Pluto* onto the mooring, about 600 metres away from the marina. Next day I went ashore to meet Shirley and her friends. The book launch was on that night at the marina, so I took some clean clothes ashore to change at Shirley's.

We arrived at the marina about 6.00 p.m. I couldn't believe it. The place was packed, and more and more people were arriving all the time. Because it was a belated book launch, most of the people had already read *The Light-house Keepers* and wanted to talk to me about the characters and events in the book. It was a buffet supper, with numerous ladies handing out the most delicious savouries. Des and Betty also owned the fishing charter vessel *James Cook*, so many of the dishes were seafood, including some of the tastiest seafood mornay I had ever eaten. At first, while people were speaking to me, I politely refrained from eating, but eventually, after seeing and smelling plate after plate of delicacies pass me by, I weakened and interrupted the conversation whenever I wanted to refill my plate or my mouth. One particular person, with a wink and a nod, kept supplying me with rum. So much for my quick cup of tea and a sandwich. And if the old man and his dog passing by did call in, I didn't see him, because he was probably lost in the crowd.

Somehow or other, Betty had found out it was my birthday, and during the evening produced a huge birthday cake with a magnificent iced replica of Bustard Head lighthouse on it.

Around 11.30 p.m. the crowd began to thin. I thanked Betty and Des for a wonderful evening.

"I can't believe how many people were here tonight," I said to Betty.

"Now you know, Stu, when Seventeen Seventy says it's having a party, we mean it."

I walked outside with Shirley and her two friends.

"Are you staying at the house with us tonight, Stu?" Shirley asked.

"I'd love to, but I'm not too happy about the mooring I'm on. Last night a motor cruiser broke away from its mooring and ended up in the mangroves. It was lucky it didn't end up on the rocks. No, I'll stay aboard *Pluto* and see you tomorrow after breakfast."

Shortly before midnight I climbed into the rubber duckie and started the outboard. The tide was well into the ebb, and a large exposed sandbank lay between *Pluto* and me. To reach the yacht meant I had to go downstream a fair way and around the bank before heading upstream again. It was almost pitch black and being the middle of July it was freezing. As I motored downstream the outboard stopped. Checking that the fuel tap was on, I pulled the starting cord again and again. Nothing. The tide was rushing out at a good 2 to 3 knots, taking me further and further away from *Pluto*. I lifted the leg of the outboard and began to row. After ten minutes I knew from lining up on a street light I hadn't gained a metre. Again I tried to start the outboard, but without success.

I decided to row with the tide to the opposite bank, from where I could walk along towing the tender upstream well above *Pluto*, and then let the tide take me back to the yacht. It sounded practical and easy. What I hadn't considered was the unevenness and steepness of the bank. I stumbled along in the darkness, dragging the tender behind, stepping into deep potholes, tripping and sinking over my head, as unknown things splashed frantically to get out of my way. I was saturated and shivering. On and on it went — stumbling, falling and sinking.

I eventually boarded *Pluto* about 2 a.m. I took off my wet clothes and still shivering uncontrollably climbed into my sleeping bag, thinking how pleasant it would be at the house, cuddled up with Shirley in a warm bed. However, I suppose there was one redeeming factor — it had been too dark for any old sea-dog who may have been lurking around the marina to witness this display of expert seamanship.

Chapter 5

WHAT A LARC!

The powerful diesel motor of the brightly painted amphibian LARC thundered into life, and with its hazard lights flashing, Des drove *Sir Joseph Banks* onto the main road and headed for the nearby public boat ramp. Amazed onlookers watched as the 10 tonne monster, filled to capacity with thirty-two passengers, bounced down the steep concrete slope and splashed into Round Hill Creek. Des had invited Shirley, our two friends and me to accompany him on the tourist day trip to Bustard Head lighthouse. It was a glorious day — the sky was cloudless and a light cool breeze made it comfortable to be in the sun. Ahead, the curving golden beach of Bustard Bay, broken by four creeks, stretched 24 kilometres to our destination.

Halfway along the first beach, Des stopped the LARC and indicated the place where Lieutenant James Cook anchored the *Endeavour* on 22 May 1770.

"The following morning," Des told us, "Cook, accompanied by Joseph Banks, Dr Solander and a party of men came ashore about where we are now, setting foot on Australian soil for the first time since leaving Botany Bay. They shot a plains turkey, which Cook called a Bustard. It weighed 17½ pounds. In his log, Cook described it as the best bird they had eaten since leaving England, and in honour of it, called this inlet Bustard Bay."

We continued on, surf crashing on the sand beside us, sending shallow foam-topped waves high up the beach to meet the LARC's huge balloon-like tyres, which sprayed out sparkling arches of sunlit droplets.

Des stopped *Sir Joseph Banks* again, and pointed out to sea.

"There're some dolphins out there, playing in the breakers," he said. "Would you like to go out and join them?"

A resounding "Yes!" from the excited passengers had Des heading *Sir Joseph Banks* into the ocean. The LARC ploughed effortlessly through the surf until we reached the calm water just outside the last line of breakers where the LARC stopped, wallowing low in the water like some huge mammal. The dolphins circled the amphibian, leaping out of the water and frolicking about as they investigated what strange thing had invaded their territory.

We made two more creek crossings before reaching Middle Island Beach. Des explained that in 1907, shortly after the death of Captain Frederick Bowton, Superintendent of Bustard Head lighthouse, the Captain's widow and her three children took up the grazing lease on the 3,432 hectare island. By 1940 only two unmarried sisters Bertha and Elsie were left to run the property.

"They were known as 'the maids'," Des said. "They lived on Middle Island until 1977, when ill health forced them into a nursing home. During their seventy years here, the younger maid Elsie made only two short visits to the mainland, the last visit being forty-six years before they finally left the island. Hardships were taken philosophically — broken limbs were mended by bark splints bound with twine; and in later years when Elsie became blind, she kept at her chores, chopping firewood for the wood stove, and finding her way from building to building by means of a strand of fencing wire strung at waist height."

As Des continued to describe the pioneering lifestyle of the maids, the tourists on the LARC listened intently as though he was talking of ancient history. For Shirley and me it didn't seem all that long ago that while we were stationed at Bustard Head we made regular visits to the maids, delivering their mail by dinghy and listening to their stories over lunch in the small corrugated iron hut where they spent most of their time. In those days, Shirley and I were continuing a tradition of communication between the lightkeepers and the maids that had been ongoing for seventy years. As though Shirley had been reading my thoughts, she said:

"It doesn't take very long for the present to become history. Does it Stu?"

Halfway along Middle Island, Des stopped *Sir Joseph Banks* at a huge sand blow. We followed him over the frontal dunes to inspect some Aboriginal middens that had been exposed by the wind.

The calm water of Jenny Lind Creek was our final crossing before reaching Bustard Head. We pulled into the bank beside a shady camping spot where Des served billy tea and homemade damper topped with rosella jam and fresh cream.

"When everyone's ready we'll start the climb to the lighthouse," Des said.

In single file, strung out like Brown's cows, we made our way up the steep slope to the top of the headland. The view was spectacular: pristine beaches, winding creeks and coastal flats with undulating hills that extended to the mountain ranges 50 kilometres away.

"Although we've seen this view a thousand times," I said to Shirley, "it's still magnificent."

"It's the best I've seen on the Queensland coast," Shirley replied.

We walked along the ridge to the lightstation. What had once been 2 hectares of manicured lawn was now overgrown with long grass and weeds. The two cottages and other station buildings, which had always been kept well maintained and freshly painted by the lightkeepers, were now vandalised beyond belief. Windows were smashed, wall panels kicked in, doors torn from their jambs, awnings and guttering ripped from their brackets and the rainwater tanks holed. The lighthouse, although rusty with fading paint, remained undamaged; most likely because the 40 millimetre thick cast-iron panels of the tower had proven too much of a match for the vandals. Shirley and I walked into the cottage that had been our home for five years. Cupboards were reduced to matchsticks and porcelain bathroom fittings smashed to smithereens.

"What is it in the human psyche that makes some people want to destroy?" I said to Shirley.

"I don't know," she replied. "But I know what I'd like to destroy."

Some tourists entered the cottage and looked around in amazement.

"How was this ever allowed to happen?" one of them asked. "This is part of our maritime history. It should have been preserved."

"It's the result of bungling bloody bureaucratic ineptitude," I said angrily. "A caretaker was left on the station after the light was automated in 1986. But six months later it was decided to withdraw him."

"Who decided that?" the tourist asked.

"Some clown in the Commonwealth Department of Transport."

"So really, he's responsible for all this?"

"That's right."

"Surely someone would be prepared to refurbish the buildings in return for a lease on the place."

"Des has been making that offer since 1986," I said, "but without success. Anyhow, it's little more than a demolition site now. It would take an awful lot of money to return the place to its original condition."

Still seething, I left the ruins and followed Des and the tourists down to the small cemetery a few hundred metres from the lightstation. Amazingly the nine gravesites remained unscathed. Superintendent Captain Frederick Bowton was buried here, alongside his wife Katherine, who had survived her husband by thirty-five years. Des explained to the tourists that three of the graves were the tragic result of the lighthouse dinghy overturning in Pancake Creek on 15 May 1889. Lightkeepers Nils Gibson and John Wilkinson, accompanied by Nils' daughter Mary and John's wife Elizabeth, were taking telegraph line repairer Alfred Power up to the Middle Creek crossing when the capsize occurred. Only Nils and John survived. Mary's body was never recovered.

"Nils' family was plagued with misfortune," Des continued. "Two years before his daughter drowned in Pancake Creek, his wife Kate took her own

ashing her throat with her husband's cut-throat razor. Her daughter
und her next day in the bush just a short distance from where we're
Nine years after Kate's death, Nils died from cirrhosis of the liver.
.....ı years, as you can see, a headstone was erected in memory of the
three Gibsons."

We returned to Jenny Lind Creek for lunch, before going for a swim and
a walk around the creek entrance. Tourists' footprints in the sand led in all
directions.

"I know you can't stop progress," I said to Shirley, "but it's only now I
realise how privileged we were as lightkeepers to have had Jenny Lind
Creek and Bustard Head to ourselves for months at a time. Apart from *our*
footprints in the sand, there wasn't a sign of another person."

"Yes, we were fortunate, Stu. Those days are certainly gone forever. But
it's all relevant. If you were used to popular tourist beaches, this would seem
like an isolated paradise."

"Mmm," I replied, unconvinced.

"All aboard who's going ashore!" shouted Des.

Everyone climbed back onto *Sir Joseph Banks.* Soon we were homeward
bound, the LARC slowing every so often as we passed groups of kangaroos
and wallabies grazing on the sand-dune grasses. We arrived back at Seventeen Seventy just as the late afternoon sun lit the western sky with a spectacular blazing red and gold sunset. It was obvious by the rousing round of
applause for Des, that everyone had thoroughly enjoyed their day.

Shirley farewelled her two friends at Seventeen Seventy and joined me on
Pluto. We sailed across Bustard Bay, passed between the dangerous rocks
that lay off Bustard Head, and turned towards the entrance of Pancake
Creek. I had to suppress the urge to jump for joy as I steered *Pluto* around
Clews Point and into the mouth of the creek we knew so well. After all those
years, here we were, sailing our own yacht into Pancake Creek, the place
where my dream had begun. I dropped anchor 2 miles upstream beside
Middle Bank, in full view of the lighthouse high on the headland.

Each day we went ashore to prowl through the bush and along the
beaches and coves, visiting our old haunts. We picked oysters, caught
whiting and mud crabs; and each evening returned to *Pluto* for a sundowner
and to watch the Bustard Head lighthouse begin its nightly vigil. After
dinner we sat in the cockpit, listening to a favourite opera as the beams from
the lighthouse swept the black, star-laden sky, flashing its warning to those
at sea, a ritual it had performed each night for the past 127 years.

"There's only one thing missing," I said to Shirley. "We can't visit the
lightkeepers at the station."

"Yes, it's tragic to think of those empty cottages sitting up there in the
darkness. So many lives have passed through them, and suddenly it's all

What a LARC!

gone. Do you remember the last night you lit the light twenty years ago? We walked along the road just on dusk for a final look at the view from the Jenny Lind headland. It was drizzling and blowing a gale. We were both sad about leaving 'the lights', and we spoke of the bond that we felt existed between us and Bustard Head. Well, I still feel that way. Of all the places where we've lived or visited, I still think of Bustard Head as 'home'."

"So do I," I replied, "and I don't think those feelings will ever change. Even though the area has become much busier."

The weather was so pleasant we delayed our departure from Pancake Creek a couple of times. After ten days we were out of ice and fresh food, and the last of the bread had developed so much black and green mould we could have established a profitable penicillin manufacturing business. We still had a little of what I called the basics — eggs and potatoes, and of course there was plenty of tinned food that I had made a rule not to use unless we were in dire straits; not so much as a matter of principle, but because I didn't like the taste of tinned food. I did all the cooking on board, which I admit wasn't overwhelmingly imaginative, partly because the two-burner methylated spirit stove had neither a griller nor an oven. After four days of fried fish and egg for breakfast, fried fish for lunch, and fried fish and potato for dinner, Shirley declared enough was enough and demanded at least a tin of baked beans for her next meal. It was time to go. A juicy steak and a hot freshwater shower were looking good.

Assisted by the flood tide and a fresh south-easterly breeze we made good time on the 32 mile sail from Pancake Creek to Gladstone. For the last 8 miles up the harbour I steered tiny *Pluto* just metres away from bulbous-bowed giant bulk carriers loading coal delivered from the Central Queensland coalfields, and offloading bauxite shipped from Weipa on Cape York Peninsula. The wharves, the cranes, everything was massive. The harbour throbbed with the sound of heavy industry — rattling conveyor belts, the hissing of escaping steam, and the rumble of millions of moving parts from gargantuan machines. A convoy of three huge tugs forged their way across the harbour to assist a bulk carrier approaching a wharf. A helicopter, with the word PILOT painted on its side, thundered overhead, heading for the fairway buoy; obviously to disembark a ship's pilot onto another bulk carrier ready to enter the harbour.

"And you reckon the Bustard Head area is busy," Shirley said.

Gladstone Marina was like an oasis within a desert of industry. Constructed and owned by the Gladstone Port Authority, it was surrounded by hectares of parkland and boardwalks, and only a twenty minute walk from the town centre. The marina complex had a large amenities block as well as a restaurant, hairdresser, and various other small shops. But what we enjoyed most about Gladstone was the friendliness of the people; they weren't obsequiously friendly, just naturally friendly as though they were talking to the bloke down the road.

After the fiasco with the outboard motor in Round Hill Creek, the motor had run reasonably well. Every now and then it would stop for no apparent reason, but would immediately start again when the starter cord was pulled. But "reasonably well" meant unreliable, so I dropped it in to an outboard mechanic for an overhaul. I also wanted a few spare parts for *Pluto*, which was going to mean a long walk around the outskirts of Gladstone to the various shops. As I was heading off, I passed "Trader Pete's", a secondhand boat chandlery shop in the marina complex. In the window there was an old pushbike for sale. Gee, I thought, that would be handy for running around town today. I went into the shop.

"G'day," I said to the man behind the counter. "I don't want to buy that pushbike in the window, but would you be interested in renting it to me for a day?"

"I'm afraid I can't do that. When I first opened the shop I looked into the possibility of hiring pushbikes to yachties, but the high cost of public liability insurance made it impractical. What did you want to use the bike for anyway?"

"Just to get some parts for the boat."

Trader Pete put his hand in his pocket, took out a set of keys and threw them on the counter.

"Here," he said, "I've got an old green Kombi outside. Take that."

We found Gladstone to be that sort of place.

One of our greatest finds in Gladstone was the Gladstone Yacht Club. The menu was extensive, the meals were reasonably priced and of excellent quality. Mine hosts Paul and Sallyanne provided lunch and dinner seven days a week. Chef Paul, a Frenchman, could easily have been mistaken for the twin of tenor Luciano Pavarotti, and as he made his rounds of the tables, radiating his flamboyant bonhomie, I would not have been in the least surprised if he had suddenly burst into "Come Back To Sorrento".

It was enjoyable to set off from the marina most evenings in anticipation of a pleasant evening at the yacht club. The stroll along the boardwalk and through the parkland of the waterfront whetted the appetite on the way to dinner and gave us hope of losing a few calories on the way back to the yacht.

It was a surprise to discover that many of the people in Gladstone had read my book. Word had somehow got around that Shirley and I were at the marina, and hardly a day passed when we weren't paid a visit by someone who had been associated with the lighthouse service.

"Don't get swelled-headed about it," Shirley remarked. "They probably just want to check that you're still alive before they sue you for what you said about them in the book."

After about a week, the desire to head north into new territory became too strong to ignore. Even Shirley appeared quite happy to be leaving the comforts of Gladstone.

Chapter 6

NIGHT OF THE PRAWN

It felt uncanny to be sailing along in the deepest part of the channel and yet I could have leant over and touched the mainland mangroves lying off *Pluto*'s port side. We had left Gladstone shortly before dawn to catch the flood tide through The Narrows, a 27 mile-long mangrove-lined waterway that snakes between the mainland and Curtis Island. So far, we had successfully followed the numerous beacons, even though at times the depth sounder had shown less than half a metre beneath the keel. The chart showed we were now approaching the shallowest section of The Narrows, parts of which dry out at low tide to heights of 1.8 metres. Opposite Monte Christo Creek the reading on the depth sounder dropped to 0.5 metre . . . 0.4 . . . 0.3 . . . then a worrying 0.2.

"It's not looking good, Stu," Shirley said, bracing herself for a grounding.

"It seems to have steadied," I replied. "Anyhow, it's well over an hour before high tide. If we do hit bottom, we'll get off pretty quickly."

We passed two red beacons to port and then came to a set of leads positioned on Curtis Island.

"Look at the depth now," I said, "it's almost 8 metres."

It soon shallowed again to about a metre, but we were over the worst of it.

I had read that The Narrows was first used by shipping in the early 1850s, and soon became a popular protected waterway for shoal draft vessels running at high tide between Rockhampton and Gladstone. First beaconed in 1867, an attempt to dredge the shallowest parts was made in 1890. But the rocky nature of the bottom made dredging a slow and difficult exercise. After sixteen months the project was abandoned. Six years later, a private contractor won the tender to dredge a channel through The Narrows to a width of 24 metres and a low water depth of just under a metre. However, he met with the same difficulties and had to abandon the contract. Soon afterwards, twenty men were employed to dig out part of the channel with pick and shovel. At the same time, ten beacons between Monte Christo Landing and Black Swan Creek were lit to provide night access to shipping. The lights were attended by a lightkeeper living on Monte Christo Island. But over the years, as the size of coastal vessels increased, The Narrows became less frequently used and the lights were discontinued.

A short distance before a second set of leads we came to some stockyards built on the bank of Curtis Island. Two parallel fences ran steeply into the water.

"This has to be what's called the Cattle Crossing," I said to Shirley, "where stock is driven across to the mainland at low tide."

"It's hard to believe that in a few hours this place is going to be bone dry," Shirley said. "We should anchor *Pluto* in a deep hole, motor down in the dinghy at low tide, and walk over to have a look at it."

"I tell you what — I'll drop you off in the dinghy now, along with a dozen cans of Aerogard, and *you* can wait to have a look at it. I'm not staying around this place at low tide, the mosquitoes and sandflies will carry you away."

For years I had been aware of The Narrows' reputation of harbouring these pests. In 1802 the explorer Matthew Flinders, while investigating The Narrows, made mention in his log of the "musketoes and sandflies" which made sleep impossible for all but one of the boat's crew camped overnight in the "mud and mangroves". And in the early 1900s, the Southern Protector of Aborigines, Archibald Meston, during a trip across The Narrows to visit Monte Christo cattle station described the mosquitoes as the worst he had ever encountered. He said: "A stockman rode over to us. The seat of his saddle was covered by a paste of dead mosquitoes. The seat of his riding pants was in the same condition and the mosquitoes had crowded in under the shoulders of his coat and had smothered there in the hundreds." He went on to say that the residents of Monte Christo homestead took not only their sleep but also their meals under mosquito nets.

While living at Bustard Head, Shirley and I had been told by visiting lighthouse mechanics that even the manned lightstation situated on the high, exposed, treeless headland of Cape Capricorn at the north-eastern end of Curtis Island was plagued by mosquitoes. To avoid being attacked by these voracious bloodsucking insects, the lightkeepers' wives often hung out the washing dressed in overalls with the legs tucked into their socks. Over their hats they draped mosquito net, which was then pushed into the neck of their overalls, and they wore gloves to protect their hands.

Years ago, Shirley and I flew by Cessna to Cape Capricorn to spend a few days photographing the station. We landed on the beach during early afternoon and set up camp below the cape. Shortly before sunset we climbed the headland to take some night photographs of the lighthouse. We hadn't sighted a mosquito since our arrival.

"I think those stories the mechanics told us about the mosquitoes are a load of codswallop," I remember saying to Shirley.

I set up the camera on the tripod, and as the sun dropped below the horizon I began shooting away. Suddenly, billions of mosquitoes appeared from nowhere and attacked us with a vengeance on the face, legs and arms. A dousing in Aerogard made little difference. In between shots we both danced around, hopping from leg to leg while continuously brushing our face, legs and arms with both hands. After a while we developed a rhythm that was akin to a sort of primitive jitterbug. We found some respite when we returned to our tent, but when we awoke in the morning the insect screen was black with mosquitoes. They cleared about midday — probably for a few hours sleep to renew their energy — before returning again at sunset.

"Before I drop you off in the dinghy," I said to Shirley, "do you remember our trip to Cape Capricorn?"

"On second thoughts, I'll give it a miss," Shirley said.

With the second set of leads well astern, the waterway began to widen and deepen. There were no beacons now, and I steered *Pluto* along the centre of the channel. A number of creeks branched off the main channel and ran far into the island. Named Badger, Mosquito, Barker and Maria, the chart showed that the creeks, although narrow, had good depth for most of their length.

"These would be great creeks to shelter in during a cyclone," I said to Shirley. "Just tie off on the mangroves on either side of the creek and sit it out."

"Yes, Mosquito Creek sounds charming," Shirley replied. "I wonder why it was called that?"

We eventually arrived at the mouth of Pacific Creek, the last creek on Curtis Island before entering Keppel Bay. The entrance to the creek almost dried out at low tide, but with four hours to go before that happened, we followed a set of leads, crossed the bar and anchored 500 metres upstream. Well before sunset we rigged up insect screening across the hatches in readiness for the evening's onslaught of mosquitoes and sandflies. To our surprise, there wasn't a one. After dinner we threw out the ultimate challenge and sat in the cockpit for an hour or two, but didn't feel a bite.

"I thought we'd be eaten alive here tonight," I said to Shirley.

"I know, so did I. I can't understand it. There's not even a breeze blowing to keep them away."

Next morning we launched the tender and headed towards the mouth of the creek, where there were some old buildings and the remains of a jetty. We knew that this was once the site of a pilot station, used for accommodating boat crews and the pilots who guided ships across Keppel Bay and up the Fitzroy River to the town of Rockhampton. We landed on a small beach beside a boatshed and followed a track that ran past the old pilots' cottages. One of the cottages appeared occupied. In the yard, a man was working on a long trawling net; beside him sat a huge rottweiler dog. As we passed, the dog rose stiffly to its feet and glared at us. The man looked over and waved, but immediately turned back to his work.

"The State government must have leased out the cottages," I said to Shirley. "The one where that bloke is working looks in good condition, but the other two are in a pretty sad state."

"Yes, they look locked up though. They must be weekenders," Shirley replied. "I wonder what that steel tower near the man's cottage is for, Stu?"

"I'm not sure. It could be radiotelephone."

We followed the steep track to the summit of Little Sea Hill where there was an automatic lighthouse. Far in the distance we could see Great Keppel Island. We continued on, down the other side to a grassy flat. A short distance in from the beach we came to a fenced grave. The headstone read:

SACRED
TO THE MEMORY OF
THE THREE BELOVED CHILDREN OF
JAMES AND JESSIE AIRD
AGED 4 MONTHS, 3½ YEARS
AND 15 MONTHS

"That's strange," I said to Shirley, "there are no dates, or names of the children."

"It is odd," Shirley replied. "I researched the Aird family for the Lighthouse Historical Society about a year ago. James Aird was a lightkeeper at Sea Hill from 1876 until 1896 I think. The two eldest children on the headstone, Colin and Angus, died in 1889, within a day of each other. Their Death Certificates show they died from gastroenteritis. But it was reported in the paper that the doctor who did the post-mortem examination, thought the gastroenteritis could have been caused by the children eating poisonous berries or shellfish. The four month old baby died years before Colin and Angus."

We walked through to the beach, which curved around for about 2 kilometres until it met a headland. We beachcombed for the rest of the morning and had lunch on top of the headland.

Later in the day when we returned past the cottages, a second man was working on the trawling net. As we motored back up the creek we passed an anchored trawler. No-one appeared to be on board.

"That other bloke working on the net is probably from the trawler," I said.

"Looks like it," Shirley replied.

We motored past *Pluto* and continued on upstream. On rounding a bend we saw another yacht anchored ahead. Named *Equinox* from Hobart, her dark blue hull was faded and had a few rust streaks. As we passed, a man came out on deck. He was tall and thin, and wore only long baggy shorts.

For a yachtie his skin was unusually white. With his dishevelled black hair and stubbly beard he looked quite a desperado.

On our return downstream a while later, we noticed that a large Jolly Roger flag had been hoisted to one of *Equinox*'s spreaders. The man was still on deck, and as we passed he smiled broadly and pointed vigorously up to the flag.

I gave him a restrained wave.

"Blackbeard the Pirate looks a bit weird," I said quietly to Shirley.

Later in the afternoon we were sitting in the cockpit having a sundowner when a dinghy appeared from upstream and headed directly towards us. It was the man from *Equinox*.

"Oh no!" Shirley said. "It looks as though Blackbeard is coming over to see us. I hope he hasn't got pillage and plunder on his mind."

The man slowed his dinghy and pulled up alongside *Pluto*.

"Hello," he said in a pleasant, refined English accent, and pointed to the flag we were flying from the starboard spreader. "What's the flag?"

"It's the emblem of the Lighthouse Historical Society of Queensland," I replied.

"Are you Stuart Buchanan?"

"Yes, I am."

"I've just finished reading your book. I really enjoyed it."

"Thank you very much," I replied, rather taken aback. "Would you like to come aboard and join us for a sundowner?"

"I'd love to."

The man introduced himself as Paul Chapman, and told us he was spending the school holidays in the area with his wife and three children.

"Are you from Hobart?" I asked.

"No, we live in Gladstone now. Cate and I bought *Equinox* in Hobart a few years ago and sailed her up to Queensland. She's showing her age a little now, and needs a bit of maintenance — *Equinox* that is, not Cate — but with three young children it's hard to get much spare time to work on the boat."

Paul was extremely affable and had a sharp sense of humour. I felt embarrassed that I had declared him "a bit weird" before meeting him. At my age, I should have learnt not to judge people so quickly.

Normally I would never enquire about someone's occupation. But Paul intrigued me. He didn't seem to belong to any stereotype group.

"Do you work in Gladstone, Paul?" I asked after a while.

Instead of answering "None of your bloody business, mate." He said:

"Yes, I'm a harbour pilot with the Gladstone Port Authority."

"Oh dear," I replied, "I wrote a few uncomplimentary things in my book about the Torres Strait pilots."

"I know," Paul said with a laugh, "and there's not a pilot in Gladstone who didn't find that hilarious."

We chatted away over a few rums.

"I'd better be getting back," Paul said eventually, "I promised the children I'd take them for a ride in the dinghy before dark."

"Well, Stu," Shirley said as Paul made his way back to *Equinox*, "contrary to Gilbert and Sullivan's *Pirates of Penzance*, Paul is a pilot and not a pirate."

That evening we were once again spared the wrath of mosquitoes and sandflies. It was full moon, and the incoming spring tide was screaming past *Pluto*'s hull at a little over 3 knots. Shirley and I were engrossed in a game of Scrabble when, at about 9.30, we heard the unmistakable sound of grinding anchor chain. Our eyes met for a fraction of a second, then I jumped up and leapt out into the cockpit. Assisted by the light from the full moon, it didn't take long for my eyes to become adjusted to the darkness. What I saw gave me the shock of my life. An unlit trawler was swinging towards us, its massive steel port outrigger less than a metre away. The trawler swept past, missing *Pluto*'s hull by a hair's breadth; then it stopped and hung beside us, its bow swinging back and forth, towering ominously over me like some great disaster waiting to happen.

"What's happening?" Shirley asked, as she joined me in the cockpit.

"I think it's the trawler we saw anchored down at the mouth of the creek this afternoon. It must have dragged anchor and picked up *Pluto*'s anchor chain."

"Anyone aboard!?" I shouted out, at the same time leaning over and banging my fist hard against the trawler's hull. "Anyone aboard!?"

"There can't be anyone on board," Shirley said. "The trawlerman must still be ashore with his mate from the pilot's cottage."

"Shit!" I exclaimed. "I think we're both dragging up the creek now."

I checked our movement against the mangroves on the creek bank. We were definitely on the move — it was slow, but we were moving.

"The trawler must have dislodged *Pluto*'s anchor," I said. "Look Shirl, I'll have to go ashore and get the bloke who owns this thing. But first I'll go and see if Paul from *Equinox* will come down and give you a hand to fend off the trawler while I'm ashore. Whatever you do, watch your hands, don't get them squashed between the two boats."

I launched the tender and sped round the bend to *Equinox*. Her lights were still on.

Paul must have heard my outboard, as he was already on deck when I pulled alongside. I explained the situation.

"Of course I'll come down and give Shirley a hand, but I wouldn't be too keen on going ashore to get the trawlerman if I were you, Stuart. Did you see the dog his mate has? It's a rottweiler the size of an elephant."

Paul was right. I had forgotten about Fido. He wasn't the type to welcome a stranger creeping around his territory in the dead of night.

"If we knew the name of the man who lives in the pilot house, I think I could phone him on VHF radio, because I'm sure that tower near his house is for radiotelephone." I said.

"Aha! You've given me an idea," Paul replied enthusiastically, reaching over to the cockpit and picking up a mobile phone. "I'll ring the coxswain at Port Alma, he's sure to know who the chap is."

Within a minute, Paul was nodding his head to me and scribbling down a number.

"Alan Warner is his name," Paul said as he stabbed at his mobile phone once again.

In less than a minute after Paul explained the situation to Alan, I heard an unmuffled vehicle roar into life over a kilometre away.

"It sounds like they're on their way. Thanks Paul. I'll get back to *Pluto* and wait for them."

"I'll come back with you."

Just as Paul spoke, I saw *Pluto* and the trawler appear from round the bend. Obviously they were still moving slowly upstream.

"It's probably best that you stay here, Paul, just in case *Pluto* and the trawler crash into *Equinox*."

"Yes, you're right."

As I climbed back on board *Pluto* I heard an outboard motor in the distance. It was screaming at full throttle.

"How did you get on, Shirl?" I asked.

"Not too bad. The boats haven't hit. But it's just luck, not my doing. The tide's too strong to do any fending off."

Before I had a chance to explain what had happened on *Equinox*, an aluminium dinghy with two men in it careered round a bend and pulled up beside us.

"We're both dragging up the creek!" I shouted to them. "Your anchor has picked up our chain! Have you got a spare anchor and line!?"

"Yes!"

"Well, buoy your anchor line and let it go — you can pick it up later!"

As I spoke, a large aluminium dinghy with a powerful looking outboard motor swept past on the tide. There was no-one in it.

"Is that your dinghy!?" I shouted, indicating behind the men.

They both turned round.

"Christ!" one of them said.

The man at the tiller of the outboard dropped his mate off on the trawler and then sped up the creek after the other dinghy.

The trawlerman buoyed the end of the anchor line, untied it from around the samson post and threw the lot into the water. The trawler took off up the creek at a great rate of knots.

"Shouldn't he have started the motor first before he let the anchor line go?" Shirley asked.

"He certainly should have."

We watched the trawler disappear round a bend bouncing off the mangroves as it went.

"I don't know where it's going to end up, but at least it didn't hit *Equinox* on the way," I remarked.

With the weight of the trawler removed from *Pluto*'s anchor chain, we had stopped moving up the creek.

"We seem to be holding OK, I'll unravel the mess in the morning," I said.

Half an hour later, the dinghy returned with the man from the pilot house in it.

"Thanks for that," he said. "I'm Alan Warner. My mate from the trawler's safely anchored further up the creek — and I got his dinghy as well. Here's a bucket of prawns for your trouble."

"Thanks very much," I said, "but it wasn't all my doing. Paul on *Equinox* had the mobile phone."

"Well, jump into your dinghy and we'll go up and share them."

"Are you coming over, Shirl?" I asked.

"No, I'll stay here in case *Pluto* drags again."

We climbed on board *Equinox*. Paul got out a bottle of port as Alan began to divide the prawns.

"Here," Alan said to me, "try some of these prawns. They're beauties — caught and cooked today."

I had hardly finished my first prawn, when I saw the repeated flashing of a torch from *Pluto*.

"*Pluto* must be dragging!" I yelled. I leapt into the tender and motored back down the creek.

"We're dragging again!" Shirley shouted as I approached.

It took over an hour and a half to untangle a mass of anchor chain, lines and anchors. It was well into the early hours of the morning before we were securely anchored much further up the creek. All the prawns were still on *Equinox*, but I wasn't leaving *Pluto* again that night.

Oh, well, I suppose I got one more prawn than Shirley did. And Alan was right, damn him — it was a beauty.

Chapter 7

IT'S BEAUTIFUL, BUT . . .

Halfway across Keppel Bay the muddy water that had been with us since entering The Narrows four days earlier changed to a clean, deep blue. It wasn't a gradual change. It was muddy one second and clear the next, as though a line of demarcation had been drawn on the surface. It was one of those days when it was a delight to be on the water. The sky was cloudless and the seas were slight with little swell; a light, crisp southerly breeze made for relaxed sailing.

A mishmash of islands lay ahead in the distance. It was impossible for me to identify from the chart which island was which, but relying on the compass as always, everything gradually fell into place as we sailed past each island in turn.

"Are you going to anchor off the resort?" Shirley asked as we approached Great Keppel Island.

"No, not with this southerly breeze predicted to increase overnight. It would be pretty uncomfortable anchored there. I was going to anchor off Svendsen's Beach on the northern side of the island — there are a number of walking tracks we can follow from there to the resort."

As we rounded a steep headland the resort came into view; it was as though we had been suddenly thrust into another world. The past few days of quiet, lonely creeks and uninhabited beaches were replaced by the scream of outboard motors as water-ski and para-sail boats zipped between and around some of the yachts at anchor. Brightly coloured sails from a number of small hire catamarans made a striking contrast with the blue water and the deep green foliage of the coconut palms that lined the beach in front of the resort.

"There's a lot of activity, but the place looks very pleasant," Shirley said as she handed me the binoculars.

We sailed through the narrow Half Tide Passage between Great Keppel and Middle Island towards Great Keppel's northern beaches.

"This looks better," I said to Shirley. "All the action must take place at the resort."

I anchored *Pluto* in 6 metres of water so clear we could see every detail of the anchor and chain lying on the sandy bottom. Only one other yacht was at anchor. Named *Kestrel,* she appeared unattended.

Next morning we motored ashore and walked along Leeke's Beach towards the resort. At the end of the beach we found a foot-track that led over a headland and down onto another beach. It was low tide, so we strolled along on the hard sand at the water's edge. I was miles away, thinking about the beauty of the island, when Shirley asked:

"Didn't you see that?"

"See what?"

"All those girls sunbaking in the nude — quite impressive they were too."

"Where?"

"On the beach, up near the dunes. We've just passed them."

"Oh, thanks for telling me now."

"I thought you would've seen them. You *are* slipping."

We left the beach and followed a paved walkway that ran through groves of coconut palms and along the beachfront to the resort. An area, separated from the main buildings, catered for boaties and day visitors. It had a bar, swimming pool and open air cafe overlooking the beach; and joy of joys — it also had hot freshwater showers. We ordered some coffee and sat at a table shaded by a large umbrella, while gazing at the passing parade of skimpily clad resort guests. My eyesight seemed to be making a remarkable recovery.

A map of the island, which we purchased from the resort's boutique, showed a maze of interesting looking walking tracks crisscrossing the island.

"You could spend weeks here," I said to Shirley, as I continued to study the map. "How about we walk out to Bald Rock Point tomorrow and have a look at the automatic lighthouse? It's about a 10 kilometre return walk. We can take some lunch and make a detour down to Wreck Beach for a swim on the way back."

"Sounds great," Shirley replied enthusiastically.

Shirley appeared to have really enjoyed herself since boarding *Pluto* at the Town of Seventeen Seventy. I knew there was no way she would sail full-time with me, but deep down I still had some hope that she might grow to like the lifestyle and prolong her stays on board.

The southerly breeze didn't increase overnight as predicted; in fact the breeze died out completely. Next day we motored ashore and walked along to the northern end of Svendsen's Beach, where the map showed a track leading across the island to the lighthouse. As we left the beach we saw a house nestled behind a thick barrier of large oleander shrubs and coconut palms.

"What a beautiful spot," Shirley remarked. "A true tropical island paradise."

"It certainly is. According to the map this is the Svendsens' property."

The track passed close to a shed; we could hear the sound of a diesel generator running inside.

"That must be the power supply for the house," I said.

We followed a steep track up the side of a hill. At its summit a large, three-bladed wind generator sat motionless on top of a stayed mast.

"No wonder the diesel generator is running," Shirley said. "There hasn't been much wind over the past couple of days to turn those blades. The Svendsens have got quite a set-up by the look of it."

The stony track followed the steep razorback of the mountain range. At various points along the way we stopped to catch our breath and gaze at the magnificent views along the island's coastline and inland across the valley. Every now and then, we caught a glimpse of our destination far in the distance. At some points the track descended sharply, before levelling and rising steeply again.

"This is the one thing I don't like about these walks of yours, Stu," Shirley gasped, wiping the perspiration from her face. "I know I've got the same damn hills to climb on the way back."

"Just keep thinking how lucky we are to be here," I replied. "Think of all the people back in the city, stuck in their offices."

"How about thinking of being back on the beach, floating in the beautiful, cool, clear water."

Just as Shirley finished speaking, we broke out of the bush onto the highest point of the range. The view was spectacular. In the distance, island after island stretched across Keppel Bay towards Curtis Island and the mainland. The headland of Cape Capricorn, 30 miles away, was plainly visible. Directly below us the dark blue ocean swells swept into Clam Bay, breaking across its extensive reef ledge. Nearby, the white sandy bottoms fringing Halfway and Humpy Islands could be clearly seen through the crystal-clear water.

"Isn't this worth a bit of sweating?" I asked.

"Yes. OK, OK."

We descended to the small, solar powered lighthouse and had lunch sitting on the nearby concrete helipad. A few metres away, a concrete slab bordered by stones was roughly inscribed with the names of some of the crew from the lighthouse supply vessel *Cape Moreton* who had constructed the light in 1975. Many of the names were familiar to us from our light-keeping days in Torres Strait.

"I wonder where all these people are now," Shirley said. "The lighthouse service is just about non-existent. The lightkeepers are all but gone, and the supply vessels are sold off. A way of life has disappeared so quickly."

"Yes," I replied, "it must have been a great life on board the *Cape Moreton*, getting paid to cruise the Barrier Reef in four star comfort — almost as good as being lightkeepers."

We sat for a while, watching a herd of goats graze the grassy slopes that dropped precipitously to the water's edge, and then set off back along the track, detouring to Wreck Beach. The kilometre long beach was delightful. Sparkling clear water spilled lazily onto the white sand, and there wasn't another soul in sight. We beachcombed its entire length, stopping every so often for a refreshing swim.

When we returned to *Pluto* late in the afternoon, although there wasn't a breath of wind, the swell had increased, making being on board quite uncomfortable. I had difficulty preparing dinner under these conditions and I could see that Shirley was becoming less happy by the minute. That night we had to fit the lee-cloths to prevent us rolling out of our bunks.

The swell lessened during the early hours of the morning, and after breakfast we went ashore to visit the old homestead and shearing shed, which were used when the island was a sheep run. We continued on to the resort for lunch and a hot shower.

Again that evening, I had difficulty making dinner because of the sea conditions. I put out a stern anchor in an attempt to hold *Pluto*'s bow into the swell, but I couldn't get it to set properly. Other yachts that had anchored nearby during the day appeared to be suffering similar discomfort.

I was just about to serve the meal when Shirley told me she wasn't hungry. Obviously the swell was beginning to upset her.

The swell worsened as I started to wash up. *Pluto* rolled from gunwale to gunwale, scattering dishes, cutlery, pots and pans from one side of the yacht to the other. It took about ten times longer than normal to complete this usually simple chore. I looked out through the companionway hatch to see how the other yachts were faring. Their masthead anchor lights were arching backwards and forwards through the night sky like shooting stars. At least it wasn't only happening to *Pluto*.

"That's it," Shirley declared, after *Pluto* was hit by a number of particularly severe swells. "I've had enough. In the morning I want to go in to Rosslyn Bay."

Any hope I had of Shirley prolonging her stay on this trip was dashed. I admit I wasn't enjoying the present conditions, but it was just one of those things you had to put up with while cruising. What made it more difficult was that I was concerned about Shirley. She wasn't happy, and that didn't make me happy.

At first light next morning we weighed anchor and headed for Rosslyn Bay Boat Harbour 9 miles away. I noticed all the other yachts were doing the same thing. The wind had picked up during the night and was now blowing at about 25 knots from the south-east. *Pluto* was screaming along on a port reach, the starboard deck periodically being swamped with water.

"I don't mind this sort of sailing, Stu," Shirley said. "But the last two nights were horrendous. I can stand a *bit* of rocking and rolling at anchor, but that . . . you yachties must be born with cast-iron stomachs to put up with it."

"Yes, I can understand how you feel," I replied. "But you will join me again though — further up the coast?"

"Of course I will. But I think that in the future I won't stay too long. You must get tired of having to consider me all the time, especially when you know I don't like rolling conditions at anchor."

"OK, fair enough."

What Shirley had said about considering her all the time was true. Because I had little idea of whether or not an anchorage would be uncomfortable, I was always apprehensive about a place before I got there; and even if it was all right when we arrived, I still remained apprehensive in case a swell came in with a change in sea conditions or tide. I was well aware that most island anchorages had some swell running into them, and I realised that in the future I would have to do some serious reconnoitring in any area where Shirley wanted to join me.

I steered *Pluto* through the breakwater entrance into Rosslyn Bay Boat Harbour. Apart from a number of pile moorings, which I had been told were too shallow at low tide for *Pluto*'s 1.4 metre draught, the harbour was a large open area with boats on moorings and at anchor. Although manoeuvring room was limited, made worse by the strong south-easter blowing, we found a space between two vessels and dropped anchor. The sailing directions warned that the harbour didn't have good holding ground; many vessels had dragged anchor and smashed into the breakwater. But after a couple of hours, during which time we received a few strong wind gusts, I felt confident that *Pluto* was securely anchored.

I had heard on the 'yachties' grapevine' that a marina for the harbour was under construction. At first this wasn't obvious, but when we went ashore we saw dozens of concrete pontoons that had been cast and more were in the process of being poured.

Shirley decided to spend a couple of days with me at Rosslyn Bay before flying back to Brisbane. Rosslyn Bay was a pleasant little settlement. Only a short stroll away, the national parks of Double Head and Bluff Point provided wonderful coastal views from their summits. The Capricorn Coast Yacht Club was built on the edge of the harbour. The club welcomed cruising yachties, and each afternoon we'd wander over for a shower and later have a drink on the verandah while watching the sun go down.

On the evening before Shirley left *Pluto* we dined at nearby Beaches Bistro. It was a good choice. The atmosphere was only surpassed by the fine food, especially the Seafood Chowder, which was a gastronomical experience of the highest order.

"This is the sort of yachting I like," Shirley said as we strolled hand in hand back to the harbour.

"Wimp," I replied.

The loneliness that descended upon me as the plane lifted from Rockhampton Airport, was much worse than when Shirley had left me at Urangan. This time I knew I wouldn't be seeing her again until I was much further up the coast — at least a couple of months. I knew from past experience that it was going to be difficult over the next few days, settling back to being on board by myself.

I drove the rental car back to Yeppoon, a busy shopping centre 8 kilometres north of Rosslyn Bay, and bought enough stores to last me a few weeks. As *Pluto*'s icebox kept ice for nine days, I was able to keep meat, margarine and cheese for that length of time. However, I usually only bought enough meat to last five days. On a few occasions I had the meat vacuum-sealed by the butcher so it would last longer, but found that when I opened the packet the meat was very wet, and when cooked, it was tasteless. Apples, oranges, lemons and limes kept for weeks, while in the vegetable line, potatoes, pumpkin, cabbage, carrots, tomatoes and lettuce fared better than any others. Rather than have the ice melt rapidly by cooling down cans of beer, I drank the beer warm, usually only one can a day with dinner. After nearly two months on *Pluto*, I still found that the inconvenience of not having refrigeration overrode the problems associated with keeping a refrigerator going. I wanted to keep things as simple as possible. The one thing I did miss in the culinary line was a home-cooked roast dinner. I had yet to find a restaurant capable of producing a roast that could even come close to what Shirley made at home.

At first light next morning, I weighed anchor and set off for Svendsen's Beach at Great Keppel Island. I wanted to return there, as there were still many places I wanted to see on the island. I anchored *Pluto* at almost the same spot where I had been with Shirley. The swell had dropped off and it was reasonably comfortable — for me at least. As before, the only other yacht at anchor was *Kestrel*, and she still appeared unattended.

One afternoon when I was motoring back to *Pluto* in the dinghy, I saw a strange-looking craft with a single green and gold sail heading towards Svendsen's Beach. She looked Indonesian. Next morning she was still anchored there and through the binoculars I could see two people sitting in the cockpit. The vessel's name was *Troppo* and she looked to be about 9 metres long. Later in the morning on my way ashore I passed close to them.

"Hello," I said with a wave. "That's an interesting boat you've got there."

"Come aboard," the man replied.

51

I climbed onto the deck and tied the tender's painter onto a cleat.

"I'm Ken Mills and this is my wife Sue," the man said.

I introduced myself, shaking hands with both of them.

"What type of vessel is she?" I asked.

"She's a St Pierre fishing dory," Ken answered. "She was designed for launching off Newfoundland's surf beaches. That's why she has an exaggerated shear and a flat bottom. With the help of a friend I built her on Magnetic Island in 1978 and spent ten years fishing commercially for mackerel. She had a wheelhouse and a large freezer in those days and no sails. A couple of years ago, Sue and I sailed to Indonesia on a friend's yacht. We were really impressed with the rig of the Indonesian fishing boats, so we decided to rig *Troppo* the same way."

Ken went on to tell me that the single unstayed mast was made from an old aluminium spinnaker pole, and the boom and yard attached to it were bamboo that he had cut from the bush in North Queensland.

Sitting in the cockpit was a small, uniquely designed pottery wood-fired barbecue.

"Is that where you do your cooking?" I asked.

"Most of it," Sue replied. "We have a small metho stove below as well. Ken built the barbecue — back home in the Blue Mountains he's a potter."

Next day I invited Ken and Sue over to *Pluto* for a cup of coffee. While we were talking in the cockpit I noticed someone in a dinghy rowing strongly towards *Troppo* from the direction of the Svendsens' property. Then the dinghy diverted and came towards *Pluto*. As it drew closer, I saw the rower was a woman who looked to be in her early thirties.

"Ahoy there!" she shouted. "I *thought* it was you two on board!"

"Hello Lyndie!" Sue replied, waving and smiling broadly as she stood up. "We went ashore to see you yesterday, but Daphne said you were working over at the resort."

"Yes, she told me," Lyndie replied.

"Permission is granted by the captain if you wish to come aboard, ma'am," I said to Lyndie.

"Thank you kind sir," Lyndie replied, giving an exaggerated bow.

Lyndie was no size twelve, but she leapt aboard with the agility of a cat. There were many hugs and kisses between the three friends.

"Lyndie lives with Carl Svendsen over there in paradise," Sue said as she introduced me. "I thought you might have already met Lyndie, she owns the yacht *Windana*."

"I did know a yacht called *Windana*," I replied. "It belonged to Mike and Teddy Shaw. I met them in Pancake Creek while Shirley and I were living at Bustard Head."

"It's the same yacht," Lyndie replied. "I've had her for five years, but I've got her up for sale now. She's just too expensive to maintain when I'm not using her very often. When I sell her, I want to buy a 7 or 8 metre long catamaran to use around the Keppel Bay Islands — something that's fun to sail and which we can moor in shallow water in front of the house, or even let sit on the beach."

"It certainly looks a terrific spot where the houses are built," I replied. "Coconut palms, white sandy beaches. In fact, all the Keppel Islands are outstandingly beautiful."

"They are," Lyndie said. "If you're ashore later in the day, call in to the house. Carl should be home by then."

While I made coffee, Lyndie, Ken and Sue chatted away bringing each other up to date with what they had been doing since last meeting.

"I must be going," Lyndie said eventually. "I'm due at the resort soon. I just called over to say hello, we'll have a good chat later on."

"Lyndie seems to enjoy life to the full," I said to Ken and Sue after she had left *Pluto*.

"Yes," Sue replied, "she's certainly tried it all. She used to be a schoolteacher in South Africa — she taught Zulu and geography. She's backpacked around Europe, lived on an Israeli kibbutz for six months, sailed in the Cape Town to South America Yacht Race, cruised the east coast of South America for a year, then later on returned to cruise the Caribbean, continued on through the Panama Canal and across the Pacific to Sydney."

"Gee, is that all," I laughed.

Later in the day I went ashore and followed a narrow track from the beach up through some coconut palms to a small cottage. A slim, fit looking man in his thirties was unloading some packages from a quad motorbike.

"G'day, are you Carl?" I asked.

"Yes, and you'd be Stuart from *Pluto* wouldn't you? Lyndie said you might drop in. I'll just finish unloading, then we'll have a cup of coffee."

I gave Carl a hand to unload, then he invited me into his cottage. The lounge room led onto an enclosed verandah, which had timber shutters hinged at the top and held open by timber props. Through the openings, the blue water of the bay glistened behind a screen of green, tropical foliage, highlighted by bright red and purple flowers. Original paintings of different parts of the island hung in each room, together with wall and ceiling hangs comprising of a combination of multicoloured wool, driftwood, shells and birds' feathers. Shells and other nautical bric-a-brac adorned timber cupboards and shelves.

"You have a beautiful setting here, Carl. Lyndie told me you've spent all your life on the island, I can understand why you've never had any inclination to leave."

"Yes, I did schooling by correspondence," Carl replied. "And I do go ashore occasionally, but Lyndie jokes that I don't go any further than the Mitre 10 store in Yeppoon."

Carl told me that his mother and father — Daphne and Punch — moved to the island in 1950 to run sheep and catch fish. They built the house where Carl and Lyndie now live, but some years ago moved into a larger house, which they built about 50 metres away.

We walked back down to the beach, where Carl showed me some light-weight dinghies he had built. Moored further out was a dory fitted with out-riggers, which Carl used around the islands for commercial fishing.

"The yacht *Kestrel* that's moored out there, is that yours?" I queried.

"It's Punch's," Carl replied. "He built it himself, all with hand tools."

"That's one hell of an effort," I said. "By the way, what's the word written on the stern below the name *Kestrel* — Woppo . . . something or other?"

"Woppaburra," Carl answered. "It's the Aboriginal name for Great Keppel Island — it means 'home of the islanders'."

"I remember someone telling me years ago that the Aborigines who lived on the Keppel Islands were pygmies. That wouldn't be right though, would it Carl?"

"No, but there is *some* truth in that statement," Carl said. "Early accounts describe the Islanders as a 'diminutive race'. It's been proven that island groups such as the Tasmanians or Mornington Islanders were certainly smaller than the mainland tribes. That's probably where the pygmy story originated."

Carl went on to tell me that the Keppel Islanders had been shockingly treated by the early pioneering mainland settlers, who occasionally visited the islands to 'disperse' the Aborigines. During 1867, whites landed on Great Keppel Island and drove eighty-four Aborigines into a cave. It is suspected that none of the eighty-four survived. Later on, Aborigines were forcibly removed from the islands by pioneers to work on sugar and coffee plantations. Some escaped and tried to swim back to their islands; a few made it, but most drowned or were taken by sharks. As cattle, sheep and then goats were introduced to Great Keppel, the remaining Aborigines became fringe-dwellers around the homestead, most of them women, who received a few handouts in return for labour and sexual favours to passing fishermen and visitors from the mainland. Eventually, in 1902, after much bureaucratic argument and indecision, the remaining Islanders, most of whom were suffering from venereal disease, were removed from the island and taken to Aboriginal reserves.

"Tragedy in paradise, eh?" I said thoughtfully to Carl.

"Yes, it's an ugly part of the history of the Keppel Islands that not too many people know about," Carl replied.

Next day I returned to Rosslyn Bay to reprovision with ice and cold goods in preparation for the next leg north. I was quite apprehensive about this sec-tion of the trip. I knew I was entering the most rugged and isolated section of Queensland's central coast — Shoalwater Bay and Broad Sound, an area of 5,000 square miles littered with islands, rocks, reefs and sandbanks, made more difficult to navigate than usual because of its 9 metre tidal range and currents of up to 7 knots. But over the past couple of months I had learnt that the best way to overcome apprehension in regard to sailing, is to do your navigation homework accurately and just get on with the thing that you're apprehensive about. I couldn't have asked for a better weather forecast — 15 knots from the south-east, with little change predicted for the next few days.

Chapter 8

LOO WITH A VIEW

Shortly before dawn I motored *Pluto* out of Rosslyn Bay Boat Harbour and headed north. There wasn't the slightest breeze, so I engaged the autopilot and continued to motor while I went below to cook some breakfast, returning to the cockpit every five minutes or so to check for approaching vessels, but *Pluto* appeared to be the only boat in the area.

When the predicted 15 knot south-easterly came in during midmorning I hoisted the main and genoa, stopped the motor, disengaged the autopilot and took over at the tiller. I had developed the habit of using the autopilot while motoring, but under sail I would hand steer for about an hour then connect the autopilot for a short break while I marked *Pluto*'s position on the chart, or walked around the deck to check the sails and stretch my legs. Sometimes I'd go out on the bowsprit and lean over the pulpit to watch the bow cut and dip its way smoothly through the clean blue water; often, a pod of dolphins would swim beside the bow, their heads and backs clearing the water every now and then as they took a gasp of air before diving below the surface to repeat the same performance over and over. At other times I'd climb the main mast-steps to the spreaders and stand there hanging on to the rigging with a bird's-eye view of the yacht heeled over, forging its way through the backs of the waves leaving a trail of foaming white water in its wake. Then I'd return to the cockpit and disengage the autopilot for another stint at the helm. There was little to beat the enjoyment and exhilaration of sitting at the tiller, feeling the yacht's every move as it made its way purposefully along the coast.

And what a coast — isolated and rugged, the tree-covered mountains dropped sharply to meet long stretches of golden sand. The only sign of habitation was high on the bald headland of Stockyard Point, 20 miles north of Rosslyn Bay, where there were a number of what appeared to be fishermen's shacks. At Cape Manifold I altered course slightly and headed for the southern entrance to Port Clinton, where I intended to anchor for a couple of days. The chart showed that the entrance to Port Clinton was 3 miles wide with a shallow bar extending across most of its width. I had calculated my arrival to coincide with the top half of the flood tide, so I had plenty of water depth; and as the sea was moderate there were no breakers over the bar. Safely behind the headland, I anchored in 6 metres of water. There were no other boats in sight.

I hadn't comprehended from the chart just how extensive an area Port Clinton was. From where *Pluto* was anchored, it was almost 5 miles across to the north-western side of the inlet and 7 miles to the south. The name Port Clinton sounded rather pretentious, considering there was no port here. In fact, there was nothing man-made here at all that I could see. I had read that Port Clinton was originally named Port Bowen in 1802 by the explorer Matthew Flinders during his exploration of the east coast. Flinders charted the waterways, found fresh water and cut pine logs from nearby Entrance Island for repairs to his ships *Investigator* and *Lady Nelson*. Flinders noted that although the area's sandy and stony ground made it unsuitable for cultivation, the waterway did offer good shelter for ships.

In 1823 Surveyor-General John Oxley left Sydney in the *Mermaid* with instructions to investigate Moreton Bay, Port Curtis and Port Bowen for the suitability of establishing convict settlements. Oxley reached Port Curtis and rejected it as a possible site, but adverse weather conditions decided him to abort his trip further north to Port Bowen. It was therefore decided that Moreton Bay should be the place for a penal settlement.

During the 1870s and 80s, settlers who had taken up land in the area for cattle production, made approaches to the government to establish a cattle-loading wharf at Port Bowen. But in 1887, although 1,500 acres in the Mt Flinders area — between Cape Clinton and Port Bowen — was gazetted as a "Reserve for Shipping Purposes", it was a private landholder who funded and built a wharf and cattle yards below Mt Flinders the same year. However, the problems in moving cattle over such extremely harsh terrain proved too difficult for man and beast. Within a few months, during which time three loads of cattle were transported south by the steamship *Delcomyn*, the project was abandoned.

The name Port Bowen was changed to Port Clinton in the 1890s to avoid confusion after an overseas vessel bound for the busy port of Bowen some 200 miles to the north, mistakenly stood off Port Bowen and fruitlessly signalled for the services of a pilot.

Port Clinton was part of a huge area of land taken over by the Army in 1965 to establish a military training base. Known as the Shoalwater Bay Military Exercise Area, it is occasionally closed to private vessels during exercises. The sailing guidebook advised that warnings of closure dates are broadcast over the marine radio and through Notices To Mariners. I had heard that most people on private vessels, especially slower moving cruising yachts, found the closures inconvenient, as it not only meant a long overnight sail from Rosslyn Bay to the nearest suitable anchorage, but also missing out on visiting a beautiful section of coastline.

Despite being a military exercise area, private enterprise proposals to establish a deepwater harbour, bulk coal–handling facility and rail link between the Central Queensland coalfields and Port Clinton were made to the government in the 1980s. After extensive commissions of inquiry regarding the environmental management of the area, it is unlikely that such proposals will ever become a reality.

I thought of all the diverse and grandiose plans that had been proposed for this solitary sheltered waterway, and yet here it was with no visible difference from how Matthew Flinders had seen it nearly 200 years ago.

Probably the only difference was the danger of unexploded ammunition lying around the military training area. The sailing guidebook warned that because of this danger the Army prohibited public access above high-water mark. I reasoned that the chance of being blown up was pretty slim; after all, during military manoeuvres, army personnel had to walk around the place. Nevertheless, next day when I went ashore, I tended to stick to the beach, rather than venture inland. The low cliffs beside the beach were covered with beautiful orchids, most of which were in flower. Never before had I seen so many covering such a wide area. Just as abundant were the sweet, fat oysters that covered the rocks. I collected a couple of dozen for dinner that evening.

I weighed anchor next morning and headed for Island Head Creek, 16 miles further north. This section of coast was also part of the Shoalwater Bay Military Exercise Area. The entry into the creek, between two, high, sparsely vegetated rocky headlands, was spectacular. Although the creek was navigable for about 5 miles, I anchored a mile in from the entrance across from a glorious looking white sandy beach that, according to the chart, ran for 5 kilometres along to Pinetrees Point. Again I was the only vessel anchored in the creek.

Next day I packed some lunch and motored ashore. Shaded by overhanging casuarina trees, I slowly beachcombed along the high-water mark, investigating the flotsam, jetsam and shells cast up by the tide. I climbed the steep slope from the beach to the top of Pinetrees Point and had lunch high on a huge boulder set amidst a forest of ancient Hoop Pine trees that looked out across the endless ocean.

Later in the day I headed back along the beach, lazy bubbling waves periodically sweeping across the glistening sand and spilling over my bare feet. The sparkling clear water, although quite chilly, was so enticing I plunged into the sea and floated weightlessly on my back. With my head arched back, and arms and legs outstretched, I gazed up at the cloudless, bright blue sky, and let the clean, refreshing salt water wash over me. I looked at my watch — almost three o'clock. Ah, I thought, I can swim for a while longer, and then by the time I walk back along the beach and return to *Pluto*, it will be just the right time to have a drink in the cockpit and watch the sun go down. Then I realised the significance of what I had so casually thought. Three o'clock on a Wednesday afternoon and here I was swimming in paradise on the Barrier Reef coast, not another soul in sight, contemplating a rum in the cockpit of the yacht, that for many years I had dreamt of owning. Sure, I had worked long and hard to be in this position, but even so, I knew that many other people worked long and hard too, but for one reason or another their dreams didn't come to fruition. I felt gloriously happy. And probably for the first time *really* appreciated just how fortunate I was.

The chart showed it was a full day's sail to my next destination — Middle Percy Island — which lay 45 miles off the coast. I decided to break the journey by anchoring overnight at Hexham Island. The tide was just beginning to ebb when I left Island Head Creek, and three hours later, when *Pluto* was halfway to Hexham Island, I found I had to steer almost 25° off the plotted course to compensate for the mass of water that was pouring out of Broad Sound Channel. The wind against the tide created confused seas, making it an uncomfortable sail. It was with some relief that I dropped anchor in the sheltered bay behind Hexham Island.

The south-easterly breeze freshened to 20 knots during the night and continued into the morning, making it a boisterous but enjoyable sail to Middle Percy Island. By midday *Pluto* was anchored in West Bay along with three other yachts.

Shirley and I had visited Middle Percy Island on a number of occasions fifteen years ago, while working as relief lightkeepers on the now demanned Pine Islet lightstation, which I could see a mile across the channel from where *Pluto* was anchored. During our visits we had got to know Andy Martin, who acquired the lease of Middle Percy Island in 1964. I knew that Andy was still living there, and had been joined by Jonathan and Lys Hickling and their two young sons. Jonathan had written to me a year ago after reading my book *The Lighthouse Keepers* in which there was a story and photograph of the Torres Strait pearling lugger *Ruby Charlotte*. Jonathan told me that he and Lys now owned *Ruby Charlotte*, which was moored at Middle Percy and used for bringing supplies from the mainland every three months or so. They had invited Shirley and me to call in and meet them whenever we were in the area.

I rowed ashore to the beach at West Bay. Little had changed at this delightful spot since my last visit; only the dozens of coconut palms planted by Andy when he first arrived on the island had grown much taller. The old telephone shed was still adorned with hundreds of plaques displaying the names of boats that had visited the island over the years. And the large A-frame structure, built by Andy in the 1970s and known as the Percy

Hilton, was still the island's 'emporium' with tables covered with bottles of honey, jam, lime juice, vegetables and goat skins, all for sale on an honour system. The only addition was a large barbecue area at the rear of the Percy Hilton, which most likely had been built by yachties for yachties.

Next day I set off along the steep 4 kilometre vehicle track that led from West Bay up to the homestead. It was an energetic but extremely pleasant walk through vegetation that varied from open forest to rainforest, with a number of spots that not only provided magnificent views across the islands in the Broad Sound area, but also provided a good excuse to stop and catch my breath. At the top of one particularly steep pinch, Andy had nailed a sign to a tree, which read:

FEELING TIRED? WELL, YOU'RE NOT NEARLY HALFWAY
THERE YET

Along the way, there were more signs written in a similar vein. I had a bit of a chuckle to myself reminiscing that one of Andy's dislikes was visitors who arrived at the homestead only to complain about how difficult the walk was. It was all right for Andy who, when I met him fifteen years ago, was an extremely fit fifty-three year old who thought nothing of carrying a 20 litre drum of fuel in each hand and a heavy bag of flour on his back from West Bay to the homestead without stopping. But for most of us mere mortals it was a different story. One overweight yachtie had told me he had found Andy's signs far from humorous. After he had huffed and puffed his way past a number of signs, he turned to his mate and gasped:

"I haven't even met Andy Martin yet, but I hate the bastard's guts already."

I arrived at the old homestead to be greeted by a couple of barking dogs with wide grins and furiously wagging tails. Andy appeared on the verandah.

"Hello, Andy. I'm Stuart. I met you when I was a relief lightkeeper at Pine."

"Yes, Stuart, I remember you. Come on up."

Andy had aged drastically since we last met. Aided by a walking stick, he hobbled through the kitchen, past a blackened wood stove and into the large dining room. Not much had changed in the house since my last visit — a young goat lay sleeping in a cardboard box near the stove, a couple of chooks walked about the kitchen, another chook sat nesting on an antiquated washing machine, while some swallows flew in and out of the house through the open shutters.

"How have you been keeping, Andy?" I asked.

"Oh, not too bad," Andy replied. "I've slowed down a bit lately. I find it difficult to get around the way I used to. Jonathan and Lys do most of the work in the garden and around the place now. I still make bread and jam, but for the last year or so I've spent most of my time writing a book."

"Oh. What's the book about?"

"About the state of the world and its future. In fact, I'd like to have a talk to you about it later. Not so much about the content, but just the layout and a few other things."

"Yes, sure Andy."

"Would you like to stay for lunch?" Andy asked. "Jonathan and Lys will be here soon. They have lunch with me most days. Jonathan's parents will be joining us too. They've flown over from England for a couple of weeks — they're going back at the end of the week."

"Thanks Andy, I'd like that."

Andy and I went on chatting about the people both of us had known while I had been working on Pine Islet. Before long I heard voices outside.

"That's Jon and Lys now," Andy said.

A group of people made their way into the dining room. Andy introduced me.

"After reading your book, I feel as though I already know you," Lys said, shaking hands.

Although Jonathan was taller than Lys, they were both thin and wiry, almost to the point of gauntness. But the muscles in their arms and legs displayed the signs of continual hard physical work. Both exuded a no-nonsense inner strength and determination. Their two sons, Jacob, seven, and Justin, four, looked even more fragile than their parents, but their eyes sparkled with an uninhibited excitement for life. Jonathan's parents looked more my type — a good covering of flesh to keep you warm on those cold, winter nights.

Lys prepared a salad for lunch while Jacob and Justin placed various plates and dishes on the table.

"Do you and Lys live in the homestead with Andy?" I asked Jonathan.

"No, we live 400 metres away in the Rondavel — just off the 'short track'."

"The Rondavel?" I queried.

"Yes, it's an octagonal building, based on the lines of an African round house. We built it from the island's stone and timber. You'll have to come over and have a look at it later."

"I'd like to."

After lunch I accompanied Jon and Lys to the Rondavel. The building oozed a rugged rustic charm. Powered by wind generator and solar energy, the family also had the comfort of a hot shower, the cold water being heated as it passed through a wood-fired heater tank on the way to the nozzle. However, I thought the toilet left a lot to be desired, especially on wet, windy nights. No walls or roof — just a seat perched over a deep hole in the middle of the paddock; I must admit though, it had the most wonderful sea views and plenty of fresh air, and you could watch the goats and horses grazing around you.

From past experience with Andy, I knew that life for Jonathan and Lys on Middle Percy wasn't just a matter of lolling on the beach waiting for the coconuts to drop off the trees. In return for island residency, Andy demanded six days a week hard work, tending the large vegetable garden, fencing, road and dam repairs, making honey, killing goats for meat and tanning the skins, looking after the ponies and the other one hundred and one jobs associated with self-sufficiency. As well, Lys had to educate Jacob through correspondence lessons. The only time off they had was on Saturday, the island's Sabbath.

"How long are you staying at Percy?" Lys asked.

"If the weather holds, I was thinking of staying about a week," I replied, "so I can have a good look around the island."

"Well, you'll have to come up for dinner some night; and make sure you call in for lunch anytime you want — we always have lunch at Andy's."

"Thanks Lys, that's very much appreciated," I replied, then went on, "It's hard not to notice a great change in Andy since I last met him."

"A lot of people who knew Andy years ago say that," Lys answered. "He's got heart, back and hip problems as well as a hernia. His hip is his worst problem because it just makes it so difficult for him to get around. He really should have a hip replacement."

"I know Andy hates doctors, but has he had any medical help?" I asked.

"Yes, he went into Mackay Hospital for tests in regard to the hip replacement, but walked out before the tests were completed. He said he's got no intention of going back to the mainland again."

"Yes, that sounds like Andy."

Each day I awoke to perfect weather. Immediately after breakfast I went ashore to explore the island. From the 221 metre summit of Castle Rock — from where there was one of the most spectacular seascapes of the Barrier Reef coast — to the magnificent sandy beaches on the island's southern side. Mostly I went alone, but sometimes I arranged to accompany Jonathan's parents and the two boys. Young Jacob and Justin knew the island backwards. At a great rate of knots they led us along barely recognisable tracks to Mt Armitage — the island's highest peak, and to the summit of Dead Sheep Hill to see the remains of a 2 metre square hole dug in hard shale by a former island resident who one night had dreamt that a treasure of gold bullion was buried at this spot. Perhaps he ran out of picks and shovels before he ran out of enthusiasm, but the treasure wasn't found.

"How would you like a sail to Marble Island with us tomorrow on *Ruby Charlotte*?" Jonathan asked me one morning while I was talking to him on the VHF radio.

Jonathan explained that because his mother had suffered severe seasickness on *Ruby Charlotte* while sailing the 70 miles from Mackay to Middle Percy, it was decided that on her return trip she would sail only 20 miles to Marble Island cattle property, where arrangements had been made for a light aircraft to land on the island's airstrip. On the incoming plane would be a volunteer teacher who would sail with us back to Middle Percy to spend six weeks with Jonathan and Lys for the purpose of teaching Jacob.

"You're on — it's an offer I can't refuse," I replied.

"OK, we'll pick you up from *Pluto* in the dinghy about seven o'clock tomorrow morning."

The 20 metre ketch *Ruby Charlotte* had undergone a few changes since I was last aboard her in Torres Strait. At that time she was engaged in the pearling industry and run by an all Islander crew using old-style hard hat diving equipment. She was still gaff rigged, but the tiller had been replaced by a wheel, and the on-deck wood-fired cooking box replaced by a gas stove.

While Jonathan and I winched in the anchor, Lys took the helm, controlling the gears by means of a length of rope and numerous pulleys that disappeared into the bowels of the engine room. To make the trip as comfortable as possible for Jonathan's parents we lashed two large cane lounge chairs, complete with cushions, to the deck.

The 15 knot breeze and sea were dead ahead, but the powerful six-cylinder Gardner diesel motor pushed *Ruby Charlotte* effortlessly along, her bowsprit dipping to skim the wavetops.

Three hours later we anchored in Homestead Bay right beside the Marble Island airstrip. We motored ashore to be welcomed by Allistair and Jillian Brice, the managers of the Duke Islands Pastoral Company and the only residents on the island.

"Well," Allistair laughed, "after all this time, it's good to meet our next door neighbours. Jillian's got some lunch ready, so let's make our way up to the homestead."

On the way, Allistair told me that he and Jillian had lived on the island for two and a half years, running a few hundred head of breeders on Marble Island and two other nearby islands — Hunter and Tynemouth.

Lunch was a sumptuous affair — plates of tender Marble Island beef and mountains of fresh Percy Island bread and salad, all spread out on a large dining table. I felt extremely embarrassed as I opened my backpack and withdrew my sole contribution — one tin of Scottish sardines.

"We understand, Stuart," Jonathan said in an affected Oxford accent, as the others let out great peels of laughter. "After all, you are a yachtie *and* a Scot."

During lunch there was much talk of bartering Percy Island bees for Marble Island turkeys, produce for calves and goats for deer.

"There's still some time before the plane's due, how about a look around the island?" Allistair offered.

There was no doubt that the Brices had every convenience — extensive farm machinery, 240 volt diesel generators, walk-in cold room and freezer and regular delivery of bread, vegetables and mail by air. The Brices were only 20 miles away from Andy and the Hicklings, but a universe away in lifestyle. But despite the differences, there was an obvious camaraderie between the two families; they were, after all, 'island people'.

"I assume that Marble Island was named because there's marble on the island," I said to Allistair.

"That's right," Allistair replied. "Our boss, Rex Jones, who holds the lease of the island, built a holiday home further along the beach — the floor's made of island marble. Come and have a look at it."

Rex's house was situated a short distance back from the beach. The marble floor and the use of quality timber complemented the uninterrupted panoramic view of the beautiful bay that could be seen through the extensive lounge room windows.

Our drooling was interrupted by the drone of a light aircraft. We made our way back to the airstrip, welcomed the volunteer teacher and farewelled Jonathan's parents and the Brices. Soon we were back on board *Ruby Charlotte* and underway. The volunteer teacher, June Schulz, appeared to be in her early sixties and had an old-world regal air about her. She wore an extremely wide-brimmed straw hat. And as she settled down in the large cane chair, which was still lashed to the aft deck, she could easily have been mistaken for actress Katharine Hepburn playing her part alongside Humphrey Bogart in *The African Queen*.

While Jonathan and I were on the foredeck hoisting the headsail, we heard a cry from Lys at the helm.

"Jon! There's smoke coming from below decks!"

Jonathan and I immediately turned round to see a stream of thick smoke pouring through the rear companionway hatch. Both of us dashed below towards the motor. Visibility was less than a metre, and the atmosphere stifling.

"I think I've found it!" Jonathan shouted after a while. "The exhaust has fractured!"

Jonathan fumbled around and brought out some sheet metal and asbestos rope. Just short of asphyxiation we managed to splint and bind the fracture, reducing the fumes by half.

"There's not much more we can do until we get back to Percy," Jonathan said.

"It seems to be holding OK," I answered. "We'll just keep an eye on it."

We returned to the deck and explained to Lys and June what had happened. June was still sitting in the cane chair, enveloped in a haze of exhaust fumes and salt-spray, holding on to her wide-brimmed straw hat which was now flapping madly in the strengthening breeze.

We arrived back at Middle Percy just on dusk, and carried June's luggage across the beach to the waiting Land Rover.

"It's all quite an adventure," June commented.

If June considered that an adventure, I thought, wait until she makes her first visit to the Rondavel's alfresco thunderbox.

"It's all quite an adventure."

Chapter 9

THAR SHE BLOWS!

West Bay was like a millpond. The weather bureau had predicted 5 to 10 knot variable winds throughout the day, with a possible 10 to 15 knot south-westerly change during the evening. West Bay, as its name implies, is open to the west. But there hadn't been a breath of breeze all day, and it appeared that the calm conditions would continue well into the night. And even if a 15 knot south-westerly did develop, I thought the anchorage would be tolerable until daybreak, at which time I planned to leave.

I had said my farewells to Andy and the Hicklings earlier in the day, and hung the mandatory plaque with *Pluto*'s name on it in the Percy Hilton. While ashore I had met a couple from the catamaran *Shalimar II*, who invited me over to their yacht for a sundowner. Compared to *Pluto*, *Shalimar II* was luxury afloat, from its powerful diesel motors and electric anchor winch, to its large dining table and glass-fronted cocktail cabinet.

Shortly after nightfall a breeze came in from the *north*-west and within a few minutes increased to 25 knots. I hurriedly left *Shalimar II* and only just made it back to *Pluto* without swamping the tender. I considered moving, but the night was pitch black, and the only nearby suitable anchorage — the south side of Pine Islet — was rock and coral strewn. I was also concerned that even if I did make it safely to Pine Islet, the wind might swing from the north-west to the predicted south-west, which would leave me more exposed than at my present position in West Bay. The other alternative was to head out to sea. I decided to stay where I was. Although uncomfortable, I felt confident that *Pluto* was securely anchored in good holding ground. I thought that perhaps a front was passing and would soon settle down.

I was wrong. About 10 p.m. the wind swung to the south-west and screamed in at 35 to 40 knots. *Pluto*'s foredeck began dipping beneath the waves. And when the bow was up, the stern was down, letting waves flood the cockpit. As well, the ketch was rolling drunkenly from side to side, flooding the port and starboard decks in turn. It was like being anchored in heavy surf.

I couldn't leave now, even if I wanted to. The strain on the anchor chain was tremendous. There was no way I could winch it in by hand; and even if I had, I doubted the motor's ability to push *Pluto* through the surf and away from shore.

Every half-hour I went on deck to be swamped by waves as I grappled my way to the bow to check the anchor chain and rope snubber. Only those few steel links stood between safety and destruction on the rocky lee shore. At first, each time I clambered out to the cockpit I put on my wet-weather jacket before making my way along the deck, but it was so ineffectual I eventually threw it to one side and wore only swimming togs.

When I returned below, I stood at each porthole in turn, checking the position of the other yachts' riding lights in case *Pluto* was dragging anchor. As the night wore on I grew progressively wearier, but sleep was impossible. Every now and then I'd wedge myself into my bunk by means of the lee-cloth and pillows, and lie for a short time listening to the wind shriek past the rigging and the waves crash against the hull. The contents of the cup-boards and lockers, which I normally made sure were secure and soundless, rattled loudly and continually as if a giant hand had lifted the yacht and was shaking it up and down like a child's moneybox.

In the early hours of the morning my heart skipped more than a few beats, when I looked through the porthole and saw *Shalimar II*'s masthead anchor light moving seaward. That meant only one thing — *Pluto* was dragging towards the shore. But I found it puzzling that there hadn't been a change in the motion of *Pluto*. I spun round and looked through the starboard side porthole at the other two yachts; their lights appeared stationary. *Shalimar II*'s anchor light was now moving quickly to seaward. Suddenly I realised what was happening — *Shalimar II* had up-anchored and was using her powerful motors to move further away from shore. By rights she should have been displaying her navigation and running lights. That way, other vessels would have known she was voluntarily underway. I relaxed a little, but my heart didn't; I could still feel it pounding away against my ribs.

The night seemed endless. As dawn arrived, the wind eased fractionally. I crawled out onto the heaving deck and made my way slowly to the mast. Amidst thick, cold sheets of spray, I steadied myself with one arm wrapped around the boom and began to set a No.2 reef in the mainsail. At times, during a succession of extremely large waves, I had to stop what I was doing and hang on with both arms, while a tangle of reefing lines swept around my legs. With the reef complete, I went back to the cockpit and started the motor, returned to the mast and hoisted the main before making my way to the bow. I knelt on the deck and began winching in the anchor. Almost instantaneously, the bow rose sharply then dropped quickly from under me. Momentarily I was suspended in midair, then my knees crashed down on top of the winch at the same time as the bow rose to meet them. I grimaced in pain as I wedged myself into the anchor-well and continued to winch. I could see streams of diluted blood running across the deck. Each time the bow dipped below the surface, waves swept across the deck and exploded against my body. In contrast to being saturated from head to foot, my mouth was so dry my tongue and palate felt glued together. With straining arms I slowly winched in the anchor chain link by link. The 40 metres of chain that I had out was marked every 6 metres. It seemed to take an interminable time for each mark to appear over the bow roller. At last I felt the anchor break free. I wound like fury to get it to deck level, then dived back to the cockpit, grabbed the tiller and gave the motor full throttle. From the moment the anchor broke free to when I returned to the cockpit, the waves had pushed *Pluto* dangerously close to shore. The motor alone wasn't anywhere near powerful enough to make headway through the breakers. Fortunately the wind had pushed *Pluto*'s bow to starboard, so, using a combination of sail and full throttle, I managed to at least hold the yacht's position on a close hauled port tack. At each breaker, *Pluto*'s bow rose towards the heavens, then plunged downwards lifting the propeller clear of the water as the motor screamed in protest. I turned the bow further away from the wind. I felt the propeller dig in, and before long I could see that we were ever so slowly pulling away from shore. Little by little we cleared the bay.

Out in open water, I checked my injured knee. There had been a lot of blood, but luckily the wound was superficial. I set a pocket-handkerchief size jib, and on a port reach plunged across a foam-streaked sea of toppling breakers towards the shelter of Digby Island 22 miles away.

Two hours later, *Pluto* was still on a port reach with the wind blowing 25 to 30 knots from the south-west. I was anticipating the comfort of being anchored behind Digby Island, just 9 miles ahead, when something towards the horizon caught my eye. It was a whale, leaping clear of the water about a mile away on my starboard side. Over the last couple of months I had seen a few humpback whales in the distance, but they had done no more than give a few tail-slaps. Until now I had never seen a whale breach, and even at a mile distant it was an awesome sight. Unlike the thousands of whale-watching tourists at Hervey Bay who can't seem to get close enough to these giants of the deep, I was perfectly happy to keep whales at a very safe distance from *Pluto*. I had read that a mature humpback weighs about 48 tonnes. My ketch weighs 5 tonnes. It didn't require too much intelligence to calculate that should those two objects collide, *Pluto* and I were going to come off second best. I had also read many accounts of yachts that had been sunk or badly damaged by whales.

It was with more than a passing interest that I tried to keep the monster in sight. A few minutes later I saw a blow; the whale was closer than before, but well behind me. I relaxed somewhat, assuming it was travelling in the opposite direction.

About thirty minutes later, a whale suddenly surfaced about 20 metres away to starboard, barrelling along on a 90° collision course with the yacht. I instinctively pushed the tiller over, turning the vessel straight into the wind. The headsail backed, the yacht stopped dead in its track as large waves pounded the deck. I hadn't felt a collision, and the whale had disappeared, but I was extremely shaken at such a close encounter. It took about ten minutes of hard wrestling with flogging sails to get back on course.

I had no idea if it was the same whale that I had seen breach earlier, but the vision of its shiny, black body erupting from the boiling ocean was etched into my memory forever.

Twenty minutes later the same thing happened, only this time the whale surfaced and lunged so close to the yacht that I didn't have time to turn the tiller. The giant disappeared somewhere beneath the centre of the boat. Again I didn't know whether or not it was the same whale, but this time it had been close enough for me to see scars and barnacles on its flesh. I was at my wits' end. What was this bloody thing trying to do? I hadn't a clue. But if it wasn't for the 30 knot wind, I'm sure my hair would have been standing on end.

I was as taut as a coiled spring during the remainder of the trip to Digby, just waiting for another performance from Moby Dick. If someone had said boo to me I would have jumped out of my skin. Thankfully, I reached the island without further incident.

Safely at anchor, and a few quick rums later to settle my jangled nerves, I opened a book about whales that I had put aside to read at a later date. It stated that during the mating period male humpbacks show aggression towards each other by lunging, fluke slapping and breaching. Other reasons for breaching were thought to be the whale ridding itself of whale lice or "inspecting the environment". Which got me thinking. Had Moby Dick lunged at *Pluto* thinking my little yacht was a competing male, or was he just preparing himself for a good look around? In the noisy, rough conditions such as we had been in, do whales have the intelligence to know what's happening on top of the water some distance away? Perhaps he hadn't known I was there at all. Or perhaps he had known, and was just having a game. What were the odds of a 48 tonne whale breaching, only to find himself on an unavoidable collision course with a yacht?

I slammed the book shut. To hell with whales. After thirty-six hours without sleep and the sort of night and day that I'd had, I was too tired to care. Although there was only a slight swell where *Pluto* was anchored, vicious bullets of wind shot down the slopes of Digby Island and swept across the bay, heeling the yacht over as it jerked and swung on its chain. But compared to West Bay it was heaven. I made an omelette and then crashed onto my bunk. The last thing I remember thinking about was slimy black whale flesh erupting from a monstrous sea.

If someone had said boo to me I would have jumped out of my skin.

Chapter 10

HELP! CALL ME A CAB

Contrary to the burst of appalling weather I had just experienced, I awoke from a deep sleep to find blue sky and a 15 knot south-easterly breeze. Feeling the need to relax for a while, I spent a couple of days exploring Digby Island before weighing anchor and setting off for Mackay. If anyone was psyched up to keep a vigilant watch for whales it was me, but I didn't see a sign of one during the 45 mile trip. *Pluto* averaged 5 knots, arriving at the entrance to Mackay Outer Harbour during midafternoon.

The man-made harbour had been built mainly to cater for large ships loading sugar and grain, but at the south-western corner of the harbour there were a number of concrete jetties to accommodate commercial tourist boats. A little further along, a series of fore and aft piles had been installed for small boats. Space was usually at a premium, as most of the piles were occupied by vessels owned by local residents. Because of this, I had radioed the Harbour Master earlier in the day to confirm that a space to suit *Pluto*'s length was available.

During our employment as lightkeepers, Shirley and I had spent a few nights in Mackay Outer Harbour on board the lighthouse stores boat *Saramoa* which, at the time, was contracted to do the Pine Islet run. On those occasions we found that the surge running into the harbour varied from uncomfortable to outright atrocious. I knew that the surge, together with the wind, was going to make tying onto the piles difficult for me as a single-handed sailor. As well, the close proximity of surrounding yachts left little margin for error. It would mean nosing the bow in at just the right spot to give me enough time to leave the tiller, run up to the bow, and with the aid of a boathook pick up the line attached to the pile — all before the wind blew the yacht out of reach of the line. Then I'd have to launch the tender, tie a long line from the yacht's stern to the pile, return to the yacht and pull in the stern.

As I was making for the narrow space between the piles, I saw two young men in a small dinghy coming towards me.

"I don't suppose you'd give me a hand to tie up in return for a warm can of beer or a rum without any ice?" I asked with a grin.

"That's why we're here," one of them answered. "Not for the booze — just to give you a hand. We heard you on the radio and calculated you'd be in about this time."

Within five harassment free minutes, *Pluto* was securely berthed.

"Thanks very much," I said to the men. "Come aboard and have that drink."

"We'll give it a miss, thanks all the same," one of them replied. "We're leaving early in the morning and we've still got a few more jobs to do on the yacht. But we're going up to the yacht club for dinner later if you'd like to join us."

"OK, I'll see you there. Is the club still just round the corner? It's nearly fifteen years since I was here last."

"Yep, it's still in the same place."

Later in the day I rowed ashore to a small sandy beach at the end of the harbour and walked over to the Mackay Cruising Yacht Club. Situated at the edge of an extensive park scattered with coconut palms, the club had undergone a few improvements since my last visit. I introduced myself to the woman behind the bar and asked if it was all right to use the club's facilities.

"Sure, luv," she replied. "The showers are along the corridor to the left. There's a washing machine and dryer at the bottom of the side stairs. Lunch and dinner are served seven days a week, and the bar stays open until only two drinkers are left."

What else did a cruising yachtie need in port?

My first shower for more than a fortnight was sublime — an endless supply of steaming hot needles of freshwater strafing my entire body. It sure beat my usual on board 'bucket bath' — 50 millimetres of water in the bottom of a bucket. Equally as good were the few icy-cold beers I had during the evening.

One other thing I was really looking forward to in Mackay was getting a haircut. My hair had grown well over my ears and was driving me mad. It was 6 kilometres from the harbour into Mackay, so I assumed there was a bus service running in to the city. I went ashore next morning and walked over to an old bloke who was sitting outside the small harbourside kiosk.

"G'day," I said. "Do you know if there's a bus service from here into Mackay, or do I have to get a cab?"

"There's no bus service, mate," he answered. "But don't worry about getting a cab, just hitch a ride — a lot of yachties do it."

Hitch a ride? It was well over thirty years since I last hitched a ride. But what the hell? I set off walking towards Mackay and, feeling extremely self-conscious, stuck my thumb out. The first car that came along stopped beside me.

"Going into Mackay?" the elderly male driver asked.

"Sure am."

"Well, hop in."

"How are you keeping?" I asked when we were underway.

"Not too good actually," the driver replied before launching into a detailed and gory description of every illness and operation he had undergone during his life. No matter how many times I tried to change the subject, the driver continued with horror stories of how the simplest of symptoms had resulted in major medical problems. I got out of his car in Mackay feeling certain I was suffering at least half the symptoms he described.

The first barber's shop I came to had about eight people waiting. Blow that, I said to myself, and walked further along the footpath. The next barber's shop I came to had no one waiting. Ha, Ha, I thought, all those stupid people waiting at the other shop. I went in and sat on the chair. The barber was a pleasant young bloke barely out of his teens.

"Is this your own business?" I asked, as he snipped away.

"No, it's Dad's business," he replied. "And before him it was Grandad's. I'm just helping out while Dad's away on holidays."

Fifteen minutes later, when a mirror was held in front of my face to inspect the finished result, I realised why there had been eight people waiting in the other shop. Where my hair should have been short, it was long, and where it should have been long, it was short. And the long tufts of hair growing out of my ears, which every other barber always trimmed, were left uncut. A mate of mine used to say there's only ten days difference between a good haircut and a bad haircut. I made a bet with myself that young Sweeney Todd from Mackay was going to prove him wrong.

On my return journey, I left the city, crossed the bridge over the Pioneer River and once more stuck my thumb out. I had hardly walked 100 metres when a rusty, battered old utility pulled up.

"Where are you going?" asked the young driver of Italian appearance.

"To the harbour,"

"Well, I'm going to the dump — that'll get you halfway there."

"Fair enough, thanks very much," I replied and got in.

The old utility was as battered inside as it was outside. In the back was a mountain of sand and gravel, bags of cement and a concrete mixer. The load was so great, the front wheels were barely touching the road. And by the variety of thumping and clunking coming from the suspension, the back wheels must have been more square than round. We moved along at a snail's pace. Pedestrians weren't actually passing us, but we weren't leaving them too far behind.

He dropped me off near the dump, and I continued walking towards the harbour. I had only taken a few steps when another utility pulled up on the verge, covering me in a cloud of dust.

"Goin' to the harbour, are you mate?" asked the long-haired driver, who was heavily tattooed and wearing a navy blue singlet.

"Yep," I replied.

"Jump in then."

The utility had been lowered so much, I had to almost crawl into it on my hands and knees. The tyres were the widest I'd ever seen; and judging by the deep gurgle coming from the exhaust, the motor was fully hotted up.

The car wheel-spun onto the bitumen and screeched along the highway. The acceleration was phenomenal. The utility shot through roundabouts with the bloke fighting the steering wheel like a Grand Prix racing car driver.

"Are you off a yacht?" he asked.

"Yes," I replied, unable to take my eyes off the road ahead.

"I'm buildin' a yacht — a trimaran," the driver continued.

"Are you?"

"Yeah. I've got kids all over the place from three marriages," he explained. "I'm goin' to pick 'em all up and sail around Australia."

"Mmmm," I answered, trying not to show fear in my voice as electricity poles and road signs swept past us in a blur. "How far have you got with building it?"

"Oh, I haven't started yet. I've got no money. I've gotta get a job first."

He dropped me off at the harbour, leaving behind a cloud of pungent, burning rubber as he wheel-spun along the road.

I returned to *Pluto*, cut the tufts of hair out of my ears and tried to rectify a hairdressing disaster.

A couple of days later when I went ashore to make another trip into Mackay, the same old bloke who had advised me to hitch a ride was again sitting outside the kiosk.

"I saw you getting a lift the other day," he said. "I told you that you wouldn't need to get a cab."

"You certainly did," I replied, as I disappeared into a phone box to ring the local cab company.

While in Mackay, I took the opportunity of phoning Ted Myers, a retired Head Lightkeeper from Pine Islet. The Pine Islet lighthouse, established in 1885, was dismantled in 1986 shortly after the station was demanned. It was then shipped ashore and eventually re-erected beside the Mackay Outer Harbour as a historic relic. Although the lighthouse wasn't open for public inspection, Ted had written to me, saying that he could arrange a visit if ever I was in Mackay.

I met Ted at the lighthouse the following morning. We swung open the heavy timber door of the tower and clumped up the well-trodden timber steps to the lantern room. Both of us had spent many lonely nights here, pumping air pressure to feed kerosene to the light and winding the heavy

The utility had been lowered so much, I had to almost crawl into it on my hands and knees.

weights to revolve the massive 5 tonne crystal lens, faithfully tending Australia's last kerosene operated light.

"Gee, Ted, they've done a remarkable job of rebuilding — especially the lens and clockwork mechanism. It's exactly how it was on Pine."

"Yes," Ted replied, "every single piece was numbered and photographed before it was removed. We've had the burner going and the lens revolving — it all works perfectly."

"It's a crying shame that the lighthouse isn't open for public inspection, Ted."

"Yes, it is. But Mackay is lucky that it's built here at all. It was very nearly taken to the National Maritime Museum at Sydney's Darling Harbour. It was only through some very strong lobbying by the Maritime Archaeological Association of Mackay that it's here. But now that it *is* here, there're just not enough local people interested in opening it to the public."

"What about you, Ted, I take it you're not interested in acting as care-taker?"

"No. Right from the start I made it clear that I'd give all the assistance I could in regard to rebuilding the lighthouse — but that would be it. After spending eighteen years looking after the light when it was on Pine Islet, I want to do a few other things during my retirement."

"That's quite understandable," I laughed. "But it makes you wonder, under these circumstances, if the lighthouse would have been more appreci-ated at Darling Harbour. I believe the lighthouse display down there is the most popular attraction at the Maritime Museum."

"No, I think the lighthouse should be here," Ted replied. "It's part of this area, and there are plans to build a large marina beside the harbour. With increased visitors there might come a time when the lighthouse will be open to the public."

"I suppose so."

"I've got an idea," Ted continued. "You and Shirl are familiar with the lighthouse — why don't you two move up here as caretakers?"

"Hey! We're retired too, remember."

Ted drove me to his home on the outskirts of Mackay, where his wife Marge had lunch prepared. The conversation was non-stop as the couple related one anecdote after another about their time in the lighthouse service. It was well after midnight when I said goodbye to Ted and Marge.

One of the necessary inconveniences of cruising is having to wash clothes. But it has to be done, as there is little more putrid than a fortnight-old pile of dirty washing that has been soaked with perspiration and salt water. I didn't consider myself a heavy user of clothes. At sea I usually wore swimming togs and a long-sleeved khaki shirt and, if it was cold, perhaps a jumper; even so, it was amazing how quickly dirty clothes built up. So far, I had found that most marinas were equipped with reasonably good laundromats. The washing machines were pretty standard, and the dryers were either gas or electric. I preferred the gas fired dryers because they could dry a heavy load of clothes in around thirty minutes, compared to nearly two hours for the same amount of clothes in the much smaller electric ones.

The Mackay Cruising Yacht Club had one electric dryer. I had used it shortly after my arrival, only to decide that if it wasn't already entered in the *Guinness Book of Records* as the world's slowest dryer, it should have been. About 4.00 p.m. on the day before I planned to leave Mackay, I went across to the yacht club to do a final load of washing. A large woman of matronly appearance had just finished using the washing machine and was putting her clothes into the dryer. I quickly calculated that the dryer wouldn't be available until at least well after six o'clock. Nevertheless, I washed my clothes, put them in a plastic bag and went up to the verandah of the yacht club to read a book and wait.

About an hour later, the woman approached me.

"Have you used that dryer before?" she asked in a rather pompous voice. "It seems to be terribly slow."

"Yes, it is." I answered. "It took a long time to dry my clothes when I used it a few days ago."

"This is *most* inconvenient," she continued, "I have to get back to the yacht and put on a roast. My husband insists that his dinner is ready on time."

"Look," I said, "if you'd like to leave some coins for the dryer, I'll keep it going until your clothes are dry, then I'll drop them in to you after I do mine. I take it you're moored out on the piles?"

My offer wasn't made entirely out of goodwill; I knew that without her here I could get her clothes out of the dryer when they were 'dry enough'. The last thing I wanted to hear her say around seven o'clock was: "They're not *quite* dry, I think I'll give them another hour".

"Would you?" she replied. "That's awfully good of you. My husband *will* be pleased."

She explained where their yacht was moored, then hurried away.

An hour later when I considered her clothes 'dry enough' I began removing them from the machine, folding each article in turn. Never before had I seen such things, never mind held them. To me, women's underclothes consisted of panties and bras. Some of the things I had folded could have harnessed a bullock team — they looked like a collection of straitjackets without sleeves. There were buckles, straps, clips and unknown things hanging everywhere. The names step-ins, corsets, girdles and stays came to mind. The worst thing was, I felt as though I was trespassing on someone's private life — rifling through the forbidden. I was relieved to get them all folded and stowed away before anyone came into the laundry and 'caught me in the act'.

By the time my clothes were 'dry enough', it was well after eight-thirty. I rowed out to the woman's yacht and knocked on the hull.

"Anyone on board?" I shouted out.

The matron quickly appeared in the cockpit.

"Oh, there you are," she said rather impatiently. "You've been so long, I was beginning to think you had run away with the clothes."

Lady, I thought, there are not too many things in life that you can be certain about, but me not running away with your knickers is one of them.

Never before had I seen such things, never mind held them.

Chapter 11

ISLANDS IN THE SUN

Like giant, green stepping stones cast higgledy-piggledy into a calm, cobalt blue lake, tropical island after tropical island lay spread out far below me, bound only by the distant shimmering horizon. From where I stood, on the summit of Brampton Island, the view was enhanced by the glorious weather conditions — cloudless sky, slight seas and perfect visibility. Situated 20 miles north of Mackay, Brampton is one of the Cumberland Islands, a group of over one hundred islands extending from Mackay northwards to Bowen. The Cumberlands were named by Lieutenant James Cook in 1770 during his voyage of discovery along Australia's east coast. On Whit Sunday 3 June 1770, as Cook sailed his bark *Endeavour* through a channel between the islands and the mainland, he named the channel "Whitsundays Passage". Although present-day charts still refer to the island group as the Cumberland Islands, they are more commonly known as the Whitsundays. The reputation of the area, within Australia and overseas, is such that many yachties who I had spoken to over the past few months were making the Whitsundays their destination — their Shangri-la. And from what I had seen so far, who could blame them. There were dozens of safe anchorages, fringed with sandy beaches and coral reefs.

I had spent the last few days exploring Brampton Island. *Pluto* was anchored a short distance from the island's jetty from where a tramway, used for transporting tourists to the resort, wound its way around the base of the island. Yachties, after registering at the resort's reception, were welcome to use the facilities. The resort had a good quality, relaxed homely feel about it. The combined bar and outdoor restaurant overlooked the water. After a day's hard work of exploring walking trails and beaches, in between snorkelling over the various reefs, it was refreshing to have a shower, then sit and enjoy a cold drink and sometimes a meal before returning to *Pluto*.

The fine weather continued as I headed north. The very light south-easterly breeze was right on the stern. With the main winged out to port and the colourful large drifter poled out to starboard, *Pluto* eased silently through the water at little more than 3 knots. But there was no rush to get anywhere, no difficulty in finding a safe anchorage before nightfall. I anchored for the night behind Goldsmith Island before continuing on to Lindeman Island the next day.

I was really looking forward to visiting Lindeman Island. I knew the island was 90 per cent national park, the remainder leased to Club Med resort. Back in the early 1980s, in the 'anything goes' days of Queensland politics, the then Premier, Sir Joh Bjelke-Petersen, tried to sell off part of the island's national park to his old mate Sir Ted Lyons for use as freehold housing blocks. Media exposure of the underhand proposal soon had thousands of people jumping up and down in anger, writing letters and attending protest meetings. I was proud to have been one of those protestors, and prouder still when the protest was successful. So, I was looking forward to seeing first-hand what I had helped save.

I anchored *Pluto* at Boat Port, a pleasant anchorage on the island's north-western side, and next day rowed ashore to a sandy beach lined with coconut palms. I followed a foot-track that led through thick, shady forest and which, a couple of kilometres further on, came out near the resort. I had heard that yachties and day visitors weren't welcome at Lindeman's Club Med; however, now that I was here, I decided to visit the reception building to see if I could get a map of the island showing the national park's walking trails. I changed my swimming togs and khaki shirt for a pair of shorts and T-shirt that I usually carried in my backpack for such occasions.

"Good morning, sir," the attractive young female receptionist said. "Can I help you?"

"I hope so," I replied. "I'm not a guest — I'm off a yacht anchored at Boat Cove, and I just wondered if you had a map showing the island's walking trails."

"Certainly, sir," she replied, as she handed me a small map. "Enjoy your walk."

Well, that was all quite harmless, I thought. Perhaps the information I had been given regarding yachties not being welcome was incorrect.

As I followed the trails through thick, lush forest and across suspended bridges to secluded beaches, I decided without doubt that my protesting to preserve the national park had been well worthwhile. I set off along the steep track to Mt Oldfield, the island's highest peak. The track snaked through cool, dark-green rainforest carpeted with bracken, before eventually breaking out onto open grassland and winding its way to the summit. The 360° view of surrounding islands was magnificent, easily surpassing the view from Brampton's highest point. This was chocolate-box scenery at its best.

I sat down on the grass to eat lunch while absorbing my surrounds. Lunch wasn't much to write home about — just two slices of buttered bread that had become a bit greasy in the heat, a banana, an orange and a drink of warm water. Just as I finished eating, a man and woman in their mid-thirties came stumbling up the track. They were both dressed as though they had just stepped out of a fashion page from *Vogue* magazine. She was wearing good casual shoes, tailored slacks and a brightly coloured blouse; she had perfectly groomed hair, full make-up and long, painted fingernails. He was wearing leather shoes, slacks and a sports shirt, which was saturated with perspiration. And no wonder; the large plastic esky he was awkwardly carrying looked as though it weighed a tonne.

"Hello," I said. "It's a beautiful view from up here."

"Oh, it is!" the woman replied with obvious delight, as her companion collapsed to the ground gasping for breath with his head between his knees.

"Look at the view, Peter!" she went on. "Isn't it delightful!"

It took Peter a few minutes before he began to take interest in anything at all.

"Are you from the resort?" the woman asked.

"No, I'm off a yacht. I take it you're staying at the resort?"

"Yes, we're from Melbourne. We're on our honeymoon. It's the first time either of us has stayed at a Club Med resort. We weren't quite sure what to expect — we'd heard it was very organised. But so far it's been quite good really. The meals have been excellent, and today when we told them we were going to climb the mountain, they packed an esky lunch for us."

Peter removed the esky lid and took out two champagne flutes and a bottle of chilled champagne. Then he produced slices of ham, chicken legs, fresh bread and salad. I was almost drooling.

"Would you like to join us?" Peter asked. "There seems to be plenty here."

After my greasy slices of bread, the thought of a chicken leg and a cold drink of anything was almost irresistible. But I controlled myself.

"Thanks very much for the offer, but I've just had my lunch. Anyhow I was about to move on when you arrived. I'll leave you both to enjoy the view in solitude. It must be quite a change from Melbourne."

On the way back down the mountain I thought it a shame to leave the island without having a quick look at the resort. The woman at reception had been very friendly and I hadn't seen any signs indicating that day visitors weren't welcome. I donned my glad rags again and began strolling through the complex. The many rows of three-storied accommodation buildings and surrounding landscaping were of pleasant design, but the overall effect seemed a bit too clinical, a bit too organised.

It amazed me how each resort attracted a different type of guest. Keppel Island seemed to cater mainly for young people, whereas Brampton Island was more family orientated. From what I had seen so far of Lindeman Island's Club Med there appeared to be a preponderance of flashy twenty-five to forty year olds. As I passed the crowded swimming pool, a man with a heavy French accent announced over the public address system that "Ze games in ze pool are now feeneeshed". He continued with times of activities scheduled for the remainder of the afternoon. I came to a large building that was obviously a lounge and bar. I've got this far, I thought, I might as well nip in and have a cold beer. Inside, a number of couples were sitting in the lounge drinking. On a nearby stage, a dozen or so women were doing aerobics, led by an extremely fit looking amazon, who was barking each movement into a microphone.

I walked over to the bar.

"A fourex heavy please," I said to the young barman.

"Certainly sir," he replied hospitably, as he deftly picked up an icy glass and filled it with froth-topped amber liquid.

I licked my lips in anticipation as he placed the glass in front of me.

"That's two reds and a green, thank you sir."

"I beg your pardon?" I queried.

"Two reds and a green, sir."

"How much is that in money?" I asked.

"We don't take money at Club Med — only tickets. Aren't you a guest?" he said, looking shocked.

I noticed the "sir" was no longer tacked on to the end of every sentence.

"No, I'm off a yacht."

He pulled the glass back across the bar.

"You'll have to buy some tickets and come back and pay for this."

"Well, where do I buy tickets?"

He directed me to a reception area a couple of rooms away, where some people were lined up at a desk buying tickets from an inscrutable Asian lady. I joined the end of the queue.

"How much are the tickets?" the bloke in front of me asked the woman, when his turn came.

Without eye contact or a word, the stony-faced Oriental nonchalantly slid a card across the desk towards him. I looked over the bloke's shoulder and read that the cheapest book of tickets was $15. What! There was no way I was going to pay $15 for a by now lukewarm, semi-flat beer. I broke from the queue and waited for the bloke to buy his tickets and walk away from the desk.

"Excuse me, but would you be interested in selling two reds and a green?" I asked, and went on to explain the situation, finishing off with an extremely generous offer, but which was much less than $15.

When I returned to the bar and handed over the tickets, I was confronted by a scrawny young man who wore multitudinous rings through his ears and sported a long, oily ponytail.

"I'm the manager here," he said aggressively. "The barman has reported that you're not a guest. You'll have to drink that beer and leave immediately. The resort is for guests only."

"Perhaps a sign indicating that, placed at the entrance to the resort, would be a help," I replied.

"This island is private property," he continued, "you can't land here without our permission."

"*Bull*shit!" I exploded. "This island is national park except for your piddling 10 per cent on the corner."

"Well — yes, I was referring to the resort grounds," he said, backing down, realising his bluff hadn't worked.

I drank the warm beer and left. My confrontation with the scrawny one was the only sour note in an otherwise great day. However, there was one redeeming factor — at the cost of only two reds and a green I had decided that Club Med resorts were not going on my holiday destination list.

The sheer 300 metre high cliffs of Pentecost Island gave the illusion of leaning outwards, poised to overbalance and topple upon me as I steered *Pluto* just a few metres away from the island's rocky shoreline. With my head stretched back to its limit, I gazed up in wonder at the towering rampart which seemed to continue upwards to the heavens. Every cave and boulder on the rugged escarpment looked menacingly close; and only when I realised that trees, which looked the size of children's farmyard models, were actually giant Hoop Pines clinging by their roots high up in the crevices, did the true scale of the island become apparent. Despite the chart and depth sounder showing there was plenty of water beneath the keel, the fact that *Pluto* was so close to shore seemed to warn me otherwise. *Pluto* was motor sailing, and although I knew it would be a million to one chance for the motor to fail and the breeze drop off at the same time, resulting in the yacht being quickly driven onto the rocks, I soon veered away to allow some leeway. But to have experienced this spectacular sight at such close quarters, even for a short time, had made any concern worthwhile.

Earlier that morning I had up-anchored from Boat Port and headed towards Stockyard Beach on Haslewood Island, diverting to Pentecost on the way. The chart showed that Stockyard Beach was reached by sailing through Solway Passage between Haslewood and Whitsunday Islands. The sailing guidebook stated that the narrow passage had tidal flows of 5 knots; the book also warned that when wind was against tide, the passage "can become spectacular, with curling waves, overfalls and whirlpools that can spin a yacht around 90°".

I had planned my arrival at Solway Passage to coincide with the ebb tide, so that wind and tide would be running in the same direction. Even so, as I steered *Pluto* past Frith Rock and entered the passage, the surface of the water became agitated with overfalls and whirlpools, which pushed and pulled the yacht off course, forcing me to continually work the tiller from side to side. To make things more difficult, a yacht was heading towards me from the opposite direction, its bow swinging erratically from port to starboard. The helmsman was steering his vessel down the dead centre of the channel. I moved well to port to give way, but he took what space I had given, forcing me towards the coral-fringed shore. I moved over further still, and he took that space too. I held my course, both vessels passing uncomfortably close to each other. The six people on deck smiled and waved energetically at me as though everything was hunky-dory. As they passed, I noticed the telltale company flag flying from the yacht's backstay, indicating that the vessel was under hire from a bareboat hire company.

Safely through the passage, I relaxed slightly and headed past Martin Islet for Stockyard Beach. Further down the coast, long-time cruising yachties had advised me to be wary of the bareboats in the Whitsundays, easily recognisable by the types of vessels and their backstay flags. Many of those who hired yachts were inexperienced with little, if any, practical knowledge of anchoring and other basic skills of seamanship. I had been especially warned to stay well clear of bareboats in anchorages, as their anchors often dragged, resulting in collisions with other vessels. Until now I hadn't encountered any bareboats; in fact, between Brampton Island and here I hadn't seen another yacht, but I knew that the area between Lindeman Island and Airlie Beach was going to be a different story.

I was surprised to find only two other yachts at Stockyard Beach, and neither of them hire boats. After some lunch I strolled along the beach and snorkelled over the coral reef a short distance offshore. At about three-thirty I was sitting in the cockpit reading, when I noticed a gaggle of yachts in the distance heading towards me. Through the binoculars I saw there were at least twenty yachts, and all were bareboats. What the hell's going on? — I thought. Is it some sort of race?

Before long, *Pluto* and the other two cruising yachts were surrounded by the bareboats all trying to anchor at the one time. The sandy shelf on which *Pluto* was anchored wasn't all that big an area. The shelf dropped off very sharply to over 20 metres of water. Because of this, those who got in first got the shallow water. The others, on finding the water further out too deep, returned to squeeze in and anchor between the yachts already anchored. Minute by minute the swinging room between the yachts decreased substantially.

A massive 15 metre yacht with eight people on board anchored in front of me. By the time the vessel hung back on its chain, it and *Pluto* were side by side only 4 metres apart.

"Do you think we're a bit close?" the young man at the wheel asked.

"Much too close," I replied.

They up-anchored and tried various other places, but ended up back beside me.

"What's the story with the mass movement of boats this afternoon?" I asked.

"The charter base recommended we stay here overnight." the man answered. "It was too rolly where we were at Whitehaven Beach. It's a condition of charter that we're anchored for the night by four o'clock. We have to check in on the radio twice a day and give our position. We're still too close to you, aren't we?"

"Yes."

They up-anchored again and moved away.

When darkness came about six o'clock, there were still half-a-dozen or so boats trying to anchor. Even when I was lying on my bunk reading after dinner, every now and then I'd hear the sound of a motor. I'd climb into the cockpit and see little red and green navigation lights weaving amongst the other yachts. Before going to bed, I took the precaution of hanging fenders along both sides of *Pluto*.

"I tell you," I said out loud to myself, "these bareboat people *are* a bit of a bloody worry."

At first light I departed the marine rabbit-warren of yachts and headed across the bay to Whitehaven Beach. Renowned worldwide for its extremely fine, blinding white sand, I was aware that this 5 kilometre long beach was the most frequently visited spot in the Whitsundays. I anchored a mile up from the southern end of the beach and later in the morning went ashore. The brilliant white sand running into the crystal-clear water was certainly an impressive sight. I followed the beach northwards to Hill Inlet, a large estuary that all but dried out at low tide. One lonely trailer-sailer was anchored in a pool of water not much bigger than a bathtub. I envied the crew's resilience, because even within minutes of entering the inlet, I was eaten alive by sandflies.

It was a relief to return to the beach and dive into the salt water to sooth the irritating bites. As the morning wore on, more and more large charter boats anchored at Whitehaven Beach, off-loading hundreds of tourists, many of them Japanese, to swim, sunbake and play netball or cricket on the sand. Some of the boats had rock music blaring from loudspeakers. Others had jet-skis, which screamed non-stop around the bay, each tourist taking their turn. Two Cessna floatplanes landed, disgorging even more people onto the beach. Fortunately for me, most of the activity was taking place at the far end of the beach, away from where *Pluto* was anchored. By midafternoon most of the large charter boats had gone, and the armada of bareboats had once more set off for Stockyard Beach. It seemed more than a coincidence that the only boats anchored nearby, were the two cruising boats that had been at Stockyard Beach the previous day.

Next day I returned through Solway Passage and sailed past the northern end of Hamilton Island, which was developed in the 1980s as a twenty-five hundred guest, high density resort, complete with jet airstrip. As I steered *Pluto* across Catseye Bay, the island's twenty-one storey apartment block stood out like a single upheld middle finger, as if symbolising the architect's contempt for any effort in trying to harmonise his building with the natural environment. Perched high on the north-west corner of the island, massive multilevel private residences flagrantly flaunted their owners' unabashed wealth. I sailed *Pluto* past the pseudo lighthouse built at the entrance to Hamilton Island's marina and tied up at a berth.

My only reason for visiting Hamilton Island was to meet Rob Nicholls and his partner Ailsa. For the past year, Rob and Ailsa, retired restaurateurs from Queensland's Sunshine Coast, had been living on nearby Dent Island lightstation as caretakers. The couple had invited me to visit them, but because there was no suitable anchorage near the lighthouse, Rob had arranged to pick me up from Hamilton Island in his small speedboat. During the early 1980s, Shirley and I had spent six weeks on Dent Island, working as relief lightkeepers. The station was demanned in 1987 and had remained unoccupied until Rob and Ailsa moved in.

I wasn't meeting Rob until the following morning, so I had time to look around Hamilton Island. It was more like a mini-city than a resort. The main street skirted the marina complex; there were numerous restaurants, boutiques, craft shops, bars, cafes, as well as a school, church, accountant, solicitor and mini-supermarket. Golf buggies were available for hire to explore the island.

I decided to dine out that evening at Spinnaker's Restaurant. Until setting off from Brisbane on *Pluto*, I had never eaten alone at a restaurant. The first time was at the Tin Can Bay marina, and I found it to be a pretty embarrassing experience; after perusing the menu and giving my order I suddenly became aware there was no-one to talk to. I read the wine list fifteen times, studied the light fittings, the carpet, the tablecloth, the salt and pepper shakers, read the wine list again and it still seemed like ages until the meal arrived. From then on I always took a book with me to read while waiting. But at Spinnaker's there was no time to read. Although the place was packed, the prawn cocktail entrée arrived before I even opened the book, and just as I swallowed my last prawn the dish was whipped away and replaced with the main meal. As I placed my knife and fork together and wiped my lips with the serviette, the waiter was instantly at my side.

"Would you care for anything else, sir," he asked politely.

"No thank you, that was a very enjoyable meal," I replied sincerely.

"I'm glad you enjoyed it," he said, as he hovered by the table.

I was aware there were other people at the bar waiting for a table, and although the waiter remained the epitome of politeness, I could almost hear him thinking: "Well, you've finished your meal, so get your 'ass' out of here, you're taking up four seats."

I obliged and paid my bill.

Every bar and café along the main street was doing a roaring trade. Hamilton Island was definitely a popular destination. As I was strolling back along the pontoon towards *Pluto*, I passed a large, luxury cruiser moored stern in. About half-a-dozen young people were enjoying a drink on the aft deck.

"Come aboard and join us for a drink!" one of the men called out to me.

"I'll give it a miss, but thanks for the offer," I replied, with an amused grin.

"Come on!" a few of them shouted. "Come and have a drink!"

"OK"

The young man who first called out, poured me a rum and offered to show me around the launch. It had every luxury imaginable.

"Is this your boat?" I asked.

"No, it's Dad's. He's in Melbourne at the moment. He leaves it here, and flies up every now and then for a week or two. I've just come up for a week with two mates. We don't do much cruising on her. We mostly just stay here and pull the chicks."

As the night wore on, every person who passed was invited on board. A lot refused, and a lot didn't. The booze flowed freely as my host 'pulled' more and more 'chicks'.

"I'd better be going," I said eventually. "I've got an early start tomorrow."

"You've picked the right night to get some sleep," the host said. "Tonight and tomorrow night are the only nights the disco isn't open. The music's so loud, no one in the marina can get any sleep. It starts at eleven and goes right through till dawn."

Early next morning Rob picked me up in his powerful speedboat and soon we were slamming from wave to wave, screaming along ten times faster than *Pluto*'s average speed.

"See that painted mark on the rock near the shore!" Rob shouted above the noise of the motor, as we almost flew down the western side of Dent Island. "That's where the *Cape Grafton* went aground!"

I had heard, that a year earlier, while the lighthouse maintenance ship *Cape Grafton* was off Dent Island, its computer steering system went haywire. No matter what frantic efforts the crew made to shut down the system, the vessel careered towards shore and ran aground. It was eventually refloated, but the cause of the computer hiccup was never found.

"I bet the skipper is still writing reports about that one!" I shouted back to Rob.

We soon pulled in to the small rocky cove below the lighthouse and cottages. I helped Rob winch his boat out of the water and then started to climb the many concrete steps that led to the lightstation.

"Isn't the crane and trolley-track working?" I asked Rob. "We used to lift the dinghy onto the concrete landing beside the crane, and transport our stores by trolley-track up to the cottages."

"No, it wasn't working when we arrived here, but I hope to get it going again soon."

Rob told me that Hamilton Island Enterprises, associated with Hamilton Island resort, held the lease of the lightstation, together with a large tract of land planned for use as a golf course. Rob and Ailsa had been 'employed' under an agreement that they would not receive a salary, but would have their stores delivered by regular helicopter flights at no charge. As well, the couple would be supplied with all the building materials required to restore the buildings since their abandonment seven years ago.

"You've got the grounds looking fantastic," I said.

"The grass was nearly over our shoulders when we first arrived here," Rob replied. "When we started cutting into it, we couldn't believe the number of stone walls and concrete paths there were. We're still finding new ones."

Rob and Ailsa were living in the old Head Lightkeeper's cottage, which had a wonderful view from the front verandah across the Whitsunday Passage.

"How about a cold drink?" Rob offered after he introduced me to Ailsa.

"Great," I replied. "You've both done a wonderful job here. The cottage looks beautiful."

"The walls were black with mildew when we arrived," Ailsa said, "and there were goats' droppings in every room. We scrubbed the whole place then painted it inside and out."

When Shirley and I lived in the cottage, the government furniture had been adequate but bottom of the range in quality. The furniture now in the rooms was Rob and Ailsa's — all good quality antique.

"The antique furniture really makes the place," I commented. "However did you get it here — considering the crane isn't working."

"Every piece was flown in, slung under a helicopter from Hamilton Island," Ailsa replied. "It took about thirty-six trips."

At the back of the cottage, the couple had built a substantial vegetable garden, enclosed by shade-screen to protect the crops from the island's numerous possums. As we walked around the station, Rob and Ailsa bombarded me with questions about how the station used to be. Their enthusiasm was infectious. I knew from experience that only a few people can live happily day after day in relative isolation. I was surprised that Rob and Ailsa, accustomed to owning and operating two extremely busy restaurants,

90

could make such a success of an alternate lifestyle. But happy they were, with no plans of ending their sojourn in nirvana.

The day seemed to fly, and before long we were heading back to Hamilton Island, my backpack filled with fresh vegetables, which Ailsa had picked from the garden.

I left Hamilton Island next day for a short sail north to Cid Harbour on the western side of Whitsunday Island. Cid Harbour was quite large, with plenty of room to anchor clear of other vessels. I anchored *Pluto* off Sawmill Beach, so named, I had read, because it was the site of a steam driven timber mill established in 1888 by John and Jeannie Withnall. Hoop Pine and Red Cedar were the main timbers harvested from Whitsunday and surrounding islands. At that time, about one hundred Aborigines lived on Whitsunday Island. The relationship between the Aborigines and the Withnalls was good; a few men from the tribe were employed at the mill, while some Aboriginal women helped Jeannie in the house. Bullock teams were used to drag the huge logs out of the thick scrub to clearings, where they were barked and slid down steep slopes to the sea. The logs were then tied together and rafted to the mill for processing. The mill closed sixteen years later, when the Withnalls decided to move back to the mainland. The mill and house were dismantled, taken to Bowen and re-erected. However, for the next fifty years, timber continued to be cut from the Whitsunday islands.

Before leaving Brisbane, I had been advised by a cruising yachtie friend to climb the 437 metre high Whitsunday Peak, the highest point of the Whitsunday island group. My friend had warned me that the track markers — mainly metal triangles nailed to trees, and stone cairns — were sometimes hard to spot. I set off along the foot-track from Sawmill Beach towards Dugong Beach keeping a watchful eye for an indication of where the track branched off to the right. I spotted a small, faded, red triangle. This has got to be it, I thought.

The rough track climbed steeply through thick forest. Sometimes the track was very obvious, and then it seemed to peter out, twisting and turning at places, where I had to bend down and push through thick undercover. At other places there were side routes off the track, which looked to be a continuation of the main track, but which led to dead ends. All I could rely on was not letting a rear marker get out of sight until I had picked up the next one ahead. It was hot, but the thick tree canopy overhead stopped the sun's intensity. Up, up, up. Sometimes the track disappeared, replaced by a carpet of lichen covered boulders. Follow the markers, follow the markers. Suddenly the track began to drop; it crossed a dry creek bed, then it was up, up, up again. The rainforest thickened, filling the atmosphere with a delicate, misty yellowish-green light. Then the rainforest became drier, gradually replaced by open forest eucalypts, grass, and huge boulders half-buried between bare rocky faces. Two hours from the start of the track, I clambered up a rock slope that flattened off to the mountain's peak. The view from Brampton Island's summit was good; from Lindeman Island's Mt Oldfield it was magnificent; from here it was stupendous. It felt as though I was floating, looking down on a miniature world. A large bulk carrier heading south through the Whitsunday Passage looked the size of a small dinghy; and the white sails of yachts appeared as mere specks. I strolled around the peak from one side to the other, absorbing as much of this majestic beauty as possible. Eventually I had to leave, realising that the fading afternoon light would make it difficult finding my way back through the rainforest.

I found the steep descent much harder than the morning's climb, mainly because my toes were constantly squeezed against the caps of my hiking boots. It was sheer pleasure to reach Sawmill Beach, remove my shoes and shirt and wallow in the salt water.

Even before I went ashore, and for reasons I couldn't explain, South Molle Island, 5 miles west of Cid Harbour, had a good feel about it. I had anchored *Pluto* in the shadow of Spion Kop and its nearby conspicuous peak The Horn. To avoid any altercation with the resort's management, similar to what I had experienced on Lindeman, I visited reception and told the girl behind the desk I was off a yacht.

"What we do here," the girl replied cheerfully, "is charge yachties a small fee for the use of the resort's facilities; and that includes just about every-thing — showers, restaurants, swimming pool and the bar."

"That seems very fair," I said, as I paid the required amount.

The girl gave me a map of the island and wished me a pleasant stay.

Most of the island was national park, with numerous walking trails. Each day I went ashore to walk the tracks, or play golf on the lovely but tricky nine-hole golf course, and then finish off with a shower and a few cold beers at the bar. My favourite walk was to the top of Spion Kop. One Friday I was up there admiring the view when a bloke turned up beside me. He was very tanned and his clothes were quite faded; not the usual colourful and well-ironed clothes of a resort guest.

"You've got to be off a yacht," I said.

"Do I look that bad?" he replied with a laugh.

He introduced himself and said he was off a 13 metre yacht, which he pointed out to me in the bay far below us. It was anchored a short distance from *Pluto*.

"Are you sailing single-handed, Dave?" I asked.

"No. There're six of us on board — my wife and two other couples."

"Don't they like walking?"

"A couple of them do, but I just had to get away by myself for a while."

I realised he wanted to expand on his statement, so I played along with him.

"Why's that?" I asked.

"I built the yacht on the Gold Coast with the idea of sailing to the Kimberleys with my wife, my best mate and his girlfriend. But before we set off next year, I thought it would be a good idea to have a sort of shakedown cruise to see how we got on together living in close quarters. My wife and I and the other couple sailed the boat up to the Whitsundays, and my mate and his girlfriend flew up to Hamilton Island to join us for a fortnight. They've only been on board four days, and already I can't stand her."

"Why?"

"She's the laziest bitch I've ever met. She takes no interest in the sailing of the boat. Never offers to cook or wash up. All she does is loll around the deck or lie in her bunk. I told her yesterday that she'd have to pull her weight and help around the boat if she still intends going to the Kimberleys. But she still didn't offer to help. So just before I came up here, I told her I'd had enough. I'm dropping her and my mate off in Airlie Beach tomorrow."

"How did your mate take that?" I asked.

"He wasn't too happy. And I'm not too happy either — after all, we've been really close friends for nearly fifteen years."

"What about his girlfriend? Have you known her for long?" I continued.

"A couple of years," Dave replied. "My wife and I have often gone out with them. She seemed all right. It just shows though — you don't really know someone until you've lived with them twenty-four hours a day. It's certainly wrecked our plans — but I suppose it's better finding out now than a few days after setting out for the Kimberleys."

We spoke about other things for a while, and then Dave asked:

"Are you going to the seafood smorgasbord at the resort tonight?"

"I didn't know about it," I replied.

"Oh, it's a beauty," Dave said. "The Friday night South Molle smorgasbord is renowned throughout the Whitsundays."

"No, I don't think I'll go," I answered thoughtfully. "I always feel a bit of a wet blanket going to something like that single-handed."

"Well, *we're* all going. Why don't you come with us?"

"What about your mate and his girlfriend? Won't the atmosphere be a bit strained?"

"Ah, they'll be sweet. See you at the bar about six o'clock."

"All right, I'll be there."

They weren't "sweet" at all. The pair looked decidedly sour. But my interest in their problems was quickly swept away by the food. Top quality oysters, prawns, crab and slabs of baked fish, complemented by fresh salad, all temptingly displayed by a gang of chefs wearing sparkling white clothes. And just when I thought I couldn't eat another thing, out came the pavlova and cheesecake.

"They have a floorshow here too that's included in the price of the meal," Dave said, as he stuffed another spoonful of pavlova into his mouth. "Are you going to that?"

"Why not," I replied enthusiastically.

Later that night, it was not with my usual steadiness that I rowed the rubber duckie back to *Pluto*.

Before heading into the marina at Airlie Beach, I decided to visit Butterfly Bay on the northern end of Hook Island, and Cateran Bay off Border Island, both places reputed to have good snorkelling sites for coral viewing. I arrived at Border Island about 2 p.m., intending to stay overnight. But when I entered Cateran Bay there were about fifteen yachts anchored between the shore and *Pluto*. To protect the coral, the Marine Parks Authority had placed a series of buoys some distance from shore, indicating that vessels couldn't anchor past the line of buoys. Without anchoring dangerously close to the other yachts, the shallowest depth of water I could find was 14 metres, meaning I'd have to let out at least 70 metres of chain. To hell with that, I thought, I'd be winding in anchor chain for the rest of my life. I decided to sail straight to Butterfly Bay, which I calculated I would reach shortly before nightfall.

Just on dusk I turned into the bay. I couldn't believe it. It was chock-a-block with yachts and cruisers; I counted at least eighty. I weaved *Pluto* around the vessels, trying to find a suitable space in which to anchor. Again the Marine Park's buoys prevented vessels from anchoring too close to shore. The only spot I could find had a depth of 15 metres. I let out all the chain that *Pluto* carried.

A nasty swell swept into the bay, rolling every vessel from side to side. It was too late to move now, especially in unfamiliar territory. Although there was a swell, there wasn't a breath of wind. The sound of people carried from every boat: the noise of television, different types of music, someone playing a guitar, people singing, guffaws of laughter, a dog barking, outboard motors. It was like being in the heart of one star suburbia — stacked in like sardines. I had seen some wonderful places in the Whitsundays; and I was aware one has to take the bad with the good. But living en masse like this was not my idea of cruising. The Whitsundays certainly weren't *my* Shangri-la.

Even before the first sign of dawn, I winched in the seemingly endless anchor chain and headed for Abel Point Marina at Airlie Beach, the hub of the Whitsunday tourist trade. The marina was different to any I had been in. Occupied mainly by charter boats and bareboats, people on the pontoons rarely acknowledged one and other as they passed. They were all too busy cleaning and re-provisioning their vessels ready for another load of tourists.

The main street of Airlie Beach was filled with backpackers, many of whom were studying travel brochures trying to decide which island tour to take.

I re-provisioned *Pluto* with fuel, ice, fresh meat and vegetables, did my washing and made ready for departure. The night before leaving, I went out to dinner. A yachting couple had told me of a hotel in the main street that served T-bone steak, chips and salad along with a pot of beer for $4.50.

"The hotel isn't much, but the food is good," they had said.

When I arrived at the pub, it was filled with backpackers, most of whom were in their early twenties. Although the thirty year age difference made me feel out of place, I still went up and ordered a meal.

"What sort of sauce would you like with your steak?" the young girl asked, then rattled off a number of sauces.

"Mushroom, please," I answered.

"Good choice," she replied with a wink and a nod, as she handed me a docket with number sixty-two written on it.

She seems extremely friendly, I thought.

The meal wasn't bad at all. I returned to *Pluto*, made a cup of coffee and went to bed. Rarely did I dream, but that night I dreamt of things demoniacally bizarre. Armed with a huge, gleaming sword I found myself fighting three-headed, fork-tongued, fire-breathing, green monster dragons, which reared and clawed in a flaming pit of hissing, writhing serpents. The more dragons I fought and beheaded, the more that magically appeared. Around the edge of the pit, an array of ugly, weird, twisted, multi-limbed demons and ghouls stamped, shouted and waved as though urging on this grotesque contest. The battle continued on and on relentlessly. Suddenly I awoke to find myself panting breathlessly, my mind racing and heart pounding. Perspiration streamed down my face and body. I felt utterly exhausted. I could feel the pillow and sheets saturated with sweat. I lay panting in the darkness, trying to gather my senses. What the hell was going on? Could it have been something I ate? It took some time before it dawned on me.

Wink, wink, nod, nod, good choice — magic mushroom sauce for the old bloke with docket number sixty-two.

Chapter 12

A BREATH OF FRESH AIR

After the crowds and razzle-dazzle of the Whitsundays it was a welcome relief to be sailing along without another vessel in sight. I had left Airlie Beach that morning on course for the narrow Gloucester Passage, which runs between Gloucester Island and the mainland. The 15 knot south-easterly breeze made the 22 mile sail a delight. Keeping well clear of the dangerous reef that extends quite a distance from the mainland, I changed course and headed for the red buoy at the entrance to the passage. Although *Pluto* was battling the flood tide, I knew the rising water would give me the advantage of making a quick recovery should the yacht run aground. But I had no need for concern, as the passage was well beaconed by a combination of cardinal and lateral marks. I rounded Cape Gloucester into Edgecumbe Bay and anchored close to the beach in almost lake-like conditions.

Behind a grove of coconut palms I could see a few small buildings, which were described in the sailing guidebook as Monte's Reef Resort.

After lunch I rowed ashore and walked up a concrete boat ramp through the grove of coconut palms towards what appeared to be the main building. Inside was a dining room, lounge and bar. Through a large plate glass window, which overlooked the bay, I could see *Pluto* swinging gently at anchor. On the walls, old sepia photographs in antique timber frames displayed the history of the resort and surrounding area. An upright piano stood in the corner of the dining room, its worn appearance testimony to frequent use. There wasn't a soul in sight, so I rang a bell that hung on the wall beside the bar. A few minutes later a young man entered.

"Hello," he said, "would you like a drink?"

"I'm not a guest — I'm off a yacht," I replied warily.

"Yes, I know. I saw you anchor. Yachties are very welcome here."

"Gee," I said, after I had taken a sip of beer, "this place is like a breath of fresh air after the Whitsundays."

The young man laughed.

"It's amazing how many yachties say that," he added.

We began talking about the various resorts in the Whitsundays. While describing my stay at Hamilton Island, I mentioned that I had left *Pluto* there during my visit to the lightstation on Dent Island.

"I used to live on a lightstation," the young man said. "My father was a lighthouse keeper."

"Was he!" I replied with surprise. "What's your name?"

"Greg Daniels."

"So your father would be Lloyd Daniels?" I said.

"That's right. Did you know him?"

"Not when he was a lightkeeper. I met him after he retired — he was at Middle Percy Island on his yacht. That would have been about fifteen years ago, when my wife and I were relief lightkeepers at Pine Islet."

"You were a lighthouse keeper too?" Greg said. "What's *your* name?"

I told him.

"Well, you're the bloke who wrote the lighthouse book — it's a small world."

"Is your father still sailing?" I asked.

"No, Dad died a few years ago. He was on his yacht in Hervey Bay when someone found him dead in the cockpit — he was just sitting there with a half-spliced length of rope in his hand. I suppose it wasn't a bad way for an old yachtie to go — he always loved the sea."

As we were speaking, a young woman walked in.

"This is my wife Georgina," Greg said, and introduced me.

"Do you both work here?" I asked.

"Yes," Georgina replied, "there's usually only the two of us. We're the managers, receptionists, bar attendants, cooks, cleaners, carpenters, plumbers and everything else it takes to run a small resort. Sometimes when it's busy we get another couple in."

"Ah, here's Harry," Greg said, as a solidly built man walked in. "Harry and his family are our only guests at the moment. They've been coming here every year for the past seven years."

"Is that your ketch out there?" Harry asked. "It's a beautiful little yacht."

"I'm very happy with it," I replied.

Harry continued asking questions about *Pluto*, so I invited him out to the yacht. When I returned him to the beach later, Harry said:

"We're having a barbecue tonight. Would you like to come?"

"I'd love to. What would you like me to bring?"

"Nothing. I've got a mate who owns a trawler, and at the moment he should be anchored over at Bona Bay behind Gloucester Island. I'm going over there in my runabout to get some prawns. Do you want to come with me?"

Within ten minutes Harry and I were rocketing along at 40 knots.

"Yep, there he is," Harry said, as we rounded Bluff Point and turned into Bona Bay.

Harry exchanged a carton of fourex for a 20 litre bucket filled with beautiful fresh green prawns.

"Dianne and the kids have gone over to Shag Islet to get some oysters," Harry said. "We're having oysters kilpatrick tonight as an entrée."

The night was balmy. A slight breeze rustled the coconut palm fronds around the barbecue area, as the full moon floodlit the silvery waters of the bay. Greg and Georgina joined us for the meal. Harry and Dianne's four children were in their teens, and certainly appeared to be relishing their stay at Monte's.

"The kids love it here," Harry said. "We've done quite a bit of travelling overseas, but this is their favourite place. They make their own fun. The resort has a Laser sailboat and a tennis court, and you can walk for miles along the beach — there's always plenty for them to do. I suppose they'll be going their own way soon, so we're making the best of it while we can."

It was nice to see a family getting genuine pleasure out of just being together. None of the children were stand-offish, or gave the impression of being the slightest bit bored; they were just part of the group, joining in with the conversation and laughter.

The meal was superb. I bought a few bottles of white wine to complement the seafood, while Harry and Dianne's eldest daughter produced a large dish of lasagne. Possums in the nearby trees climbed down to investigate what was on offer; they turned up their noses at the oysters kilpatrick and barbecued prawns, but were enthusiastic about the lasagne.

Next day, Georgina showed me through one of the six, separate units. It contained two bedrooms, was fully self-contained and spotlessly clean; and like the others, was just a few footsteps from the beach.

"Very, very pleasant," I said to Georgina. "How do guests get here — by road?"

Georgina explained there was no legal access by land, but an agreement had been made to cross a neighbouring property to reach the nearest public road 4 kilometres away. However, guests weren't allowed to bring their vehicles to the resort; Greg would meet them with his Land Cruiser at a locked gate, transfer their luggage and food, and drive them to Monte's. Because Harry was such a regular guest at the resort, he had been given special permission to drive in with his runabout.

"Harry and Dianne are leaving tomorrow," Georgina continued. "We'll be going in with the Land Cruiser to help with some of the luggage. Why don't you come with us for the drive?"

"I'd love to," I replied.

We set off next day, bouncing along a rough, dusty dirt track. At the top of one excessively steep hill, which looked only slightly less than a vertical wall, Greg stopped the Land Cruiser.

"I'll just wait here to see that Harry makes it to the top OK. The weight of his runabout might be a bit too much for his vehicle. By the way, this is called 'Oh God Hill', because guests always say 'Oh, God!' when they drive down it for the first time."

Harry's Land Cruiser bounced and wheel-spun as it clawed its way slowly but successfully to the top.

"It's all plain sailing now," Greg said, as we climbed back into the vehicle.

We farewelled Harry and his family and drove back to Monte's.

The following day I motored *Pluto* around Shag Islet and anchored a mile further along the beach. There was no wind, so I spent a few lazy days doing a bit of maintenance to the yacht.

From where *Pluto* was anchored it was 12 miles across Edgecumbe Bay to the town of Bowen. I had been waiting for a brisk south-easterly to take me across this leg of the trip. In those conditions, the offshore breeze would flatten the waves, allowing for a smooth, express-like sail across the bay. But the calm continued, so eventually I weighed anchor and began motoring to Bowen. I connected the autopilot and went below to look at the chart. A couple of minutes later, when I came back on deck, *Pluto* was heading well over 90° off course. I took over on the tiller, went back on course and reset the autopilot, but the yacht slowly veered away as before. I tried all the usual things with the autopilot — shaking it, giving it a bit of a tap, talking nicely to it, but it still didn't work.

On closer inspection I discovered that one of the control buttons was stuck, effectively shorting out the whole system. I unscrewed the panel from the back of the control unit and looked inside. I could see that a new button would rectify the problem; but even if I had a replacement it would need a professional technician to fit it. I rang the Australian distributor of the auto-pilot on VHF Seaphone to order a new button; I hoped I could have it installed by a television or video repairman in Bowen, as I didn't think the town would have an authorised repairer. But the distributor surprised me by saying there was one, and gave me his name.

Although Seaphone calls were quite expensive, the VHF radio had proven itself invaluable on this trip. A couple of times a week I would give Shirley a call to make sure she was all right, and to let her know that *Pluto* and I were still above water. The radio reception was usually very good. There were a few blind spots along the coast; in fact, the reception during the call I had just made to the autopilot distributor was the worst I had experienced so far — everything I said had to be repeated at least three times. The biggest problem with Seaphone was that anyone who was listening in on the frequency being used, heard the land end of the conversation, and sometimes both ends. Anything of a private nature that Shirley or I wanted to discuss had to wait until I had access to a landline. A further inconvenience was that the caller and the receiver couldn't speak at the same time; the word "over" had to be used to signify the end of saying something. While I was at Lady Musgrave Island further down the coast, I overheard a passenger on a nearby charter boat call his wife on Seaphone. The woman raved on about their "horrible next-door neighbour and her brood of brats", disclosing the most intimate details of what she would like to do with them. Eventually her husband managed to break in and tell her she was being overheard along 100 miles of coastline. There was a shocked silence before the poor woman hung up. In the same area, a deckhand from a trawler regularly called his tarty girlfriend. In a sultry voice, she purred sensual innuendoes about what was waiting for him at home. I'm sure it was a set-up to drive the deckie's mates into a testosterone-charged frenzy; or perhaps she just wanted him home quickly to mow the lawn.

Until now I hadn't realised just how much I relied on the autopilot. If there had been a breeze I could have connected the Fleming wind vane to the tiller; but as there still wasn't a breath of wind, I had to hand steer to Bowen, hoving to each time I went below to check *Pluto*'s position on the chart.

I steered *Pluto* along the narrow, beaconed channel leading into the boat harbour. Immediately to port were a few pontoon berths in front of the North Queensland Cruising Yacht Club. The centre of the harbour was filled with pile berths, most of which were occupied. I tied up at the only empty pontoon berth and walked up to the yacht club.

"I've just tied up at a berth — two along from the walkway," I said to the woman behind the bar. "Is it all right to stay there, or do I have to move?"

"That's Fred's berth. He'll be back in tonight. How long are you staying?"

"Probably four or five days," I replied.

"Well, why don't you go over to the duck pond? It's quite nice over there."

"The 'duck pond'?" I queried.

The woman explained that the duck pond, part of Magazine Creek and attached to the harbour, had been dug out for a marina. But the project had been abandoned and was now used for mooring boats.

"They have fore and aft drum moorings over there. When you've tied up, go and see the Harbour Authority — they're just up the road."

The woman was right — it was quite nice in the duck pond. It had a very open feel, and was out of the way of trawler traffic and the public boat ramp.

I paid my mooring fees at the Harbour Authority next morning on the way uptown to drop in the autopilot. The town centre was only a ten minute walk away from the harbour. With its extremely wide streets and old colonial homes, Bowen had the relaxed, quiet atmosphere of a country town. I agreed with the autopilot repairer's recommendation to replace the six control buttons on the one circuit board rather than the one faulty button. He told me it would be a few days before he received and fitted the parts. That suited me fine, because I had been invited to stay with a couple who lived on a few hectares an hour's drive from Bowen. Barry and Margot Laver were former lightkeepers, who left the job to buy a yacht and cruise the Barrier Reef coast. After a few years they sold the yacht and built a mud-brick house on their property.

Barry picked me up from outside the yacht club the following day and drove me to their home. It had a rustic, rambling design with wide verandahs shaded by climbing shrubs. Coloured glass set into one wall of the lounge room admitted the sunlight, filling the room with a serene tinted glow. The bathroom, a separate building connected to the house by a covered way, consisted of an old 18,000 litre rainwater tank, whose bottom had been removed and the tank placed on a metre high circular stone wall. The floor was paved with large flat stones, while a leadlight window set into the side of the tank admitted natural light. Vines and plants covered much of the internal and external walls. It was like having a shower in the middle of a rainforest. The guest bedroom was also a separate building, placed at the end of a little walking track that meandered through a forest of shrubs and trees.

Margot had a workshop where she made jewellery, mostly out of silver. Like their house, her jewellery was of innovative design.

It was late when I retired to the guest bedroom. Outside, not a leaf stirred on a tree, not an insect made the slightest sound. There was a deathly silence. On *Pluto* there was always some sound. I had got to know every slight creak and groan, the funny little noises that only yachts can make: the rumble of the anchor chain, the slight vibration of a halyard, the slap of a wave against the hull, the rippling sound of the running tide, and more predominant than all — the hum of the wind sweeping past the rigging. Even in the calm of marinas there were constant gurglings and the occasional tug of a mooring line. It felt eerie to hear absolutely nothing. Nevertheless, it didn't stop me from quickly falling asleep.

When I returned to Bowen I went to pick up the autopilot.

"The parts are here, but they're not fitted yet. Peter had to go to Collinsville," I was told. "It should be ready in about three days."

I tried again three days later.

"Peter hasn't had a chance to do it yet. And he won't be in this afternoon — this is his golf day."

Bowen is a nice place. But after a few days, during which time I visited the museum, walked around town numerous times to admire the civic murals painted on some of the office buildings, studied every real estate office window to see what was for sale, and climbed Flagstaff Hill each afternoon for the exercise, I was more than ready to leave.

One morning I was sitting in the cockpit deciding whether I should visit the museum again or have another look at the murals, when a man approached in an aluminium dinghy.

"Hello," he said. "I'm handing out the Commonwealth Government's Census Form Kit. There's an information sheet to show you how to fill out the form on the appropriate day."

"You're keen," I replied, "rowing around handing out census forms."

"The government's pretty well organised for this census," he said.

When he had gone, I had a quick look at the questions, then threw the packet down below and didn't give it another thought. After all, questions like "By what means did you travel to work today?" and "How many rooms does the house contain in which you are presently residing?" were hardly relevant to my situation.

Eventually the autopilot was repaired. I re-provisioned at the local super-market, finalised my mooring fees with the Harbour Authority, hanked on the headsail and removed the sail covers ready for an early departure next morning.

Chapter 13

THE BILL

It seemed like the middle of nowhere. Dusk's encroaching veil made it look a lonely and forbidding place. The rugged, tree and boulder-strewn cape rose steeply from the sea, the overall gauntness relieved by a few small sandy beaches lying between stony headlands. There wasn't another boat in sight. The only sign of civilisation was a number of cottages built along the narrow strip of beachfront. Unlit and obviously unoccupied, they added to the eeriness.

After a slow, full day's sail from Bowen, I had just anchored behind Cape Upstart. The wind had been fluky all day; always from the south-east, but varying from 5 to 15 knots. Every time the wind had picked up, I was sure it was going to stay, but within ten or fifteen minutes it slowly dropped off again.

I was rigging the anchor light and looking forward to a belated sundowner when I heard the distant sound of an outboard motor. It seemed as though it was heading my way.

"Who the hell would be out in a runabout at this time of night in this isolated place?" I said out loud.

Before long, a runabout appeared out of the darkness and came alongside.

"G'day," said the boat's sole occupant. "My name's Joe Linton, I'm the census collector. Have you filled out your census form yet?"

"What! You've got to be joking?" I exclaimed.

"Do you want to see my identification?" the man replied.

"No, no, I believe you," I laughed. "I just can't believe that anyone would be running around out here collecting census forms. I mean, you wouldn't have many customers, would you?"

"No, not really, it's just that I volunteered to cover this area," Joe replied.

"Look," I said, "I was just about to have a rum when you came along — would you like to come aboard and join me?"

"Don't mind if I do," Joe replied enthusiastically.

"Do you live around here?" I asked Joe after I had poured him a drink and put out some cheese and biscuits.

"We've got a family holiday shack further along the beach — you can't see it from here, it's round the corner. But I live at Home Hill — we've got a cane farm there."

Joe told me that the holiday house, built on one of the freehold beachfront blocks adjoining Cape Upstart Wilderness National Park, had been in his family since 1947. Although there was mains power to the settlement, there were no roads; access was by boat, with most residents travelling from Molongle Creek 5 miles away.

"Ninety per cent of the houses here are cane-cockies' holiday homes," Joe said.

During my recent pastime of staring into real estate office windows in Bowen, I had seen a sun-faded photograph of a Cape Upstart beachfront property which, the sign said, had been "reduced from $600,000 to $195,000". I mentioned this to Joe.

"Yeah, that's the Yank's place," Joe replied. "He's been trying to sell it for quite a while. It's almost directly across from where you're anchored — it's an odd looking place, but worth a look if you go ashore."

"Is he a cane-cocky?" I asked.

"No," Joe laughed, "but he certainly keeps the cane-cockies here amused — he's always involved in one sort of drama or another. He bought a yacht a couple of years back and was always getting into trouble — for a while he was one of the Coast Guard's best customers. He ended up wrecking the yacht in the bay — you can still see the smashed up hull on the beach in front of his place."

Joe told me that only a few weeks ago, while the American was riding along the sand on his three-wheeled motor bike, he stopped to talk to someone near the swimming enclosure. It was school holidays and there were quite a few parents and children swimming there. When the American was ready to leave, he started the bike, but he had forgotten it was still in gear. The bike shot forward, throwing him off before careering across the beach and plunging into the swimming enclosure. The heavily ribbed balloon-like tyres of the bike not only allowed it to float, but propelled it helter-skelter amongst the swimmers.

"It was like a scene from the movie *Jaws*," Joe said, "there were kids and parents screaming and running out of the water everywhere. He's not a bad bloke, the Yank — but things just seem to happen to him. It's a bit like having a resident court jester."

Over a few more drinks, cheese and biscuits, Joe told me that some years ago he had left the cane farm for nine months to cruise aboard his 9 metre flybridge cruiser.

"My wife Margaret and the two kids came too," Joe said. "It was a great trip. We cruised from the Gold Coast to Cape York's Princess Charlotte Bay."

We went on comparing notes about the places we had visited along the coast.

"Hell!" Joe said, a couple of hours later, after looking at his watch. "I was supposed to be going home to the farm tonight, but I think I'll just bunk at the hut. Do you mind if I use your VHF radio and let Margaret know — we've got a VHF radio at the farm."

"Sure Joe, go ahead," I replied, turning on the radio to the appropriate channel and handing him the microphone.

"Margaret," Joe said, when his wife answered the radio, "I'm on a yacht called *Pluto*. I'll spend the night in the hut and come home tomorrow afternoon."

"All right," Margaret replied stoically, as though this was an everyday occurrence.

I motioned to Joe that I wanted to speak to Margaret.

"Margaret, this is the skipper of *Pluto*. Your husband is depleting the ship's stock of rum, cheese and biscuits at a great pace."

As quick as a flash and as dry as a Gibson Desert gibber, Margaret replied:

"Well you know what to do — throw him overboard."

An hour or so later, with the tide level in the rum bottle dropping at an alarming rate, Joe and I finally got down to the serious business of filling out my census form. Another hour or so later, Joe, clutching my completed form, clambered into his runabout and zoomed off into the darkness. Now that was a census collector serious about his job.

I motored ashore in the tender next morning to have a look at the 'Yank's place'. It was like a fairytale castle. Almost every type of material had been used in its construction. The main house was three storeys high; some of the walls were stone stuck over brickwork, some were brick waiting for the stone to be stuck onto them, while others were timber. The expansive window openings were filled with battered, aluminium framed plate glass panels that looked as though they had spent their past life as entrance doors to a pub. Through the ground floor window I could see that the lounge room had a 9 metre high cathedral ceiling; in one corner of the room there was a two-storey waterfall and rock-pool built of huge boulders. A bathroom, which opened onto the back verandah, had a giant clamshell as the vanity basin; the tap was a cast brass fish that obviously spewed water out of its mouth. There were separate guests' quarters and lookout gazebos supported high above the ground on stilts. All the buildings were connected by bridges and walkways that curved around trees and meandered past a salt-water swimming pool designed to look like a swimming hole in the rainforest, and which contained just as many rotting leaves as a swimming hole in the rain-forest.

The real estate blurb in Bowen had stated that the house was 90 per cent complete. What it hadn't stated was that every part of the house was 90 per cent complete — nothing was finished. It was as though the American had thought of an idea, put it into action, tired of it before completion, then moved on to the next idea. It was a shame, because done properly the house would have been magnificent — a maintenance nightmare perhaps — but nevertheless magnificent.

Compared to the 'Yank's place', the cane-cockies' houses were pretty humdrum, but still interesting. It was obvious that the cane-cockies had spent many happy hours down in their sheds on the farm fabricating a variety of utilitarian items from bits and pieces of scrap metal and discarded spare parts; there were rotary clothes hoists, barbecues, boat trailers, solar hot water systems, tables, chairs, water tanks and a multitude of other items, all designed and built with typical farmers' ingenuity.

Two days later, contrary to the Bureau of Meteorology's prediction of a continuing spell of light winds, I awoke to a 15 knot south-easterly breeze. I decided to continue on to Cape Bowling Green, 35 miles to the north-west. Ten miles into the journey the breeze dropped out and I had to start the motor — it appeared the Bureau was right after all. The coast was low-wooded with no reference marks. The chart showed that Cape Bowling Green was a narrow spit of sand only a few metres high, which jutted 8 miles out to sea. The first sign I saw of the cape was a solitary coconut palm sticking high above the horizon. Soon afterwards, the steel lattice-framed automatic lighthouse built 3 miles from the end of the cape came into view. It was easy to see why this low, barely distinguishable sand spit had been a danger to shipping in the days before a lighthouse was built there.

The original Cape Bowling Green lighthouse was established in 1874 and manned by a Superintendent, three assistant lightkeepers and their families. It was soon discovered that the fragile sand spit on which the lighthouse and cottages were built was subject to constant change, especially during easterly winds at spring high tides. By 1879 the sea had eroded so much sand from around the lighthouse footings, the structure had to be moved. This was done by dragging the 16 metre high lighthouse on a timber raft to a new site 109 metres away. The cottages were shifted at the same time and positioned beside the tower. In 1892 the cottages had to be moved again — this time 334 metres away from the lighthouse. The erosion was so severe that at spring high tides the lightkeepers had to use a punt to reach the lighthouse. Two years later the lightkeepers built a raised footway, which provided access at all stages of the tide between the cottages and the tower. A heavy easterly gale in May 1908 undermined the footing of the lighthouse with such severity that the whole structure had to be supported with stays to prevent it from collapse. It was decided to move the lighthouse 355 metres, to the area where the cottages had been rebuilt. But the undulating nature of the sand ruled out the possibility of moving it on a timber raft as was done previously, so the structure was dismantled and reassembled at the new site. The station was demanned and automated in 1920, but remanned between 1942 and 1944 for wartime use; by that time the cottages had been removed and the two lightkeepers had to live in the lighthouse. A retired Head Light-keeper, seventy year old Mick O'Meara, volunteered to run the station. There was very little spare room inside the tower; the ground floor was taken up with acetylene cylinders used for operating the light, and on the first floor there was a wireless telegraph set. The men were provided with a kerosene stove in an outside kitchen which, in anything but a strong south-easterly wind, was under constant attack from hordes of sandflies and mosquitoes. Stores were delivered by boat to the lightkeepers every three months, but each week one lightkeeper was allowed to ride a pushbike provided by the lighthouse department 20 kilometres along the beach to the small settlement of Alva, where fresh food was available. The present steel lattice-framed structure with a solar powered light was built in 1987; the original light-house was dismantled, transported to Sydney and rebuilt at the Australian National Maritime Museum at Darling Harbour as a historic relic, where it has become the Museum's most popular attraction.

It was dead low tide when I rounded the cape during midafternoon and steered *Pluto* into Bowling Green Bay. The bay was extremely shallow and discoloured with muddy silt; at the spot where I anchored, *Pluto* was over 2 miles from shore with only half a metre of water beneath the keel. Normally I wouldn't anchor in such shallow water in this relatively exposed position, but the Bureau of Meteorology's latest report had predicted a continuation of light winds and calm seas. Also, as I intended going ashore next morning to visit the original lighthouse site, I didn't want to be too far away from the beach.

Two other yachts were at anchor in the large bay. Through the binoculars I saw one vessel was flying the American flag; the other had a dark blue hull. Both yachts looked about the same size as *Pluto*.

Just on dusk I noticed a few dark storm clouds far over the land to the west. They were moving south, so I didn't consider them a concern. But shortly before 8 p.m., without the slightest warning, the wind blasted in at 45 knots from the south-west, churning the water around me into a cauldron of boiling waves. As the short, steep seas increased in height, *Pluto* was battered and slammed up and down and from side to side, as the wind screamed incessantly past the rigging, reminiscent of my last night at Middle Percy's West Bay. I crawled along the pitching deck to check the anchor chain, then went below, hoping the storm would soon pass. By midnight there was no change. Unlike West Bay, where I sat out the night at anchor, I knew that here I would have to move to deeper water. If I didn't, the combination of falling tide and steep waves would soon have *Pluto*'s keel pounding on the seabed.

Although the wind speed was stronger than what I had experienced at West Bay, the waves were not as high or powerful. Nevertheless, by the time I hand-winched in the anchor chain, moved *Pluto* to deeper water and re-anchored I was streaming with salt water and felt as though I had done ten rounds in the boxing ring. I went below to dry off; again, sleep was impossible, and for the remainder of the night I could do little else but keep watch on the lighthouse and the American yacht's riding light to make sure *Pluto* wasn't dragging anchor. Earlier in the night, I had noticed that the blue-hulled yacht wasn't displaying a riding light. Despite the *International Rules for Prevention of Collision at Sea* stating that vessels at anchor *must* display a riding light at night, it's only commonsense and courtesy for the skipper of a vessel to do so. It's difficult enough approaching an anchorage in the darkness without having to worry about unlit vessels and whether or not you're going to run into them. In this case, if the blue-hulled yacht had been displaying a light, it would have given me another position to check if *Pluto* was dragging.

At the first hint of dawn I up-anchored and headed west-north-west towards Cape Cleveland. My planned visit to the old Cape Bowling Green lighthouse site was postponed indefinitely. The wind had swung to the south-east and steadied off at 35 knots. As I left the bay I could see the American yacht's navigation lights behind me; obviously it was leaving too.

Pluto screamed along, surfing down the wave crests and then slowing slightly as the bow ploughed into the backs of the waves ahead, sending thick sheets of water high in the air before they erupted into millions of heavy drops that drenched the entire length of the yacht. I was certainly making up for the light, fluky winds and motoring of the last few legs. After a three hour roller-coaster ride, Cape Cleveland and its offshore rocks and reef lay only a few miles ahead. In good conditions, when sailing into strange territory, I'm always alert. Add a few rocks and reefs that have to be negotiated and I become seriously concerned. But with 35 knots of wind and rough seas on top of those conditions I found myself bordering on controlled panic. The chart showed that half a mile offshore from the cape was Twenty Foot Rock, three-quarters of a mile further out was Four Foot Rock, and a mile further out again was the submerged Salamander Reef. I had plotted my course to pass between the two rocks, but so far I had spotted only one rock, and I was unsure which one it was. I altered course to pass it close on the seaward side; by doing that I would miss Salamander Reef, no matter which rock it was. However, I wasn't happy — the missing rock was a worry, it couldn't have just disappeared. The charts were never wrong. Using the handheld compass I took bearings from the land to plot my position, but the violent movement of the yacht was too much to obtain accurate readings. With one arm wrapped around a shroud to steady myself, I peered through the salt-coated binoculars, scouring the steep, rocky cliffs of the shoreline. Then, perhaps because of a change of light and shadow, I noticed that one section of the cliffs appeared to be standing out to sea. Was it Twenty Foot Rock or just part of the coastline? As *Pluto* drew closer I saw it was separated from the mainland. It *was* Twenty Foot Rock. Everything suddenly fell into place. I sighed with relief, and changed course again to sail between the two rocks.

Before long I had rounded Cape Cleveland and was almost flying across the relative calmness of Cleveland Bay heading towards the conspicuous landmark of Castle Hill, which overlooks the city of Townsville. Shortly after midday *Pluto* was safely berthed at the Breakwater Marina. I had some hot tinned soup, a hot shower and collapsed onto my bunk for some much needed sleep.

Next day when I was walking around the marina looking at the boats, I came to a small yacht flying the American flag. Named *Atom*, there was an elderly man with a short white beard sitting in the cockpit.

"G'day," I said, "were you anchored at Cape Bowling Green two nights ago?"

His head shot up in surprise.

"Were you on one of the other yachts?" he replied in an American accent.

"Yes, the ketch."

"Did you know that the blue yacht was washed up on the beach?" the American said.

"No!" I replied with surprise. "It was still very dark when I left. Apart from the lighthouse, all I could see was your navigation lights."

"Yeah, it was washed up near the end of the spit. I tried calling them on the radio, but no-one answered. They seemed to be OK though — I saw three people walking around on the beach. There's a good chance they went up on the falling tide, so I suppose they refloated it on the flood. I saw you move during the night — were you dragging?"

"No, it was a bit too shallow where I was anchored, so I moved out into deeper water."

"Yeah, it was a really rotten night — I didn't get a wink of sleep. Anyway, my name's Gerry Couture, come aboard and have a cup of coffee."

"What length is *Atom*?" I asked, after climbing on board and introducing myself.

"8.5 metres," Gerry replied. "She's a Nor-Sea sloop designed by Lyle Hess. It's pretty basic, there's no refrigeration or anchor winch, but like you Aussies say — it's built like a brick shithouse."

"Did you sail it from America, Gerry?"

"Yeah, I bought *Atom* in 1991. I sailed her from Florida across the North Atlantic to the Mediterranean, via Bermuda and the Azores. I stayed there a year then returned to Florida. It was a shakedown cruise to see how I'd go sailing single-handed. It worked out OK, so a year later I took off on a circumnavigation — the Bahamas, through the Panama Canal and across the Pacific to Australia."

Gerry told me that his longest crossing was sixty days from the Panama Canal to the Marquesas Islands. During that time, a school of fish followed *Atom*, enabling Gerry to catch a fish any time he wanted to.

"It was like a living pantry, and it sure beat tinned food," Gerry said.

"Do you still like single-handed sailing?" I asked.

"On a boat of *Atom*'s size, you've got to," Gerry laughed. "But yes, I wouldn't like it any other way. It's probably a selfish outlook, but you have no responsibility for anyone else. During the tough times though, it sure would be handy to have another person on board who knew what they were doing, but somehow or other you get through OK."

"Talking about tough times, what's the worst weather you've experienced on the voyage so far?"

"Two nights ago at Cape sonofabitch Bowling Green!" Gerry replied without the slightest hesitation.

A while later, as Gerry stood up to go below and get a book he wanted to show me, he grimaced and grabbed at his waist.

"This darn pelvis is playing up again," he said.

"What's the trouble with it?" I asked.

Gerry told me that seven years ago he owned a 9 metre sloop. One night he was anchored off the South Florida coast; it was a hot, calm, peaceful night, so Gerry decided to sleep on the cockpit seat. He climbed into his sleeping bag and soon drifted off. The next thing he knew there was a tremendous explosion, a blinding white light, a searing pain in his leg and Gerry found himself in the water gasping for breath and struggling for his life. In a semi-conscious state, Gerry felt himself being pulled from the water onto another boat. The next thing he knew he was in hospital with his pelvis broken in five places.

He later discovered that about 2 a.m. on the morning of the accident, an 8 metre speedboat, powered by twin 200 horsepower outboards and travelling at 40 knots ploughed straight into the side of his yacht. The bow of the speedboat lifted over the yacht's gunwale, shattering the boom and tiller to smithereens and knocking Gerry into the cockpit well; an action which saved his life, because the outboard propellers then gouged out the cockpit seat like butter, snagged the sleeping bag and dragged it and Gerry out of the yacht into the water. Like a limp doll, he was flicked out of the sleeping bag before it fouled the propellers, bringing the speedboat to a standstill. The crew from the speedboat pulled Gerry from the water and arranged for him to be taken to hospital. The case went to court, but because the speedboat crew claimed that Gerry wasn't displaying an anchor light, he was awarded a minimal amount of compensation.

"I *was* displaying a riding light from the boom," Gerry emphasised. "I always do, but it was four of them against me. All I got was $30,000 out of it — just enough to buy *Atom*."

"What was the speedboat doing running around at 40 knots at two o'clock in the morning?" I asked.

"Well, they said they were returning from a fishing trip, but I heard they were under suspicion for drug running. A lot of it goes on in that area."

"After that experience, Gerry, you'd think a chicken farm in Nebraska would be all you'd want — as far away from the sea as possible."

"Once the sea's in your blood it's darn hard to get rid of. And anyway, I didn't want to sit around after retirement growing fat, drinking beer and watching television. I've got a small pension from the time I spent in the Marines and the Air Force — it's not big, but enough to live on if I'm careful."

A couple of days later, while doing my washing at the marina's laundromat, I saw an advertisement on the noticeboard asking for a "female adventurer extraordinaire" to accompany the skipper of a 6.7 metre catamaran to Indonesia. The name of the yacht was *Cooking Fat*. What a strange name, I thought. Later on I went down to see the catamaran. The vessel was so tiny; the two hulls were like coffins, joined by a couple of spars and a rope trampoline. Struth! Sail to Indonesia on that? You'd have to be an adventurer extraordinaire all right.

No-one was on board, but a bloke on the yacht across from *Cooking Fat* gave me a wave.

"Applying for the job," he laughed.

"No," I laughed back, "I don't think I'm quite what the skipper has in mind."

"He sailed out from England on that, you know," the bloke said.

"You're kidding?"

"No, fair dinkum, he did."

I shook my head in wonderment.

"Has he had any takers for his trip to Indonesia?" I queried.

"A few women have come down to look at her, but they walk away very quickly. I think he's going to have to go on his own."

"Do you know why he called her *Cooking Fat*?" I asked. "It's a strange sort of name."

"Yes, it's north England slang," the bloke said. "Change the C and the F around and what do you get?"

I thought for a couple of seconds and then burst into laughter.

"Fooking Cat!" I exploded. "At least he's got a sense of humour."

As I was walking back to *Pluto* I met Gerry on the pontoon.

"I was thinking of going out for a meal tonight," he said. "Do you know of any place that's cheap and reasonable?"

"As a matter of fact, earlier on I was talking to the bloke who runs the Travel-Lift at the slip, and he recommended the Sheraton Hotel Casino. Apparently on a Friday night they have an excellent seafood smorgasbord for $9.95."

"That sounds pretty good to me," Gerry replied. "With my budget I don't like to pay anymore than $10 for a meal. How about we both go?"

"Sure. Pop over to *Pluto* for a rum about six-thirty, then we can walk over to the casino — it should only be a ten minute stroll."

When we arrived at the brilliantly lit, ritzy entrance to the casino, I asked the doorman the location of the seafood smorgasbord.

"Walk straight ahead, sir, up the small flight of stairs and it's the second set of doors to your left."

We walked across a plush carpet and arrived at the door to be welcomed by a friendly looking girl standing behind a desk.

"Good evening," I said. "Is this where the seafood smorgasbord is served?"

"Yes, sir."

"Could we have a table for two, please?"

"Do you have a booking, sir?" she smiled.

"No, we don't."

"Oh, I'm sorry, but we're completely booked out tonight."

"Really?"

"Yes, I'm sorry, but the Friday night smorgasbord has become extremely popular."

I feigned bitter disappointment.

"Do you realise," I said, "that this gentleman with me has sailed a tiny 8 metre yacht single-handed halfway around the world to get here. He's battled storm and tempest thousands of miles from land, sat out doldrums for weeks, lived on bland tinned food for months and suffered privations almost too terrible to describe, all to reach this beautiful tropical wonderland of ours where he was hoping to taste the seafood delights that he's been told your establishment has to offer — and this is how he's rewarded — this is how he will remember Australian hospitality. He will sail away from our golden shores with sad memories and an empty stomach only to face more storms and lonely nights on an unrelenting sea . . ."

"All right, all right," the girl interrupted with a wide grin, "you've talked me into it, you can have a table."

As I took out my wallet to pay, the girl said:

112

"Don't pay for it now. We add the drinks on to the bill and you pay the whole lot at the end of your meal."

As we followed the girl to a table, Gerry said to me:

"And you Aussies always say it's us Yanks who are full of bullshit."

The range of food at the smorgasbord was astonishing. Not only were there top quality oysters, mussels, prawns, crab, Moreton Bay bugs, crayfish, and baked fish, there were varieties of steaming soup, roasts, casseroles, baked vegetables, salad and a dozen types of dessert.

"This is unbelievable," Gerry said. "I think I'll have some soup, then stick to the seafood."

"Exactly what I was thinking," I replied.

We ordered two beers from a waitress who came to the table.

"How can they afford to do this for $9.95?" Gerry asked as he finished off his large bowl of soup.

"It's got to be from the money they make from the gambling," I answered. "The majority of people lose, so I suppose putting on a spread like this gets them into the casino. They have a meal, then go and lose their money."

"Do you gamble?" Gerry asked.

"No, it's a mugs' game, as far as I'm concerned."

"I agree with you there," Gerry replied. "But it looks as though we're winners here tonight."

When the waitress returned to the table with the two beers, she slipped a docket between the salt and pepper shakers. Gerry and I continued with our feast.

"These prawns are superb," I drooled.

"Magnificent," Gerry agreed.

When the waitress returned later with a second lot of drinks, she took the original docket and replaced it with another.

"What's that docket the broad keeps putting between the salt and pepper shakers?" Gerry asked after the waitress had gone.

"Probably just the bill, Gerry. Every time we have a drink, she most likely brings the total up to date."

Gerry finished eating a prawn, put on his spectacles, then picked up the docket and looked at it. In one swift movement his chair was knocked over backwards as he leapt to his feet and shouted at the top of his voice:

"Jesus Christ! $92.50!"

There was a sudden, deathly silence, as everyone in the restaurant stopped eating and stared towards our table. Gerry righted his chair, sat down and handed me the docket. The two meals were written down as $39.95 each. While I was looking at the docket, a waitress came to take our soup plates away.

"I thought this smorgasbord was $9.95 each," Gerry said to her.

"Oh, no sir. The $9.95 seafood smorgasbord is in the casino area at their little café. It's not nearly as good as this."

Gerry appeared shell-shocked. Realising the 'show' was over, the other diners settled back to their meals.

"That's blown my darn budget for a while," Gerry said.

"Don't worry about it, Gerry, it's my fault that we ended up here. I'm paying for both our meals. Think of it as just some good old Aussie hospitality. Come on, eat up, don't let it spoil your night."

I could see that Gerry wasn't happy with that arrangement.

"Look," he said, "it would make me feel better if I bought the drinks for the rest of the evening."

"OK, if that's what you want."

Gerry soon reverted to his old self, and began tucking in to the remainder of the meal.

After dinner we went into the gambling area of the casino. It was fascinating walking around watching thousands of dollars of punters' money being poked through small slots with sticks, certainly a night's entertainment in itself, just watching the passing parade. It was well into the early hours of the morning when we returned to the marina. I don't know who spent the most that night — me on meals, or Gerry on drinks, but what did it matter.

"That's the best darn night I've had since arriving in Australia," Gerry said. "True Aussie hospitality."

"It's the least we could do for someone who has sailed halfway around the world in a tiny 8 metre yacht, battling storm and tempest, sitting out doldrums and suffering privations almost too terrible to . . . "

Chapter 14

LAND OF PLENTY

The 25 to 30 knot south-easterly wind had rarely faltered since my arrival in Townsville a week earlier. Each day the Bureau of Meteorology had issued a strong wind warning for coastal waters between Cardwell and Bowen. Assuming the weather would have to improve soon, Shirley flew up from Brisbane to spend a week or so with me. We planned to sail over to Magnetic Island, which lay only 5 miles from Townsville and where, according to the chart, there were a number of interesting looking bays protected from the prevailing winds. But the weather didn't improve, and Shirley made it clear she wasn't leaving the marina on *Pluto* in these conditions, and for once I totally agreed with her. It didn't matter all that much anyhow, as it was enjoyable just being in each other's company again.

The very pleasant walk from the marina to the city was through a beautifully maintained park and past many of Townsville's historic buildings. We did all the touristy things — visited the Maritime Museum, the Museum of Tropical Queensland, the Art Gallery and together with yachties Anne and Lawrie from the catamaran *Red Cloud*, explored Townsville and its surrounds in a hire car.

Even strolling around the marina complex itself was entertaining. Next to the marina was a block of just completed high-rise apartments, in which one resident spent an hour or two each evening playing the saxophone. It may not have been too entertaining for his immediate neighbours, but the deep soulful sounds wafting through the night air certainly added atmosphere to our after dinner walks. The marina, high-rise apartments, casino and entertainment centre had all been built on reclaimed land in the harbour. The whole area had been extensively landscaped, predominantly with mature coconut palms. What had previously been a rarely visited part of Townsville was now a focal point for the community — some event or other was always happening there.

"It doesn't seem as though this wind will ever stop," I said to Shirley one morning. "How about we go across to Magnetic Island on the ferry? That'll be better than not seeing the island at all."

"Sounds like an excellent idea to me."

Even on the large ferry it was quite a boisterous ride across the bay. We disembarked at the jetty beside the small settlement of Picnic Bay. Our ferry tickets included free use of the island's bus service, which ran from Picnic Bay through a number of small coastal settlements to Horseshoe Bay on the other side of the island. Most of Magnetic Island was national park and the roads were confined to the south-eastern side of the island, so we had time to stop off at each place, including having lunch at the Nelly Bay Hotel. Each beachside settlement had its residential area, small tourist resort and a few shops. Perfect places for a relaxed family holiday away from the hustle and bustle of the city. Nelly Bay had a partly developed marina and boat harbour; the breakwater had been built, but the whole harbour needed extensive dredging. We were told that the developers had run out of money.

After ten days in Townsville, it was time for Shirley to fly back to Brisbane. The wind had dropped to 20 knots from the south-east, so I decided to continue my journey north. Freed of mooring lines and with the breeze directly astern, *Pluto* rode jauntily over the waves as if he was pleased to be back in his rightful environment. Referring to *Pluto* in the male gender instead of the universally accepted female form wasn't an error. Since the first time I boarded *Pluto*, I did not think of the yacht as a "she". Even Shirley surprised me shortly after we bought *Pluto* by saying:

"*Pluto* is a he, not a she."

I don't know whether tampering with the accepted gender of vessels is supposed to be unlucky or not, but I had got this far unscathed and was prepared to stick to my decision.

About four o'clock in the afternoon I rounded the south-western end of Great Palm Island and anchored *Pluto* in Casement Bay, a short distance from the island's Aboriginal township. The settlement was recorded as being one of the most violent communities in the world. Domestic violence and murder, mostly fuelled by alcohol, were common. The sailing directions warned that crime was rampant on the island and recommended that visitors should not go ashore. In Townsville, a trawler skipper told me he had recently visited the settlement to collect some emergency engine parts that had been flown in to the island's airstrip.

"It was like another world," he recalled. "There were drunks staggering around, and while I was walking down the road, groups of Aboriginal teenagers heckled me and shouted 'fuck off you white cunt'. Graffiti was everywhere — the word PIGS was sprayed across the front of the police station. There was rubbish blowing all over the place; the football field looked as if someone had dumped thousands of empty drink cans and truckloads of garbage over it, then flattened it into the ground with a road-roller. It was disgusting. Some Aborigines on the island are trying to turn things around, but I think they're fighting a losing battle."

It certainly didn't sound good, but I had two reasons for anchoring in Casement Bay — it was reputed to be the best anchorage during strong south-easterlies in the whole Palm Isles group, and it was only 15 miles away from the southern entrance to the Hinchinbrook Channel, which I wanted to negotiate at the top half of the flood tide within the next few days. The anchorage proved to be excellent, because that night the south-easterly wind increased with gusts of well over 30 knots, accompanied by heavy rain squalls. The lousy conditions continued for two days, but I was perfectly comfortable and there wasn't the slightest swell. The only disturbance occurred each evening when an assault of loud rock music blasted across the bay from the island's community centre. I retaliated with a selection of operatic arias sung by Maria Callas. Maria won, but not by much.

I departed Casement Bay on the third morning. The wind had dropped to about 15 knots, however the sky was still heavily overcast. I steered *Pluto* past Fantome Island and along the western side of Orpheus Island to Little Pioneer Bay, where I anchored to have some lunch. I had considered spending the night there and going ashore the following day to have a look at the island, but the swell running into the bay was atrocious. I up-anchored and headed for Hinchinbrook Channel.

The steel tower at the end of the Lucinda Point bulk sugar conveyor jetty provided a handy reference mark for the entrance to the channel. This huge structure projected 3 miles out to sea. I sailed *Pluto* past the end of the jetty and turned sharply round the fairway buoy. The short choppy seas caused the ketch to bounce around so much it was impossible to pick out the entrance leads through the binoculars. With my eyes glued alternately on the compass and depth sounder, which sometimes showed less than a metre beneath the keel, *Pluto* was carried quickly along on the flood tide. The entrance leads eventually came into view. As I passed the sugar sheds at Lucinda Point the waves reduced to a slight chop, making it easier to see the port and starboard markers ahead. Before entering new territory such as this, I always made a point of doing my 'homework'. I'd lay off the courses on the chart from one beacon or buoy to the next; that way, when I rounded a mark I'd always know which course to steer, even though I couldn't immediately distinguish the next mark ahead. It had certainly helped to keep my blood pressure in check so far.

The further along the channel I went, the calmer the water became, but every so often bullets of wind would suddenly shoot in, heeling *Pluto* over from almost upright to 20°. An hour before nightfall I anchored behind tiny Haycock Island, 7 miles upstream from Lucinda. It was still heavily overcast and hazy. The banks of the channel were lined with dense mangroves, and Hinchinbrook Island's mountains were lost in thick cloud. As darkness descended so did the mosquitoes; I hurriedly fitted the insect screens over the hatches and went below to prepare dinner. Later that night as I sat reading in my bunk, I heard the strange, deep bark of a crocodile close by in the mangroves. So far, Hinchinbrook Island looked a lot less appealing than its World Heritage listed reputation.

But next morning I awoke to a different world, a world of majestic grandeur, comparable in Australia only to Tasmania's rugged south-west wilderness. The sky was cloudless and brilliant blue, the dark water of the channel was like a millpond, reflecting its mangrove-lined edges like a mirror image. There wasn't a breath of breeze, and the only sounds were made by small birds chirping away as they flitted through the mangroves in search of food.

I cooked the last of my bacon for breakfast, up-anchored and began motoring along the remaining 18 miles of twisting channel. Flanked by the mainland's Cardwell Range to port and Hinchinbrook Island to starboard, each bend presented a magnificent vista of the island's mountain range. The thick mangrove forests were overshadowed by dark green rainforest covered slopes that stretched dizzily skywards for over 1,100 metres to jagged mountain peaks. Waterfalls, glistening like silver in the morning sun, tumbled down the mountains' sides and cascaded into deep precipitous gullies. Dozens of small creeks branched off the main channel, snaking their way inland.

After motoring for about 8 miles the channel widened and a 12 knot south-easterly breeze came in. I hoisted sail, stopped the motor, and with only the slight sound of tiny waves slapping against the hull, *Pluto* cut gently and swiftly through the water.

A cluster of tall coconut palms behind a small sandy beach at Scraggy Point, near the north-western end of Hinchinbrook Island, looked too tempting to pass. I dropped anchor and went ashore with my machete, thinking how nice some fresh coconut milk and kernel would be. At the end of a short track that passed through thick undergrowth, I came to a grassy clearing dotted with coconut palms. Nearby, a national park sign stated:

WARNING. ESTUARINE CROCODILES INHABIT THIS AREA

I had no sooner finished reading the last word, when right behind me I heard an urgent heavy thrashing in the undergrowth.

"*Shit!*" I cried out, instinctively leaping in the air before running for my life into the clearing. I stopped and turned round to see what monster I had to do battle with. What I saw was a 2 metre long goanna scrambling up a tree.

"You rotten bastard!" I shouted at it, brandishing my machete. "You nearly gave me a heart attack!"

The goanna stopped climbing and looked down at me as if to say:

"Ha, ha. Scared the pants off another one."

I'm sure it was grinning.

I collected a few coconuts, de-husked them, drank some of the milk and broke up the kernel ready to take back to *Pluto*. Then I followed a walking track through the rainforest and came to a fresh water stream that was running quite rapidly after the recent rain. The water tasted deliciously pure, so much better than the town water on board *Pluto*. I found a deep, clear pool and plunged in; the water was so cold it took my breath away, but it was beautiful to bathe in the soft, fresh water.

The wind had dropped off again, so I decided to stay anchored at Scraggy Point overnight. That evening I grated some of the coconut kernel and squeezed it through a handkerchief to obtain some coconut cream to pour over my tinned fruit. The cream was rich and sweet, and although it took a lot of effort to obtain very little quantity, the result was delicious. It didn't taste too bad either, mixed with a dash of rum. One old beachcomber who I met in my lighthouse days, reckoned the coconut cream tastes even better when squeezed through a woman's black silk stocking — straight off the leg of course. That was something I had yet to confirm.

On the mainland at Oyster Point, just 2 miles across from where *Pluto* was anchored, a marina and resort were in the early stages of construction. Conservationists had been against this development for years, claiming that the dredging of the channel into the marina would have a detrimental effect on the habitat of the region's dugong. Work on the project had been halted on a number of occasions because of legal and physical battles. Considering the huge area of the Hinchinbrook Channel compared to the tiny dot of the Oyster Point development, it didn't appear that the dugongs would have much of a problem. By law, Aborigines and Torres Strait Islanders are permitted to hunt dugong and turtle for food, as has been their tradition for centuries. But over the years, bark canoes have been replaced by aluminium dinghies with powerful outboards, and native spears replaced by rifles, giving an unfair advantage to the hunter and extinguishing any claim to tradition. It crossed my mind that perhaps the dugongs would have more chance of survival if the conservationists tried to change *that* law.

The glorious weather conditions continued. I set off next morning for the 25 mile trip to Dunk Island, the largest of the Family Islands. I had eaten the last of my fresh meat the previous night, so I let out a trolling line as *Pluto* sailed across Rockingham Bay. Within a minute the elastic shock cord went taut. I reeled in the line and pulled aboard a Spotted Mackerel about three-quarters of a metre long — enough to last me for at least three days. After filleting the fish and storing most of it in the icebox, I dusted a few fillets with flour and fried some for lunch. With a squeeze of lemon they were delicious.

The country had now changed — on the mainland, a canopy of thick rainforest descended sharply from the mountains right to the beachfront, and each island I passed was steep and densely wooded with similar vegetation.

121

This was the start of the true tropics — the Far North, where the rainforest meets the sea. The atmosphere seemed to emanate nirvana: no rush, no deadlines, tomorrow will do. Clear sky, a fair breeze, a tiller in my hand, fresh fish and coconut cream in my rum. What more could I ask? — well, perhaps Shirley and a pair of black silk stockings.

Chapter 15

STEP TO THE MUSIC YOU HEAR

"Do you sell ice here?" I asked the glum-looking man behind the bar at Dunk Island's day visitor centre.

"Yeah," he replied.

"What size are the bags?"

"Just the normal size."

"Well, I'll have two bags please."

"I'll have to go out the back and get them."

When he returned he dumped the bags unceremoniously onto the bar. They looked quite a bit smaller than "normal" size.

"That's $10," he said.

"$10!" exploded his cocky young male assistant, who was serving a beer to a bloke beside me. "$5 for a bag of frozen water! You can get a bigger bag than that for $1.50 down south!"

The glum-looking man's eyes narrowed, as he ignored his assistant's remarks. But the young bloke didn't let it rest.

"I can't believe it!" he continued, gesturing to the half-dozen or so people at the bar and pointing to the ice. "$5 for a bag of frozen water! What a rip off!"

"Shouldn't you be on *this* side of the bar, when you make statements like that?" I said jovially. "I think you've been reading the wrong books on how to improve your promotion prospects."

"It's easy come, easy go with me, mate," he replied. "If I lose this job, I'll just get another one. I hate rip offs. $5 for a bag of water! It's unbelievable!"

As the young assistant walked away to serve another customer, the glum-looking man gave him a look that would have instantly withered most people, but it was like water off a duck's back to the young bloke.

I must admit, $5 for a bag of ice was the most I had paid so far, but I had learnt to accept that most island resorts had a fairly high mark-up on everything they sold. You either accepted it or you didn't buy it; there was little purpose in making a song and dance about it.

123

Despite the high cost of ice, Dunk Island was a really pleasant place. *Pluto*, along with half-a-dozen other yachts, was anchored in Brammo Bay, just a short distance along the beach from the resort. Behind the beachfront, directly opposite where the yachts were anchored, there was a small bar and outdoor cafe that catered for yachties and day visitors. Further along, under a canopy of trees, was a national park camping area and a brand new toilet and shower block. Although yachties, day visitors and campers were not permitted in the resort area, they were welcome to make a booking for lunch or dinner in the resort's dining room.

I thought that having a separate day visitor centre was an excellent idea. It provided an income for the resort and kept the hoi polloi away from the resort guests, who had paid a substantial tariff and were entitled to their privacy.

Thick rainforest covered most of the island; a number of walking tracks led across gurgling streams to mountain tops and quiet beaches. There were also some cleared paddocks covered with lush grass where a herd of contented-looking cows grazed, which, I was told, provided all the milk required by the resort.

But Dunk Island is probably best known for being the home of Edmund and Bertha Banfield, who settled on the island in 1897 and spent twenty-five years there living a peaceful, hermitic existence. During their time on Dunk, Edmund wrote four books, the best known being *Confessions of a Beach-comber* published in 1908. It was obvious that the Banfields had no intention of struggling with the real hardships of self-sufficiency, as they arrived on the island with a boat, a prefabricated cedar dwelling, a workman and two "faithful black servants". Nevertheless, they developed a deep bond with the island, which is obvious from Edmund's writings. Edmund died in 1923 and was buried on his beloved Dunk Island.

Through the rainforest, only a short distance from the back of the resort, I climbed a steep track to Banfield's grave. The epitaph on the weathered headstone read:

> *"If a man does not keep pace with his companions, perhaps it is because he hears a different drummer. Let him step to the music which he hears."*

Those words came from the book *Walden* written by Henry David Thoreau who, from 1845 to 1847, lived a solitary existence in a self-built hut on the banks of Walden Pond in Concord, Massachusetts. While living there, Thoreau wrote *Walden*, which remains one of the classics of American literature. There is little doubt that Thoreau's philosophy was responsible for inducing the Banfields to take up residence on Dunk Island.

As I stood by the grave in the shadowy rainforest, pondering on Thoreau's wise words, I wondered what Banfield would think of his island if he was here today. The house in which the Banfields lived has long gone, replaced by the resort's staff quarters. A few mango trees and coconut palms are the only evidence of the couple's past life on the island. Now there's a luxurious resort with its own airstrip, para-sailing and jet-skiing on Brammo Bay, hot meals, cold drinks and bags of ice for sale at the beachfront bar, and regular daily ferry services from Mission Beach and Clump Point a few miles away on the mainland. I imagine Banfield would be horrified. Or perhaps he wouldn't — perhaps he'd be down at the beachside bar, admiring the bikini-clad campers and selling his books to the tourists.

After a day exploring the island, the beachside bar was a great place to sit, have a cold drink and a chat to other yachties or sometimes campers, most of whom were backpackers from overseas. Then, before returning to *Pluto*, call in for a shower at the amenities building. The male and female toilets and showers were under the same roof, but entry to the men's was on one side, the women's on the other. Early one evening I walked into the amenities building to have a shower. The two shower cubicles were in use, but suddenly I heard female voices coming from both. Oh, no! I said to myself. Don't tell me I've been using the wrong side of the building for the last two nights. You read about this sort of thing in the newspapers, with headlines like:

DIRTY OLD MAN FOUND LURKING IN WOMEN'S TOILETS
CLAIMS HE THOUGHT IT WAS THE MEN'S

Oh yeah, we've heard that one before, mate. I hurried outside and looked at the sign. It plainly said MEN. I walked back inside and found a young woman in her late teens combing her wet hair in front of the mirror.

"Excuse me," I said, "but do you realise this is the men's?"

"Yes, we know," she replied casually. "It's just that the showers here seem to work better than in the women's."

I went into the spare cubicle and began to shower. The partition between the two cubicles was a short distance off the floor. Suddenly there was a sharp bang on the floor tiles and a hairbrush shot under the partition into my cubicle. Next thing a woman's hand appeared and began feeling around. I gave the brush a deft kick with my foot and sent it flying back under the partition.

"Thanks," a voice called out, and then broke into song.

It's not fair on us men, I thought. There will never be real equality between men and women. I mean, you just don't see headlines saying:

DIRTY YOUNG WOMAN FOUND LURKING IN MEN'S TOILETS
CLAIMS SHE THOUGHT IT WAS THE WOMEN'S

Apart from the Banfields, another name synonymous with Dunk Island is Bruce Arthur. For years I'd known that Bruce lived on a hectare or two in

125

the rainforest about 2 kilometres from the resort. Bruce, a former wrestler who had competed in the Olympic and Commonwealth Games, was now renowned worldwide for his woollen tapestries. For thirty years, Bruce has lived in relative seclusion; firstly on Timana Island — a tiny island 2 miles south of Dunk, before moving to Dunk Island ten years later.

I set off one morning to visit his studio. About halfway along the track, I suddenly felt, rather than heard, the presence of someone behind me. I quickly turned round to see an attractive woman in her early thirties. She was tall and slim, and had long, straight, honey-blonde hair. She wore a blouse and jeans, but was barefoot, and carried a decorative woollen bag slung on a long strap over her shoulder.

"Hello," she said, "did I startle you?"

"Just a little," I replied. "I don't see many people walking by themselves, and those who walk in groups are usually pretty noisy — you can hear them kilometres away."

"Are you going to Bruce's?" she asked.

"Yes, are you?"

"Yes, I'm helping out there today. This is one of the two mornings each week that guests from the resort visit the studio."

"Are you from the resort?" I asked.

"No, I live on the mainland. I came over on the ferry this morning."

"Are you off a yacht?" she enquired.

"Yes, I've sailed up from Brisbane."

As we walked along the track, the woman told me her name was Liz Gallie and that she lived at Bingil Bay in a house she had built herself in the rainforest. Liz sometimes came over to the island for the day to help out and at the same time visit her friend Sue who lived at Bruce's.

"I've been helping out quite a bit lately," Liz told me. "Bruce has been away on the mainland having a hip operation. He's well enough to travel now and will be coming back to the island in a few days."

"It's a shame to see these legendary island dwellers like Bruce growing old," I said. "They've been such a unique part of the Barrier Reef islands for decades, you almost think of them as immortal. And there aren't many of them left now."

"No, that's right," Liz replied. "Noel Woods has only recently left Bedarra Island. He first went there to paint in 1936. He sold his property and it's now been subdivided into seven exclusive house blocks."

"Do you know Andy Martin from Middle Percy Island?" I asked.

"I've heard of him, but I've never met him."

"He's got hip problems too, amongst other things," I continued. "He can't manage by himself anymore — he's got a young couple on the island doing all the hard work now."

"Yes, I heard that he had."

We came to a narrow walking track that branched off to the left.

"Bruce's place is in here," Liz said.

We climbed some stone steps and eventually came to a semi-cleared area where there was a geodesic dome structure built on a stone base.

"That's the studio," Liz said. "Feel free to go inside and look around. I'm going over to the house to help Sue prepare some cold drinks and nibbles for the resort guests — they'll be along soon."

The atmosphere inside the dome was quiet, almost cathedral-like. Bruce's vibrantly coloured tapestry wall hangs, along with original paintings of the island were hung around the wall; there were sculptures, items of pottery and glass-topped cabinets containing an array of beautiful jewellery, each display showing the artist's name. Some of the prices took my breath away, but there was no doubt that the people who had created these pieces were highly talented. One cabinet of jewellery really appealed to me. It contained a selection of bracelets and necklaces of simplistic, elegant beauty, made from a combination of silver, black coral and bone. I looked down at the card that displayed the maker's name. It read: "LIZ GALLIE".

A short while later, Liz came into the dome with another woman.

"Stuart, this is my friend Sue Kirk," she said.

"Ah, Sue Kirk," I replied. "That's another name I recognize. I've just been looking at both your jewellery displays — they're superb."

"Thank you," Sue replied. "How many pieces would you like to buy?"

"That depends on whether you're interested in taking a small ketch as a deposit."

Sue laughed and continued:

"The guests from the resort are just coming up the track, so after they've gone would you like to come over to the house for a drink?"

"Yes I would. Thanks very much."

When I went over to the house later, Sue answered my call.

"Come in," she said. "What would you like to drink — a beer?"

"Thank you — that would be great."

The room we were in was large and rambling with different floor levels. There were bookcases and cabinets filled with books, and coffee tables covered with even more books. A number of Bruce's tapestries hung on the walls; and a huge uncompleted one was still in its loom, its bright colours a severe contrast to the rest of the room's dark décor. A large dining table and an assortment of well-used lounge chairs were placed haphazardly around the floor. This was a house used for living — completely utilitarian.

"Sue," I asked, "I noticed a few buildings further up the hill — are they a part of Bruce's place?"

"Yes," Sue replied, "they're usually occupied by artists who Bruce invites to the island. Bruce has done quite well out of his tapestries, and for years now he's been giving something back more valuable than money, and that's inspiration and experience. Working together seems to help people who are still finding their way. Discussing each other's works and making suggestions seems to push them over accepted boundaries and urges them on to greater creativity."

"Well," I said thoughtfully, "from what I've seen in the dome, his theory certainly seems to be working."

"We've only got one person living here at the moment." Sue continued. "I don't suppose you know anyone who paints or sculpts who'd like to stay here for a few months?"

"No, I don't," I replied. "But if you put an advertisement in *The Courier-Mail*, I reckon you'd be swamped with applicants."

I was invited to stay for a delicious fresh fruit salad lunch, most of the fruit grown in Sue's garden. We spoke on well into the afternoon. There was no doubt that Liz and Sue were two very independent women who had heard a different drummer and were stepping to the music which they heard. Thoreau and the Banfields would have been proud of them.

It certainly wasn't great weather for sailing — calm seas and not much over 5 knots of breeze. But it was perfect weather for what I had planned — motor sailing slowly along the coast, anchoring overnight behind islands where it would have been insufferable during even moderate winds and seas. I left Dunk Island early in the morning, motoring northwards close to shore. Although I could see a number of houses partially hidden by trees near the foreshore of Mission Beach, the thick, dark-green cover of rainforest that swept up the range to meet Mt Tam O'Shanter looked impenetrable. It was this type of country that had greeted the ill-fated explorer Edmund Kennedy and his party when they arrived in Rockingham Bay during May 1848 on board the vessels *Tam O'Shanter* and *Rattlesnake*. Kennedy and his twelve men landed 2 miles south of Mission Beach, and after unloading a heavy square cart, two spring carts, twenty-eight horses, one hundred sheep and tonnes of stores, set off to find an overland route to Cape York.

The expedition was plagued with disaster right from the start. The party immediately encountered swamps, thick scrub, stinging trees and entanglements of impassable lawyer-vine — so named because once its hooks are into you, it never lets go. After weeks of hacking their way through jungle to find a suitable track, the party found themselves further south than when they had first begun. The horses and carts repeatedly bogged in muddy creeks, forcing the men to offload the stores and carry them on their shoulders to the other side. The first attack from spear-throwing Aborigines occurred a month into the expedition; the men managed to scare the blacks away by firing shots, which killed one and wounded three. Eventually Kennedy decided to abandon the carts and much of their gear. During August, Kennedy discovered that the storeman Niblet had been falsifying food records, taking larger rations for himself; there was little that Kennedy could do but reprimand Niblet and put someone else in charge of provisions. Arrangements had been made for *HMS Rambler* to wait for the party in Princess Charlotte Bay until the end of August in case they needed assistance; but by the end of August the party was nowhere near the bay, and shortly afterwards the ship departed.

Only fifty sheep remained, all in poor condition. Some of the horses were so weak that when they fell they couldn't get back on their feet; they were shot and eaten. Attacks from Aborigines became more prevalent. When the men reached Weymouth Bay, Kennedy realised that all their stores would be eaten well before they reached their destination. So, leaving eight of the men behind with two horses and a small amount of flour, Kennedy and four men set off for Port Albany, where they knew a ship would be waiting. One night, while camped at Shelburne Bay, one of the party accidentally shot himself in the arm and shoulder. Kennedy left two men with the injured man and pushed on with his native servant Jackey Jackey. With Port Albany almost in sight, Kennedy and Jackey Jackey were attacked by Aborigines. Kennedy was speared in the back; Jackey Jackey cut off the shaft and dug out the spear, then helped Kennedy stagger on. Kennedy was soon speared in the right leg above the knee, and shortly afterwards took a fatal hit in the side. While the Aborigines temporarily retreated, Jackey Jackey buried Kennedy in the scrub, then pressed on across the crocodile infested Escape River to Port Albany, all the while wary of being stalked by blacks.

Jackey Jackey arrived at Port Albany on 23 December and told his story to Captain Dobson of the *Ariel.* They set sail that evening for Shelburne Bay, but on their arrival the only trace of the three men was a cloak found in an abandoned native canoe. They could only surmise that the men had been killed by Aborigines. The *Ariel* continued south to Weymouth Bay; only two of the eight men left there were still alive, and they were all but skeletons. The other six had died of exhaustion and starvation. One of the survivors told how some of the Aborigines had at first appeared friendly, and brought them small amounts of food. However, most were openly hostile, threatening them with spears and boomerangs, and throwing spears into the camp. It appeared that the *Ariel* had arrived just in time to save the two men from certain death. Of the party of thirteen who set off from Rockingham Bay seven months earlier, only three survived to record one of the greatest disasters in Australia's exploration history.

Over the next week I made my way along 60 miles of rainforest covered coastline, making short hops between the small, uninhabited islands that lay 2 or 3 miles offshore. For much of that distance the coastline was overshadowed by the lofty Bellenden Ker Range and Queensland's highest peak Mt Bartle Frere. Fresh fish was always on the menu; every few days I'd let out a trolling line, and as before in Rockingham Bay I'd soon have a Spotted Mackerel on board. The weather remained perfect, and the breeze never exceeded 10 knots.

After a week of not seeing another vessel, it was a bit of a shock to motor *Pluto* into Welcome Bay off Fitzroy Island and find at least twenty or so vessels anchored in front of the resort. Situated only 15 miles from the city of Cairns, it was obvious that the island was a popular destination for local residents. I had last been to Fitzroy Island in 1981 to visit some friends who worked there as lightkeepers. Shirley and I had travelled from Cairns on board the fast catamaran *Fitzroy Flyer*, which did a daily run to the resort. Ten years after that visit the lighthouse was decommissioned and replaced by a solar powered automatic light built on tiny Little Fitzroy Island, a stone's throw from the north-eastern side of its big brother.

I left the beach and made my way up a very steep, winding vehicular track that led through thick rainforest towards the lightstation. The track had been cut into the side of the island, and at some places the edge of the track dropped sharply to the sea over 100 metres below. When the light was first established in 1943, the lightkeepers lived in huts beside the beach where the resort now stands. Each evening the lightkeeper on duty would drive the station jeep up to the lighthouse and put on the light. At times, especially during wet weather, or when the vehicle was carrying a heavy load of fuel for the generators that powered the light, the lightkeepers had to reverse the jeep up the track, taking advantage of its lower gear ratio.

As I climbed higher, the bush thinned and the ground flattened off to a plateau where the track curved round to the lighthouse cottages. The lightstation was now controlled by Queensland Parks and Wildlife Service. One cottage looked as though it had just been renovated and was being used for ranger accommodation.

The original lighthouse was established in 1943, and replaced by a more modern tower in 1973. Although no longer operating, the modern lighthouse still remained, just a short distance from the cottages. Built of stainless steel and concrete sheathed with ceramic tiles, it had an attached lookout office at its base that provided 300° views to seaward. I returned a few hundred metres along the vehicle track and branched off up a steep pinch to the site of the original lighthouse. Apart from a concrete slab and a few piers, there was little evidence that it had once been an important navigational aid.

The light was installed to help guide ships through an opening in the Barrier Reef and along the Grafton Passage into Cairns. The design of the light was the only one of its kind in the world; it consisted of two bullseye lens panels positioned side by side, synchronised to pivot by means of a single driving motor. If a vessel approaching Cairns kept close to dead centre of the narrow passage the light would read group flashing (4) every 16 seconds. However, if a vessel veered too far to the north of centre of the passage, the light would read a long flash followed by two short flashes, which in morse code means the letter D, and indicated to the ship's skipper *go Down to be in the centre of the passage*. Conversely, if a vessel veered too far to the south of centre of the passage, the light would read two short flashes followed by a long flash, which in morse code means the letter U, and indicated *go Up to be in the centre of the passage*.

In 1994 the Australian Maritime Safety Authority (AMSA), the government agency which at that time controlled all Australian coastal lighthouses, made the unprecedented move of auctioning many of its surplus lighthouse lenses. Shirley and I attended the auction and bought the original Fitzroy Island lenses and machinery. It wasn't so much that we wanted it, it was just that we didn't want it disappearing into someone's home who had no idea of what it was. This was a museum piece, which we thought should be on public display. When we got the five, large, heavy timber crates home, we found a note attached to one that read:

KEEP FOR LIGHTHOUSE MUSEUM

We had no idea of its significance and quickly forgot about it. I contacted the Queensland Maritime Museum in Brisbane and offered to donate the light to them, but their indifference disappointed me, and made me decide not to give it to them. Then one day shortly before I left Brisbane on *Pluto* for my trip north, I received a telephone call from a woman in Cairns who said she was from the Queensland Parks and Wildlife Service.

"I've just finished reading your book *The Lighthouse Keepers*," she said, "and I wonder if you have any old photographs of the original Fitzroy Island lighthouse or lightkeepers who served there. Next year we'll be setting up a permanent display in the lighthouse lookout office on the island. We'd be very grateful if you'd allow us to display any photos you have. We'd pay for printing costs, of course."

"I haven't got many photographs," I replied, "but how would you like the original Fitzroy Island light? That would look pretty impressive in the lookout office."

There was a stunned silence, so I went on to explain. The offer was enthusiastically accepted and I sent the crates up to Cairns, where a retired lighthouse mechanic, John Spearritt, who had maintained and overhauled the light when it was operational on the island, offered to reconstruct it. John was probably the only person alive with the knowledge to do so. We discovered later that AMSA had mistakenly included the light in the auction, as it was supposed to have been kept for the National Maritime Museum in Sydney. Perhaps it is fate that the light is going back to its rightful home on Fitzroy Island.

I continued on along the steep foot-track, past huge boulders and gnarled old trees to the island's highest peak. Not a leaf stirred, but a developing line of heavy cloud on the horizon indicated that wind was on the way.

Next morning I awoke to a stiff south-easterly breeze. I hoisted sail and headed for Half Moon Bay Marina at Yorkeys Knob, 8 miles north of Cairns. As I approached Cape Grafton, just 5 miles from Fitzroy Island, the seas became choppy and confused. Every so often a bullet of wind would heel *Pluto* over, as the sheets strained and creaked on their winches. During one gust I heard a sharp, metallic explosion from the vicinity of the main mast, and at the same time saw the mainsail drop slightly in the mast track. I connected the autopilot and quickly went to investigate. I found that the block, which led the main halyard into the mast, had shattered, leaving the rope end of the halyard to chaff on the sharp edge of the mast opening. I wedged a piece of rubber under the halyard and took up the slack; it was a running repair, but would last until I reached the marina.

It was a very impressive sight sailing into the two hundred berth marina. A huge, elevated clubhouse, with a wide verandah running its full length overlooked the berthed yachts. Everything looked spotlessly clean and ship-shape. As I was tying up, I heard a bloke call out to me:

"G'day Stuart!"

I looked up. It was Don McCleod from the yacht *Leasar*. I had met him at Hamilton Island in the Whitsundays. Don had been the cameraman for Alby Mangles' television series *World Safari*, filmed in Torres Strait and South America.

"G'day Don!" I replied. "What are you doing up here? I thought you were well and truly entrenched in the Whitsundays."

"Ah, one morning I woke up and just decided it was time to go. This is a great marina. They've got a courtesy bus that runs into the shopping centre at Smithfield each day, and they have lunch and dinner at the club seven days a week. Anyhow, I'll let you settle in. I'll be up at the club about five if you want to join me for a drink."

"OK, see you up there, Don."

Don was right — it *was* a good marina. The girls in the office were very friendly and helpful, the meals at the clubhouse were excellent, enhanced by the nautical atmosphere of the surrounds. There were quite a number of yachties in the marina who I had met further down the coast, and it became customary most evenings to have a sundowner or two on someone's yacht or at the clubhouse. But like most things that are too good to be true, there had to be a bad point. And it didn't take me long to find out what that was. At about 2 a.m. on my first morning there, I was torn from a deep sleep by a roaring, screaming mechanical noise that made me levitate from my bunk in terror. It sounded as though a Jumbo jet was landing in *Pluto*'s cockpit. I was partly right; I discovered later it *was* a Jumbo jet, but instead of landing in the cockpit, it had landed at Cairns airport a few kilometres down the road. When my heart stopped pounding I managed to drop off to sleep again reasonably quickly. But two hours later I found myself involuntarily back on my feet when the same thing happened. Next day, I mentioned my disturbed night to Don.

"Yeah, a couple of Jumbos land most nights," Don replied. "They're full of Japanese tourists. It's a bit annoying at first, but you get used to it."

I didn't get used to it, but eventually I managed not to leap out of my bunk in fright. However, the marina's good points easily outweighed the interrupted sleep.

The yacht club's courtesy bus left the marina for Smithfield shopping centre each weekday at noon, and returned for pick-up two hours later. The shopping complex was huge and provided almost everything except yacht chandlery. Needing to replace the shattered mast fitting, I found out from the girls in the yacht club office that the nearest chandler was in Cairns. As they were giving me directions on how to get to the bus stop, Don came along.

"I need some yacht parts myself," he said. "Instead of going by bus though, there's a bloke here who lets you use his car for $20 a day. What do you think of getting that and having a look around Cairns as well?"

"Sounds good to me," I replied. "As long as the car goes. Or more importantly — stops."

"Ah, don't worry about stopping," Don laughed, "Cairns is pretty flat. OK, I'll organise it for tomorrow."

Surprisingly, the car was in quite good condition, and Don had rustled up another two yachties, which cut the price we each had to pay to almost less than a bus fare.

I still got a real kick out of the contrast of being at sea for a week or two, living on pretty simple fare and not having much company, and then suddenly thrust into a city with an almost endless supply of shops, restaurants and people. The delicatessen and fruit and vegetable sections in the supermarkets never failed to attract me. The array of food was almost too much to comprehend; I felt like a young boy in a toyshop — I wanted one of everything. It made me appreciate just how fortunate I was to be living in a country like Australia.

For months now I had been associating mainly with people who, like myself, wore little else but shorts and T-shirt. Even the residents of the small towns and cities dressed very casually. Yachties were usually suntanned with a definite wrinkled, weather-beaten look, and the women wore little if any make-up. So, one Saturday evening while a few of us were having a meal at the yacht club, it was quite a shock to see a parade of men and women dressed to the nines walk past our table to the club's function room. The men, smartly attired in dinner suit and black tie, looked debonair. But it was the women, with their elegant evening gowns, high heels and full make-up who were a pleasing sight for us male yachties, and objects of envy for most of the female yachties. A blonde New Zealander at our table put her head on her husband's shoulder and feigning distress, whimpered:

133

"I want to look like that too."

The formal event was to celebrate the yacht club's first anniversary. As the evening wore on and we returned to our yachts, the volume of noise from the function increased by the hour as the revellers let their hair down. Even so, I didn't take long to fall asleep; and as it happened, it was the first and only night that I didn't hear the Jumbo jets from Japan landing in the cockpit.

Despite the pleasures of the yacht club and Cairns, the urge to move on could no longer be denied. I had repaired the mast fitting, done my laundry and reprovisioned *Pluto*; it was time to leave.

Chapter 16

A COOK'S TOUR

I couldn't believe how much Low Isles had changed since my previous visit. The tiny sand cay itself hadn't altered greatly; the clear water above the fringing coral reef still lapped onto the blinding white sand, and the coconut palms, silhouetted against a bright blue sky, still stood proudly above the canopy of dark-green vegetation that covered the island. When Shirley and I were last here, Low Isles was the sole domain of two light-keeping families, and the only vessel anchored in the sheltered bay was the lighthouse stores launch *Doreen*, on which we had accompanied the skipper on his fortnightly trip from the small mainland settlement of Port Douglas 9 miles away.

Now, there were at least two dozen yachts and some huge tourist vessels from Port Douglas; hundreds of people lazed on the beach and snorkelled over the reef. Permanent beach shelters with canopies of thatched coconut palm fronds lined the foreshore.

Twenty-three years ago, the Head Lightkeeper, Ernie Lone, had taken Shirley and me on a tour of the lightstation; a tour that made us decide to become lightkeepers ourselves. I knew that the light was now automatic and the lightkeepers had been replaced by Queensland Parks and Wildlife Service personnel and University of Queensland research staff.

Next morning I went ashore, looking forward to wandering around the old lightstation precinct again. But at the start of every foot-track that led from the beach into the centre of the island I found a sign that read:

PRIVATE NO ENTRY

Like most lighthouse keepers I always felt a sense of belonging whenever I visited a lightstation, even ones I hadn't worked on. I didn't want to go into the buildings, I just wanted to walk around what I regarded as my 'spiritual land'. No Johnny-come-lately national park ranger or university academic was going to stop me from doing that — not without a fight anyway.

Ready for battle, I walked defiantly past the sign and followed the track into the centre of the island. I had gone no more than 30 metres, when I came face to face with a young man wearing a national park uniform.

"Look," I said, gruffly, "I saw the 'NO ENTRY' sign, but I used to be a lightkeeper, and . . ."

"Did you?" the young man interrupted in surprise. "Hey, that's great. Well, come and have a look around. The lighthouse is locked, but I've got the key, so we can go inside if you like."

I went down like a pricked balloon.

"Oh — thanks," I mumbled in embarrassment.

After looking through the lighthouse, the young man asked me over to his cottage for a cup of coffee. Lying on the kitchen table was a copy of my book. I picked it up and flicked through it.

"Have you read that?" the young man asked. "I've just started it. I had to wait my turn — everyone else on the island has read it but me."

The young man stared at me for a few seconds, then took the book and opened it at the photograph on the back flap. He laughed and said:

"You know, when we met on the track, I was sure I had seen your face somewhere before."

I spent a few days at Low Isles, snorkelling the vast reef that connects the sand cay of Low Isles to a much larger mangrove covered island. Just off-shore from the sand cay in the sheltered bay was a patch of clamshells bigger than any I had seen. Although the island was very busy between 9 a.m. and 3 p.m., it was pretty quiet the rest of the time. Considering the hundreds of tourists who visit Low Isles each day, the coral close to the beach looked to be in reasonably good condition. Naturally, it is in the tourist boat operators' interests to look after the coral reef, and for that reason environmental tour guides are employed to advise tourists on the do's and don'ts of appreciating the coral without damaging it. But marine biologists are worried that such large visitor numbers can only have a detrimental effect on the reef. One of their concerns is the damage to coral from urea produced by tourists urinating in the water while swimming. The biologists say it's the old, old story — just too many rats in the cage.

A brisk south-easterly breeze on *Pluto*'s beam gave me a lively sail into Port Douglas. I steered *Pluto* across the shallow bar into the narrow Dickson Inlet, passing close to small jetties, moored trawlers, slipways and a restaurant whose open deck looked out across the water. Just over half a mile along the inlet I turned into the extensive Mirage Marina. As a single-handed yachtie, I always had some concern about tying up at marina berths. If the breeze was just off the bow and pushing the yacht sideways towards the berth it was quite easy; but if the breeze was blowing the vessel away from the berth, problems could occur. Over the last few months I had seen some terrible displays by yachting couples trying to berth their boats. The man was usually at the helm while the woman stood on deck ready to leap ashore with a line. Sometimes the man would bring the vessel in too far away from the pontoon and expect the woman to jump 2 metres across the water, then scream obscenities at her when she didn't. When Shirley and I were at the Gladstone Marina we saw a well-appointed 13 metre yacht come into berth across the water from us. The woman stepped ashore with a bow line.

"Tie it onto the cleat, dear," the skipper said to her in a deep, loud and very cultured voice.

Perhaps the woman didn't know what a cleat was, because she just stood there with the line in her hand. A gust of wind began to push the heavy yacht away from the berth.

"For God's sake, tie it onto the cleat!" the man shouted with panic in his voice.

But the woman continued to stand motionless, letting the line slip slowly through her hands.

"Tie it onto the fucking cleat!" the man screamed at the top of his voice, and continued with a tirade of abuse.

Fortunately, some other yachties were close enough to lend a hand and the vessel was soon safely tied up. Ten minutes later, we saw the woman dressed in good clothes and carrying a travel-bag leave the yacht. It was obvious by her body language and the terse finality of her farewell that she wasn't returning.

Shirley shook her head and said:

"Yachting certainly brings out the best in a man."

I had no worries about such an incident happening between Shirley and me. When Shirley was on board *Pluto* she considered herself a passenger and wanted nothing to do with the running of the 'ship'. It was a very good arrangement, because I had developed my own way of doing things, and whenever an inexperienced person tried to help, everything seemed to go wrong.

Before coming in to a berth, I always ran a long bow line and stern line into the cockpit, so that I could quickly jump ashore with the two lines and have complete control of the yacht. *Pluto* weighed only 5 tonnes and was fairly easy to handle. However, if the wind was strong and I saw that it would blow me away from my allocated berth, I would abort the approach and either call the marina office and ask for a more suitable berth, or temporarily moor somewhere else until I found a couple of strong yachties who could take my lines.

But the brisk south-easter that had driven me quickly in to Port Douglas had little effect in the shelter of Marina Mirage. With *Pluto* secure, I went up to the marina office on the first floor of the two-storeyed marina complex. And what a complex; there were shops and restaurants of all descriptions that opened onto a wide boardwalk overlooking the marina. And inside the complex there was an arcade with more shops and restaurants.

When Shirley and I were in Port Douglas at the time of our visit to Low Isles, the town was a quiet little place with one shop and a couple of pubs. It had seen livelier times. In the late 1870s it had outranked Cairns to become the main port for supplying the Hodgkinson River goldfields. By 1879 there were twenty-one hotels in town. But within ten years when the gold ran out and it was decided to build a rail link from the inland to Cairns instead of Port Douglas, the town all but died. A new type of prospector was now in town. Instead of looking for gold they were looking for the tourist dollar. The main street of Port Douglas was filled with backpackers and tourists prowling the shops to buy clothes, jewellery, souvenirs, a variety of take away foods and a hundred flavours of ice-cream. Although tourist orientated, the town had a pleasant atmosphere, which was certainly helped by the fact that it had preserved a number of its historic buildings.

Since my arrival in Port Douglas, the strong south-easterly wind had rarely fallen below 25 knots. About seven o'clock one morning, a 13 metre racing yacht headed in towards the berth next to *Pluto*. I gave the two men on board a hand with their lines.

"Thanks very much," they both said.

The men looked exhausted. They had on salt-encrusted wet-weather gear; their hair was wet and matted, and beneath a few days of stubble, I could see their faces were strained and haggard.

"Where have you come in from?" I asked.

"Lizard Island," the younger one replied. "We did it in one leg. Two nights we've been out there — tacking into the south-easter — two days and nights to cover a distance of a lousy 120 miles. We were ready to leave the island two weeks ago, but the wind didn't drop below 25 knots. Two days ago it dropped to 20, so we decided to bite the bullet and go. Where are you heading?"

"Lizard Island," I replied.

"Are you coming back from there or are you continuing on to Torres Strait?"

"Coming back," I answered. "Lizard Island is as far as I'm going."

He snorted more than laughed, and said:

"You'll never do it. Not in *that* boat. How close can she point to windward?"

"Forty-five degrees."

"Well mine can point to almost thirty degrees and we had trouble."

It was just the sort of news I didn't want to hear. I was well aware that from Port Douglas to Torres Strait the south-east trade winds howl almost continuously day and night, week after week, from the beginning of April to the end of October. For the rest of the year, in between a few periods of calms and light northerly winds, the trade winds continue. I was already spooked by stories of yachties who had spent up to six weeks at Lizard Island waiting for the south-easter to drop below 20 knots so they could head south. Some of them had run out of food and survived by befriending the staff from the exclusive five star Lizard Island Lodge, who provided them with leftovers from the kitchen.

Worse still, was the story of Frank Jardine who, in the late 1800s, was Government Resident and Police Magistrate of the small settlement of Somerset near the tip of Cape York Peninsula. In July 1869 he boarded a sailing ship to return to Brisbane on leave. After three weeks of battling the south-east trade winds, the vessel had only covered 90 miles. The skipper decided to go about and head for Brisbane via Western Australia, a voyage that took three months. Circumnavigating Australia certainly wasn't on my agenda, but I was determined to reach Lizard Island.

I left Port Douglas about midday and sailed back to Low Isles, from where I planned to leave about 2 a.m. the following morning for the 60 mile sail to Cooktown. But an hour or so after I left Low Isles the wind decreased until *Pluto* was barely moving. I started the motor and cruised along at 5 knots. The weather report predicted light winds for the next two days, so I decided to anchor behind Cape Tribulation, 20 miles north of Low Isles, and wait for the wind to increase. There was a fair swell running in behind the headland, but after setting a stern anchor to hold *Pluto*'s bow directly into the swell, the movement became quite bearable.

Over the last few years, Cape Tribulation had become a popular destination for tourists. From seaward, all I could see was thick rainforest overhanging the beach, but when I went ashore I found barbecue areas and parking for buses and cars. A boardwalk led up to a lookout on the northern side of the cape, and another track wound across the headland to the southern beach. I walked along the beach for a kilometre or so, past a number of sunbaking backpackers, then followed a track that led to a huge backpackers' hostel. I continued on to the coast road that ran from the Daintree River vehicular ferry to Cape Tribulation and on to Cooktown; buses and four-wheel drives passed me in a constant stream. It seemed strange that not so long ago, Cape Tribulation was the haunt of only two families and a few hippies who lived in the rainforest. That all changed when, for no logical reason and amongst much controversy, the dictatorial State Premier of the time Sir Joh Bjelke-Petersen allowed bulldozers in to carve a red dirt road through the pristine rainforest; a road that was constantly eroded by the torrential summer rains and which caused thousands of tonnes of red dirt to stream down the precipitous slopes into the sea.

The south-easter came in as predicted. By midmorning the wind had increased to 25 knots. I put one reef in the main and kept the genoa up. *Pluto* flew along. I looked behind me. There didn't seem to be too much swell, just short, very steep waves about 2 metres high with breaking crests. The bloke on that racing yacht was right, I thought, there is no way I could sail back into that — it would be like trying to punch into one brick wall after another. Ahead of me I could see the tiny Hope Islands. It was this group of islands that Lieutenant James Cook saw shortly before nightfall on 10 June 1770. To avoid them he hauled *Endeavour* off to seaward. But Cook was unaware that not only did the Barrier Reef exist, but it was closing in on him the further north he went. The Outer Barrier Reef lay only 20 miles from the mainland and the seabed in between was strewn with thousands of huge hidden reefs and bommies. Cook later called it "the insane labyrinth". At nine o'clock that evening, Cook was summoned urgently on deck; the lead line had shown a sudden shoaling. But at the next cast of the lead the water deepened. Cook assumed they had passed over the tail of the shoals they had seen at sunset. But they hadn't. They had passed over the tail of what is now known as Pickersgill Reef and were heading for disaster.

A few minutes before 11 p.m. *Endeavour* came to a jarring halt as she struck what is now called Endeavour Reef, 18 miles north-north-east of Cape Tribulation. The sails were immediately taken in and the boats launched to examine the water depths around the ship. It was not good news. There was a depth of 4 fathoms at the stern but only half a fathom at the bow. *Endeavour* had lifted over a ledge of rock and was sitting trapped in a basin of coral which, aided by the swell, was all the time grinding away at the hull. Two anchors were laid in the deepest water that could be found and the men began straining away on the capstan and windlass, trying to pull *Endeavour* off the reef. But the ship had hit the reef at high tide and minute by minute the sea-level over the reef was dropping. *Endeavour* began to heel over. In the moonlight, huge pieces of the false keel and protective sheathing boards, specially fitted in England to protect the ship's true hull, could be seen floating away. The ship's next chance of reprieve was at high tide the following day. To make the vessel lighter, six canons, iron and stone ballast, casks and other items totalling 50 tonnes were jettisoned. The pumps were continuously manned. As the tide rose next day, water poured into the ship so fast the pumps could scarcely keep up with it. At high tide the men pushed on the capstan arms and windlass until their bodies ached, but the ship didn't budge.

However, two things were in their favour. The wind had dropped right off making the sea unusually calm for that time of the year, and the high tide that night would be much higher than the midday one. Cook's main concern was that even if the ship did pull free, the hull might be so badly damaged that once away from the support of the coral bed on which she was sitting, *Endeavour* would quickly sink. Cook later described in his journal how he felt at that time:

This was a dreadful circumstance, so that we anticipated the floating of the ship not as an earnest of deliverance, but as an event that would probably precipitate our destruction. We well knew that our boats were not capable of carrying us all on shore, and that when the dreadful crisis should arrive, as all command and subordination would be at an end, a contest for preference would probably ensue, that would increase even the horrors of shipwreck, and terminate in the destruction of us all by the hands of each other; yet we knew that if any should be left on board to perish in the waves, they would probably suffer less upon the whole than those who should get on shore, without any lasting or effectual defence against the natives, in a country where even nets and fire-arms would scarcely furnish them with food; and where, if they should find the means of subsistence, they must be condemned to languish out the remainder of life in a desolate wilderness, without the possession, or even hope, of any domestic comfort, and cut off from all commerce with mankind, except the naked savages who prowled the desert, and who perhaps were some of the most rude and uncivilized upon the earth.

At ten o'clock that night the men once more returned to the capstan and windlass. Everyone was aware that if their efforts weren't successful this time, it was unlikely *Endeavour* would survive another twenty-four hours of abrasion on the reef. With their lives depending on it, the men put every last bit of energy into their task. The ship's boats were out too, with lines attached to *Endeavour*. The men began pulling on the oars with all their might. There was a slight, jerky movement, then, slowly but surely the vessel was heaved into deep water. As it did so, the kedge anchor cable became entangled on the coral and had to be cut away; the anchor was abandoned. The men waited to see if the water level in the hold would suddenly increase, but miraculously the level appeared to be holding. For almost thirty-six hours the pumps had been continuously manned; the men were reaching exhaustion. Midshipman Jonathan Monkhouse suggested to Cook that the leak might be slowed by 'fothering' — taking a sail, sewing chopped wool and oakum to it and smothering the lot with dung and other filth, before hauling it under the hull where the water pressure would force it into the hole. Cook was unaware of this method, but immediately ordered that the lower studding sail be brought on deck and prepared. The result was so successful that instead of the water gaining on the three pumps, one pump easily kept the water level in check.

Two ship's boats were sent ahead to search for a suitable harbour where *Endeavour* could be beached for repairs. Twenty-six miles north-west of Endeavour Reef a river was found, now known as the Endeavour River where Cooktown stands. But a gale forced *Endeavour* to anchor outside the river for two days. On the third day the gale was still blowing as hard, but Cook believed he just *had* to get his ship to safety. Twice they ran aground before reaching the steep beach where *Endeavour* was to be positioned at high tide. When the tide dropped, leaving the ship's bow dry on the beach, Cook and his men could not believe how close to disaster they had been. Little of the protective sheathing remained and a large chunk of coral rock was found wedged into the true planking; if that had dislodged when the ship was pulled off the reef there is no doubt that *Endeavour* would have quickly sunk.

As the strong south-easter pushed *Pluto* relentlessly on, past Endeavour Reef and the Hope Islands, I tried to imagine the despair that Cook and his men must have felt as they headed for the Endeavour River. Though they had escaped within an inch of their lives from the reef, they did not know what further dangers lay ahead. There they were, boxed in by reefs to the east and seemingly to the north, with no hope of returning south against the strong trade winds. Cape Tribulation had been well-named by Cook. "Here we became acquainted with misfortune . . . " Cook wrote in his log.

I steered *Pluto* through the mile and a half wide gap between the mainland and Gubbins Reef, changed course to skirt Cowlishaw Reef and changed again to pass Dawson Reef before heading in towards the mouth of the Endeavour River. The charts for this area showed a minefield of reefs; so much so, that Shirley, after looking at the charts in Townsville, had bought me a handheld GPS. When I protested that I didn't need a GPS, Shirley had replied:

"Well, you don't have to use it all the time, but it will be handy for checking your dead reckoning position, especially in that area north of Port Douglas."

And now I had to admit she was right. At least once every hour I marked my dead reckoning position on the chart and checked it with the latitude and longitude on the GPS. It gave me that extra bit of assurance.

Before heading into hazardous or restricted waters, I always made it a practice to start the motor and drop all sail. First, I'd connect the autopilot and drop the headsail, then I'd turn *Pluto* straight into the wind to drop the main. But as the present short steep waves were going to make that task very awkward, I decided to wait until I had some shelter from Grassy Hill, the headland at the start of the Endeavour River. However, as I gybed *Pluto* to follow the leads into the river, the 25 knot south-easter slammed *Pluto* on the port beam, heeling him over. The autopilot couldn't handle the wind strength, which was made even worse by the occasional bullets of wind that swept down Grassy Hill and across the water. The shoaling bottom made the seas stand up and break against the side of the yacht, sending sheets of water high in the air before they crashed down on top of me. The chart had shown that the surrounding water was very shallow, allowing little manoeuvrability. I was hemmed in by the rocky shoreline on one side and a shallow sand spit on the other. There was nothing I could do but stay at the tiller, ease the sheets and forge into the river under sail. Fortunately, the sea and wind eased as I made my way further behind the headland, giving me time to go below and start the motor before returning on deck to drop sail. It was quite a tight squeeze doing all this without either colliding with the public jetty on the foreshore or the vessels anchored on the other side of the narrow channel. Even though everything turned out satisfactorily, the whole episode had been much too close for comfort.

I anchored *Pluto* in the vicinity of the other vessels, the only spot in the river that had enough water to allow a vessel to swing at low tide. There were ten yachts at anchor, most of them foreign — French, American and Swedish. I had noticed that the further north I travelled, the fewer Australian yachts there were. Most of the Australian yachties I had met on the first two months of the trip had gone no further than the Whitsundays. Of the others who had continued north, only a few were planning on going further than Port Douglas.

"Cooktown is the pits," some yachties had told me. "It's dead — it's just that no-one has signed its death certificate yet."

I found that difficult to believe. A town that was not only associated with Cook's *Endeavour*, but which, in the rip-roaring gold fever days of the 1870s, had throbbed with thousands of adventurers hell bent on making their fortunes from the Palmer River goldfields 200 kilometres inland, had to have something about it. And throb it had. Irish adventurer James Venture Mulligan started it all when he discovered payable gold on the Palmer River in 1873. He received a government reward of £1,000 for his find, and a few days later the greatest gold rush ever seen in Queensland began. Mulligan led the first party of prospectors over 320 kilometres of wilderness to the field, but a month later a settlement and port was established on the banks of the Endeavour River, from where prospectors had *only* 200 kilometres to walk. At first, the main street — Charlotte Street was lined with tents and huts, but within a year, as thousands of southerners, Chinese and Americans flooded the town, the street grew to nearly 4 kilometres long, lined by substantial timber and iron buildings. Within a few years there were ninety-four hotels — most of them two-storeyed, twenty-four restaurants, twelve large general stores, five bakers, six butchers, three banks, two newspapers, along with doctors, chemists, saddlers, wheelwrights, tentmakers and one hundred and sixty brothels.

The journey to and from the Palmer was fraught with danger. At the notorious Hell's Gates, a steep, narrow mountain pass, hundreds of gold seekers were speared and killed by cannibalistic Aborigines. Chinese were preferred because they were reputed to taste less salty than Europeans.

Many prospectors who struck it rich, died from starvation on their return journey from the goldfields when caught for weeks between flooded rivers. Aborigines who found the dead men, robbed them of useful possessions. They took the men's chamois pouches that were filled with fortunes of gold, but threw away the 'useless' yellow stones and powdery stuff inside.

And many of the prospectors who did make it back to Cooktown with their fortunes intact soon lost it gambling, drinking and womanising. There was always some conniving entrepreneur ready to take the hard-earned money any way he or she could. It was said that of the many who took their gold into French Charley's establishment, few came away with it, but what they did take away were memories of free-flowing champagne and the most beautiful whores in Cooktown, memories that would have to see them through the long months ahead while replenishing their stock of gold back on the Palmer. Palmer Kate and her girls were also in frequent demand in Cooktown. It took a fight and a large nugget of gold to be the lucky man who spent the night with the ravishing Kate.

But while the sounds of bawdy laughter, raucous music, and wild brawls swept the length of Charlotte Street, on the slopes of Grassy Hill there was another world. A world where the families of prosperous businessmen, government officials and bank officers had formal dances, dinner parties and piano recitals. Cooktown — Queen of the North — had it all. But it didn't last; within a few years, as the Palmer yielded less and less gold, the town slowly declined. It is recorded that the Palmer produced one million ounces of gold, but it is thought that the Chinese smuggled that much again out of Australia.

From where *Pluto* was anchored, just 300 metres from where Cook beached *Endeavour*, Cooktown didn't appear to have retained much of its former glory. But next day when I went ashore and strolled along Webber Esplanade and up Charlotte Street, it wasn't difficult to fall under the historic spell of the town. The streets weren't paved with gold, but the kerb and channelling were the original hand-laid stone pitching. Many of the old buildings were still there, most looking splendidly maintained. There was the brick powder magazine, built in 1874 and used for storing explosives; recognised by the National Trust as the oldest brick structure in Cape York. The Cooktown Post Office, built in 1887 was still in use, as was the Westpac Bank, originally built for the Queensland National Bank in 1890. I walked through the entrance of the bank's two-storeyed, colonnaded façade. Inside was a magnificent, intricately carved red cedar counter, upon which thousands of jubilant miners had slammed down their bags of gold for weighing. Even the bank's original gold scales were on display in a glass case.

I continued on up the street, past the West Coast Hotel and the Cooktown Hotel, both witnesses to the rollicking gold fever days. A wallaby hopped out of a side street and continued along the road before turning into another side street. In the distance, at the other end of town, I saw a shop awning painted with the words:

PALMER KATE'S

Don't tell me, I thought, that Palmer Kate's great-great grand-daughter is carrying on the family business. But when I arrived at the shop and looked inside I didn't see a ravishing beauty flaunting her wares, all I saw were a few coin-operated washing machines and dryers. If the proprietor of the laundromat was related to Palmer Kate, it was obvious she had opted for a cleaner lifestyle.

But what I had really been looking forward to, was a visit to the James Cook Museum. On display in this musty old building was one of the six cannons jettisoned from *Endeavour*; also displayed was the ship's kedge anchor, which had been abandoned as the vessel was heaved off the reef. These weren't replicas, these were the real thing. I stood, deep in thought, trying to imagine the scene that night on board *Endeavour* as she groaned and grated on the reef. The voices of men, as they hurried to obey shouted commands. Working as fast as they could and with all their strength to lighten the ship, aware they may never see England or their loved ones again. Little did they know what history they were making.

A few attempts had been made to recover the cannons over the years. In 1887 the Cooktown Working Men's Progress Association offered a reward of £300 for their recovery. Their idea was to mount the cannons around the base of the ornate Captain Cook Monument built between the riverbank and Charlotte Street, and which still stands today. That same year the Cooktown Harbour Master spent a week unsuccessfully searching for the cannons. It wasn't until 1969 that an expedition sponsored by the Philadelphia Academy of Natural Sciences located the site of the grounding using a magnetometer. Assisted by Vince Vlassoff on his vessel *Tropic Seas*, and Captain Len Foxcroft on the Torres Strait lighthouse vessel *Wallach*, the jettisoned items were recovered and transported to Cairns, where they were temporarily stored in a large salt-water tank before being taken to Melbourne for restoration.

The two-storeyed James Cook Museum began its life in 1889 as St Mary's Convent and boarding school. During the Second World War the building was abandoned and fell into disrepair. In 1969 the Catholic Church decided to sell the building for demolition, but it was given a last minute reprieve when the National Trust formulated a plan to restore it as a museum. The following year, 200 years after Cook's visit, the museum was opened by Queen Elizabeth II. The museum also houses relics from the Palmer River gold rush days and a replica of a Chinese Joss House.

One particularly pleasant place I discovered was the Cooktown Botanic Gardens, located a short walk out of town. Established in 1878 when the population of Cooktown was at its peak, the gardens were installed with complex systems of stone-pitched waterways that led down to waterfalls and rockpools and which weaved their way through colourful gardens and shady stands of trees. But as the gold ran out, the 60 hectare site was let deteriorate until it was eventually closed in 1917. For seventy years the gardens remained overgrown and neglected. Then in the late 1980s a decision was made to resurrect them; incredibly, most of the original stone-pitching was found to be in excellent condition, and the gardens are now beautifully maintained.

I spent the next few days exploring Cooktown on foot, always finding some new and varied delight. At the Endeavour River Gallery there was an exquisite collection of botanical illustrations showing the area's flowering plants; and at the Cooktown Sea Museum there was the stuffed crocodile that film star Paul Hogan carried into the Walkabout Hotel in the movie "Crocodile Dundee". Most days I climbed to Grassy Hill Lookout and stared out across the white-capped ocean that disappeared into a veil of salt haze, and most days the 25 to 30 knot south-easterly wind accelerated up the hill and almost knocked me off my feet.

On the day before I planned to leave, I went ashore to wash a few items of clothing. Rather than walk to Palmer Kate's at the other end of town I decided to have a look at the public toilet block across from where *Pluto* was anchored. I thought it might have a laundry tub. But what I saw inside left me aghast. It appeared as though someone had stacked about five hundred water-sodden toilet rolls on the floor and lit a stick of gelignite under them — the floor, walls and ceiling were plastered with dags of papier-mache. The shower was devoid of its shower-rose, and the shower tray was so thick with black filth and mould it would have kept a bacteriologist happily occupied for a lifetime. The hand-basin, without a plug of course, looked as though the local motor mechanic had been washing engine parts in it for the past few years. But I wasn't going to be beaten. There was a tap on the outside wall, so I went back to *Pluto*, got a few plastic buckets and returned to do my washing. It wasn't too bad though, I met a few people as they walked past and saw my old mate the wallaby hopping down the street.

While I was rinsing my clothes, a bloke rode up on a horse.

"G'day," he said, "I don't suppose I could borrow one of yer buckets to give me 'orse a drink?"

"Of course you can," I replied, filling a bucket with water. The "'orse" drank noisily as its owner told me in great detail about the current low cattle prices and the high cost of transporting his beasts to market — all really interesting stuff for a yachtie.

146

It was pretty hot work washing by hand, so after I finished hanging out the clothes to dry on *Pluto*'s safety lines I walked uptown and popped into the Sovereign Hotel for a cold beer. There was only one other customer there — an old bloke sitting in the corner at the end of the bar. Above him on the wall was a framed photograph of the same bloke.

"Is that you in the photograph?" I asked astutely.

"Yep, this is Bob's corner," he replied.

We started talking. Bob told me he had lived in Cooktown since 1949.

"There were no cars in Cooktown in those days," Bob said. "Even the local copper got around on horseback. The Sovereign's a new pub — it's only been built a few years. You see, the old one burnt down. Years back though, long before my time, when Harry Poole was the licensee of the old Sovereign, Sub-Inspector Townsend of the native police rode his horse into the bar. It was a huge brute of a black stallion. Wherever he went, Townsend always had his three dogs with him — they were called Jesus Christ, Holy Ghost and Virgin Mary. Anyhow, Harry told him to get his horse and his mongrel dogs out of the bar while there were ladies drinking there. Townsend objected to this — he spurred his stallion and chased Harry out of the bar and halfway up the main staircase towards the first floor of the pub. The day the pub burnt down you could still see the horse's shoe marks in the timber stairs."

Bob burst into great bellows of laughter, banged his fist on the bar and at the same time managed to order another beer.

"You wouldn't be dead for quids, would you?" Bob laughed.

"And talking about being dead," he continued, "about twenty-six years ago an old mate of mine carked it. His family arranged the funeral, but the town's funeral director wanted payment before the service went ahead. Just thirty minutes before the service was due to begin, the family still hadn't forked over the money, so the funeral director turned up, tipped me old mate out of the coffin and took it away."

Once again, Bob burst into peals of laughter before going on with another story. My washing was well and truly dry by the time I returned to *Pluto*.

Contrary to those yachties who had told me that Cooktown was "the pits" and that "it's dead", I thought the place was well and truly alive. The town was overflowing with the ambience of bygone eras. I had talked to old Bob at the Sovereign about Cooktown's chance of survival and could only agree with his parting quip:

"She's the Queen of the North, mate — she'll never die."

148

Chapter 17

THE JEWEL IN THE CROWN

With only a reefed mainsail the 30 knot south-easter drove *Pluto* along at a frantic pace; past the weird, wind-blown plateau-like headland of Cape Bedford, and on towards the narrow gap between Low Wooded Isle and Three Isles, whose encircling coral reefs, pounded by foaming white breakers, lay in wait to tear the bottom from any vessel that should stray off course. Then onwards to Cape Flattery, its peaked headland bordered on both sides by blinding white sand-dunes. For the first time since leaving Hinchinbrook Channel 200 miles to the south, the rainforest no longer met the sea. The country was now lower and drier. Dead ahead, 20 miles in the distance I could plainly see the peak of Lizard Island. Around one o'clock the wind dropped to just above 20 knots, so I hoisted the genoa and shook out the reef for the final leg along the main shipping route, before branching off to the island.

It was with mixed feelings of elation and sadness that I sailed *Pluto* into the sheltered waters of Watson's Bay. Elation that after four months and 1,300 miles I had reached my destination — sadness that it was the turning point of the cruise. But the sadness was quickly swept away by the beauty that surrounded me. Only a slight ripple disturbed the surface of the bay and there wasn't the slightest sign of swell, making it hard to believe that the south-easter was still blowing strongly out in open water. In 6 metres of water I could see the sandy bottom with such clarity it was as though *Pluto* was suspended in midair. The island's high, sparsely vegetated windswept granite ridges plummeted down to a green, central valley, fringed by the white beach of Watson's Bay.

As I motored towards shore I counted eight other yachts at anchor. A rubber duckie with two people on board left one of the yachts and headed towards me. As it drew closer I recognised the couple as Dave and Lyn from the yacht *Sapphire II*. I had first met them in Bundaberg and later in Cairns.

"G'day Dave! — G'day Lyn!" I shouted and waved.

"G'day, Stuart!" they both replied.

149

"It's all clear bottom here," Dave shouted, "except for a small bommie close to shore."

"Yep, I can see it from here," I replied.

"We're having a barbecue on the beach with a few other yachties tonight. Would you like to come along?" Dave asked.

"I'd love to."

"That's good, because there's someone who wants to meet you. Do you know David Beard?"

"I don't think so — but for some reason the name sounds familiar."

"He was Master of the marine science vessel *Lady Basten*, and an officer on the lighthouse ships. A few years ago he became the first person to sail single-handedly non-stop around Australia," Dave continued.

"That's right, now I know the name, I've got his book *I Can Sail Circles*."

"That's him," Dave said. "He wants to have a talk about the lighthouse days. He's heading north first thing tomorrow morning. Anyhow, we'll leave you to anchor and settle in. See you ashore about five o'clock."

If the south-easterly doesn't abate, I thought, meeting David could prove very handy — I could get a few tips about circumnavigating Australia.

It was one of those nights where Bob from the Sovereign would say: "you wouldn't be dead for quids". The full moon illuminated the bay and the anchored yachts with a misty, dreamlike atmosphere, transforming reality into what looked more like a painted stage setting for a grand opera. The yachts' tiny anchor lights, twinkling in the background, added an even more mystical air to the scene. A cool breeze drifted across the valley and onto the beach, as sixteen congenial yachties sat around a large picnic table eating, drinking and enjoying life to the full. Some of the yachties were continuing northwards to Torres Strait, Indonesia and Malaysia; David Beard was setting out on his second circumnavigation of the world; others like me were returning south. The conversation was lively and enjoyable, but by nine o'clock I was dead tired and returned to *Pluto*.

Next morning I set out to climb the 358 metre high Cook's Look, the island's highest peak. From Watson's Bay the track zigzagged up the first steep pinch over large grey granite slabs and rocks, and through clumps of hardy shrubs. Higher up, the track levelled as it passed through stands of kapok and ash trees. Every so often, a group of small bar-shouldered doves would explode from the undergrowth less than a metre from where I was walking. On each occasion their sudden movement and loud wing-clatter scared the daylights out of me. At various places along the narrow track, large goannas lay basking in the sun, reluctant to be disturbed from their comfortable siestas. The track opened out once more and led to the peak.

The view from the summit was almost too spectacular to be real. To the right, far below, *Pluto* and the other yachts lay peacefully at anchor in the clear waters of Watson's Bay. To the left, on the other side of the island, was

Blue Lagoon. This large lagoon, over a mile in diameter, was bordered by islands, each connected by a coral reef. Through one of these reefs, a narrow twisting passage led from the deep blue of the sea into the lagoon's protected waters. But it was the intensity of colours within the lagoon that made the view breathtakingly beautiful — the myriad shades of blue and green of its waters, the yellow and brown of its reefs, all contrasting vividly with the white of the islands' beaches, had a clarity and luminescence I had never seen before. Of all the islands I had visited so far this was undoubtedly the jewel in the crown — a marine Garden of Eden.

Ten miles to the east, the Outer Barrier Reef, edged with white breakers, extended north and south as far as the eye could see. Inside the reef, to all points of the compass, there was reef, reef and more reef. It was from where I was standing that James Cook must have desperately searched the horizon for an opening in the reef that would take him out of the "insane labyrinth" of coral and into the deep, safe waters of the South Pacific Ocean. After spending forty-eight days in the Endeavour River repairing the ship and replenishing stores hunted from the area, *Endeavour* continued northwards, this time with the utmost caution. A ship's boat always led the way, its crew taking soundings every few metres. Fifteen miles east of Cape Bedford the weather deteriorated and *Endeavour* was brought to anchor. During the night a strong gale developed. Next morning it was discovered that *Endeavour* had dragged anchor for a distance of 3 miles and was moving dangerously close towards a reef. Yards and topmasts were brought down to reduce windage, more cable was let out and a second anchor set, but the ship still continued to move. As a third anchor was about to be set, one of the anchors hooked onto something on the seabed and held *Endeavour* fast.

For four days the ship sat out the gale, with only a snagged anchor between survival and certain death. The gale abated and *Endeavour* moved slowly onwards past Cape Flattery where again the ship was confronted by dangerous reefs in every direction. With *Endeavour* once more at anchor, Cook, along with botanist Joseph Banks and some crew sailed one of the ship's boats 15 miles out to what Cook later named Lizard Island. From the height of its peak they hoped to find a safe passage through the reef-strewn waters. With "a mixture of hope and fear" Cook climbed to the island's summit where, towards the north-east through the haze, he saw a number of openings leading through the Great Barrier Reef to the ocean beyond. Cook remained on the island, while the crew of the ship's boat went out to investigate the opening Cook had chosen. Before long, *Endeavour* was safely out in the Pacific. But the crew's relief was short-lived. Within two days the wind dropped off to dead calm and *Endeavour* was pushed back towards the reef by the swell and flood tide. As the tide ebbed, the ship was taken out to sea; as it flooded, it was driven back towards the reef, sometimes as close as 100 metres from where the powerful Pacific Ocean swell reared up to crash on the deadly coral rampart. The water was too deep for anchoring — 275 metres of line was let out and still no bottom was found. Three ship's boats were launched in an attempt to pull *Endeavour* away from danger, but they had little effect against the current and tide. Cook and his crew knew that their present predicament was worse than when the ship had struck Endeavour Reef. If the ship was swept onto this reef, it would be reduced to matchsticks in seconds. Once again the ship was sucked in by the tide towards the reef — this time within a breaker's length of disaster; the crew believed the end was imminent. Suddenly, a barely noticeable breeze came in; the sails were quickly set to take full advantage of this godsend, and *Endeavour* pulled ever so slowly away from the wall of death. But within ten minutes the breeze died out and *Endeavour* was once more inextricably drawn towards her doom. Then, what at first must have seemed like a mirage, an opening through the reef was sighted; a ship's boat was launched and soundings taken. Although barely 400 metres wide, the passage was found to have good depth. The ship was driven, more than towed, towards the narrow entrance; the flow of the flood tide increased, sweeping *Endeavour* through the opening and down the centre of the passage like an empty bottle in a millrace. Before long the ship was safely at anchor behind the reef. Joseph Banks wrote in his journal:

> " . . . we came to an anchor happy once more to encounter those shoals which but two days before we thought ourselves supreamly [sic] happy to have escaped from. How little do men know for what is for their real advantage: two days ago our utmost wishes were crowned by getting without the reef and today we were made again happy by getting within it."

Cook wrote in his journal that he believed it was providence that had sent "that light air of wind", enabling his ship to beat off the reef and find a safe opening. Accordingly, he named the opening Providential Channel. *Endeavour* continued northwards within the reef, always preceded by two of the ship's boats sounding every metre of the way. *Endeavour* eventually arrived at Torres Strait, turned west into unobstructed waters and made for Batavia, where the ship was repaired before heading back to England. Providence or just plain good luck — who knows? But one thing's for certain, Australia as we know it today owes its existence to a simple breath of breeze.

I signed the visitors' book, which was kept in a box at the base of a stone cairn, and wandered around the summit. Although Cook's Look was the highest point on the island, a short distance off the track at a slightly lower level, there was a single, huge boulder perched close to a precipitous drop. From the top of the boulder there was an even more majestic outlook over both the island's valley and lagoon. I had my lunch there, while absorbing the kaleidoscope of natural beauty that I felt so privileged to be witnessing.

Next day I anchored the rubber duckie beside the large reef at the southern end of Watson's Bay and splashed overboard to snorkel. Dave and Lyn had told me the snorkelling over the reef was "very good" — they had forgotten to tell me it was unsurpassable. There were giant clams over a metre long with their beautiful orange, green and purple orifices nestled amongst the hundreds of coral species. Turtles and schools of colourful fish swam beside me, seemingly unconcerned by my intrusion upon their domain. Some of the schools were huge, each fish moving this way and that in perfect unison. As I dived and swam slowly amongst them, they didn't frighten and swim away, but parted, allowing just enough room for me to pass without touching them, as if they had a sixth sense that made them aware of the next movement I was going to make. I could plainly hear the sound of parrotfish grazing on coral algae, as their beak-like teeth grated away like a rasp at the stems of hard coral. There was colour everywhere — the bright gold, blue, purple and white bands of the Blue-banded Angel fish; the Beaked Coral fish with its strange, protruding beak, black-edged gold bands and ominous black 'eye' on its dorsal fin; the brilliant blue, black-striped, yellow-tailed Blue Tang Surgeon fish and dozens of other species all gliding effortlessly amongst the purples, browns and whites of the coral. It seemed impossible to believe that the design and vivid multifarious electric colours of the fish and coral were natural and had not been sculptured and painted by some crazed, surrealistic artist. In the reef itself there were large holes and caves that I dived into, always finding some new delight in what seemed like an underwater fantasy world.

Day after day I explored the island, crossing the central valley through stands of mangrove, ancient pandanus and paperbark trees to snorkel in Blue Lagoon and at other small coves dotted around the shore. Apart from Lizard Island Lodge and its airstrip, the only other development on the island was a marine research station, which was open to visitors on Monday and Friday mornings. The remainder of Lizard Island was national park. I joined a tour of the marine research station one Monday; there were six of us — Heather and Ron from the yacht *Pacific Haven* and three American guests from the lodge. The manager of the research station explained that the facility received no direct government funding, but operated on fees paid by visiting researchers, contributions from the Australian Museum Trust and donations from private enterprise. We were shown informative videos of the marine life around the island and then taken out to see salt-water tanks containing living coral, beche-de-mer and Crown of Thorns starfish, a species renowned for depleting entire hard coral reefs. I had seen a couple of Crown of Thorns starfish on the coral while snorkelling in Watson's Bay, and so I asked the manager if the starfish was as much a threat to the reef as it was purported to be.

"After all the research that's been done," he replied, "no-one can say for sure why there has been an explosion of Crown of Thorns. We don't know if the depletion of entire reefs by the starfish is a natural cyclic phenomenon, or is the result of man changing the natural balance of the reef, either from over-collecting its natural predators such as the Giant Triton shell, or over-fishing or fertiliser run-off being flushed into the sea."

The manager went on to say that the Crown of Thorns starfish was originally catalogued by the famous Swedish zoologist Linnaeus in 1758. The starfish was first found at the northern end of the Barrier Reef in 1946. During 1959 the Crown of Thorns was found feeding on the coral reef surrounding Green Island off Cairns. By 1965 the starfish on the Green Island reef had reached such plague proportions that skindivers were employed to remove an estimated 27,000 before destruction of the reef was stopped. Gradually the plague moved southward along the Barrier Reef. Some believe that the starfish has always been present in Barrier Reef waters, but has only recently been discovered because of the growing popularity of skindiving. Whatever the theories, no-one really knows.

Along with the rest of the visitors, I did my little bit to help future research by buying a couple of T-shirts and a book on marine biology.

At the end of the tour I asked the three Americans if they were enjoying their stay at the Lizard Island Lodge.

"It's beautiful," one of them replied. "Low key, but has everything you could ask. The meals are superb — five star silver service."

Lizard Island Lodge was situated over Chinaman's Ridge at the far southern end of Watson's Bay. For years I had heard that boaties were definitely not welcome at this small but luxurious resort. Even in the 1970s there were reports of yachties who had anchored directly in front of the complex being physically threatened by staff if they didn't move. Before leaving Brisbane I had telephoned the manager of the lodge to enquire about his policy in regard to yachties visiting the resort.

"I'm entertaining guests at the moment," the manager had answered rather gruffly, "but write to me with your request."

I did write, and received a very polite letter in reply advising that although yachties weren't allowed to visit the resort any time they wished, they would be welcome to attend lunch or dinner as long as twenty-four hours notice was given.

At the beachside barbecue on my first night at Lizard, one couple told how they had anchored their yacht in the small bay in front of the resort. Before long, two staff motored out in a dinghy and asked the couple to leave.

"You might own the lease of the resort's land," one of the yachties replied, "but you don't own the sea in front of it. We're not leaving."

The two staff returned to shore. A short while later the manager of the lodge came out to the yacht and presented the couple with a food hamper and a bottle of wine. He apologised, saying that the yachties were right — the resort couldn't force the couple to move. However, if they and other yachties kept clear of the bay, keeping it solely for resort guests, the manager in return would assist yachties in times of emergency, by providing the services of the resort's nurse, telephone and the delivery of food by air from Cairns at a nominal charge of $10 a carton. The couple decided to weigh anchor and move to the northern end of Watson's Bay. I thought it a reasonable compromise, especially as the bay in front of the resort was coral-strewn and not as pretty as the accepted anchoring area.

The resort's offer to fly food in during an emergency made the thought of a forced lengthy stay at Lizard Island much less of a concern. Running out of fresh water wasn't going to be a problem, because just 250 metres inland a hand-pump drew abundant amounts of water out of the ground.

This permanent supply of fresh water was no doubt the main reason why Captain Robert Watson and his business partner Fuller established a small beche-de-mer processing base on the island in the 1870s, just 100 metres inland from Watson's Bay. Little evidence of it remains today — just a few stone walls of what was Watson's cottage. In May 1880, Robert Watson married twenty-one year old schoolteacher Mary in Cooktown and immediately took her to live on Lizard Island. By September the following year, Mary had given birth to son Ferrier, and was living on the island with two Chinese servants, while her husband Robert and Fuller were away investigating a site for a new fishing base further north on Night Island.

Aborigines from the mainland frequently visited Lizard Island by canoe, and often appeared hostile to the settlers. On 29 September 1881 during one of those visits, Chinese servant Ah Leong, while working at "the farm" 400 metres from the cottage, was speared and killed by Aborigines. Next evening, just on nightfall, the Aborigines grouped on the beach near the cottage and made threatening gestures with their spears, but were scared off when the remaining Chinese servant Ah Sam fired some shots over their heads. But next day the blacks returned and attacked Ah Sam, spearing him seven times. Still alive, but in severe pain, Ah Sam's wounds were tended to by Mary. Fearing for her son Ferrier's life, Mary decided that, although they didn't have a boat, they had to somehow get away from the island. The following afternoon Ah Sam and Mary rolled and dragged a steel beche-de-mer boiling tank across the beach to the water's edge. They loaded some tinned food, rice and preserved milk and paddled out to sea. There was little wind and the sea was calm, and after four days they landed on an island in the Howick Group, 28 miles north of Lizard. Ah Sam went inland to search for water; he was unsuccessful, however, he did discover that some Aborigines were camped on the island. Next day they again took to the sea and paddled 5 miles to No. 5 Howick Island, now known as Watson Island. No water could be found there either. Later that day a steamer was sighted heading north. Mary hoisted her son's white and pink wrap to attract the crew's attention, but her signal went unheeded and the vessel sailed on.

Next day a strong south-easter developed. Any move to leave the island now would result in the immediate capsize of the tiny steel tank. Although the castaways had adequate provisions, they had no water. Each day their throats became more swollen to the point they couldn't swallow any food. They were slowly dying of thirst. On 11 October Ah Sam, knowing that he was about to die, staggered away out of sight of Mary and Ferrier. Mary knew her time had come too; she climbed into the steel tank with her son, and wrote a final entry in her diary:

> " . . . Ah Sam preparing to die. Have not seen him since 9. Ferrier more cheerful. Self not feeling well at all. Have not seen any boat of any description. No water. Nearly dead with thirst."

Mary, cradling her baby, then lay down in the tank to wait for death.

Three months later, the beche-de-mer schooner *Kate Kearney* anchored off No. 5 Howick Island. While some of the native crew went ashore to search for eggs, they found Ah Sam's decomposing body and further away the remains of Mary and Ferrier still in the tank which, ironically, was half-filled with fresh water.

It was later assumed that the hostility of the Aborigines on Lizard Island was due to the beche-de-mer settlement being built on sacred ground. The remains of Mary, Ferrier and Ah Sam were buried in the Cooktown Cemetery on 29 January 1882. The beche-de-mer tank in which the three escaped from Lizard Island is now on display in Townsville's Museum of Tropical Queensland, and Mary Watson's diary is held in the John Oxley Library in Brisbane.

So far, during my eight days on Lizard Island, the wind hadn't dropped below 20 knots from the south-east. However, the weather bureau predicted that on the following day the wind would drop to 15 knots and swing to the east. In case they were right, I climbed Cook's Look for a farewell panoramic view, and snorkelled once more over the reef in Watson's Bay. I had considered staying a while longer, but if I missed the opportunity of the easterly now, the strong south-easterly might return and stay for weeks. As one yachtie, who had been caught here for six weeks, had said: "There's only so many times you can climb Cook's Look without it becoming a chore."

At first light I awoke to find a steady breeze from the east. I hurriedly cooked some breakfast, weighed anchor and set off about 7 a.m. Clear of the influence of the island, the breeze pushed *Pluto* along on a beam reach at a comfortable 5 knots. It was 140 miles from Lizard Island to Half Moon Bay Marina at Yorkeys Knob. If the present conditions prevailed, I would arrive at the marina around noon the next day.

Just on nightfall I was 9 miles abeam of Cooktown, passing Egret Reef to port. Three miles further on, as I came abeam of Cowlishaw Reef to starboard, I saw the navigation lights of a large vessel approaching from the south. According to the *International Rules for Prevention of Collision at Sea* a power-driven vessel shall give way to a vessel under sail, unless the former is operating in a narrow channel or restricted waterway. I had my own rule: keep out of the way of any vessel, especially 100,000 tonne bulk carriers. If *Pluto* and the large vessel kept to their present course, we would pass port to port, the accepted procedure for two vessels heading in opposite directions. However, I always made it a practice in such situations to call the ship, just to confirm that *Pluto* had been seen. Better to be safe than sorry. I called the vessel on VHF channel 16:

"Large vessel heading north approaching Archer Point, this is the yacht *Pluto*, do you receive? — over."

The vessel immediately acknowledged my call.

"I'm a few miles ahead of you, heading south and under sail," I continued. "I can see your port light. Do you intend keeping to your present course?"

"Romeo, *Pluto*, we see your red — we'll pass red to red."

"Romeo, red to red it is, *Pluto* standing by on 16."

A short while later, the huge vessel rumbled past about 300 metres away.

The wind increased slightly as I sailed towards Gubbins Reef, where I had to pass between it and the mainland. As I approached the mile and a half wide opening I saw the starboard light of another large vessel heading northwards along the channel. I became concerned, not only because the channel was narrow, but because there was a dogleg in it as well. I knew that the vessel's present green light would soon change to red as she altered course, but when that would happen I had no idea. If I took *Pluto* to seaward and the ship changed course sharply, we could collide. If I held my present course or tended towards the shore and the ship took a slow turn, we could also collide.

I connected the autopilot and went below to call the ship on the radio.

"Large vessel heading north approaching Gubbins Reef light, this is the yacht *Pluto*, do you receive? — over."

There was no answer.

I waited a short time and called again. Still no answer.

I called repeatedly without success. I dived back into the cockpit. The vessel's light was much closer and still green.

A few weeks ago in Cairns I had spoken to a Torres Strait pilot who had related a similar situation during daylight hours. He was almost beside himself with mirth as he told how he had stood on the ship's bridge, not acknowledging the yachtie's frantic radio calls.

"The poor bastard was changing course all over the place," the pilot had laughed. "You could almost feel the fear coming from the yacht."

Very funny. Perhaps this was the same sick pilot getting his turn-on on the bridge.

The safest evasive action I could take was to gybe *Pluto* 90° and head as fast as possible towards shore, where I knew the large vessel wouldn't go. According to my dead reckoning position, *Pluto* was about 2 miles from the rock and reef-strewn Forsberg Point. It was the "about 2 miles" that was my main concern. At *Pluto*'s present speed of 6 knots, I had probably somewhere between ten and twenty minutes of clear sailing before *Pluto* hit the reef. It was imperative that I knew exactly how much safe time I had. Maybe I was much closer to shore than I realised. The depth sounder couldn't help me in this situation, because the chart showed that the water depth didn't gradually decrease as the shore was approached, but went almost immediately from 12 metres to zero metres on the reef. Even in my present panic, I thought how ridiculous it was to be trying to evade destruction by sailing as fast as possible towards destruction.

I dived below and hurriedly brought 'Shirley's GPS' into the cockpit and turned it on. It seemed to take forever for the satellites to appear on screen one by one, slowly increasing in intensity until at last the latitude and longitude clicked in. I went below again and marked the position on the chart, rechecking it twice. It showed *Pluto* had 1 mile, or ten minutes grace before hitting shore. I returned to the cockpit. Now I could see the red and green navigation lights of the large vessel, and knew by the position of its fore and aft white steaming lights that it was changing course away from me. I continued on for a while, before gybing *Pluto* again and heading away from land. A few minutes later the huge black wall of the leviathan rumbled past a few hundred metres away.

I stood in the cockpit, gesticulating and shouting a stream of abuse directed at the pilot on the bridge. I doubt if he heard me, because if he had, I'm sure he would have turned the ship around and run me down. Or perhaps he wouldn't — he might have been too busy rolling around in laughter on the bridge. Having spent my anger, a wave of relief swept over me as I thanked Shirley out loud for her foresight in purchasing the GPS.

Just to keep me on my toes, four other ships passed *Pluto* during the night, every one of them answering my radio call.

By dawn I was abeam of Low Isles — 110 miles down, 30 to go. I had considered anchoring at Low Isles for some sleep, but the night's events had left me extremely alert, so I decided to sail on to the marina. The wind was still blowing a 15 knot easterly, but four hours later it slowly dropped off until there wasn't a breath of breeze. I started the motor and dropped all sail.

Perhaps it was the steady beat of the motor, or the fact that I no longer had to concentrate on sailing the boat — whatever it was, I suddenly began to feel the effects of nearly thirty hours without sleep. To try to wake myself up, I made a cup of very strong black coffee and walked around the deck a few times, stretching and yawning; but within seconds of sitting back at the tiller, I felt my head drop as I started to drift off. The next hour seemed the longest of my life. I was scared to sit down in the cockpit in case I went to sleep, but even standing up, hanging on to the rigging, my eyes kept closing and I felt myself drift off time after time. All I wanted in the world was to lie down, fully relax, and sleep. It was all I could think about — sleep, beautiful sleep.

Eventually, shortly after noon, I steered *Pluto* down the leads and turned into the marina. Despite what the pessimistic yachties in Port Douglas had said to me: "You'll never do it. Not in *that* boat . . . ". *Pluto* had done it. The circumnavigation of Australia was definitely off.

Chapter 18

TITBITS

"Would you like to fly up to Lizard Island with me?" Shirley asked one evening while we were having dinner at the Half Moon Bay yacht club.

"*Fly up to Lizard?*" I replied in surprise, almost choking on a prawn cutlet.

"Well, you haven't stopped raving about the place since I arrived here, so I thought I might hire a plane and go up there for the day to see it for myself. If it's as good as you say, we could go back sometime and stay at the lodge."

"Yes, sure, I'll go back to that island anytime."

"All right, we can organise a charter flight tomorrow."

Since arriving in Cairns ten days ago, Shirley had sailed up to Low Isles with me where, to her delight, we had spent a few 'swell-free' days at anchor, before going into Port Douglas. Like me, Shirley found her stay in the small town very enjoyable. We hired pushbikes to see the sights, and travelled on the small steam train that ran from the marina to the Mirage Resort. Unlike the shocking weather Shirley had experienced in Townsville, the weather here had been magnificent.

Next day I telephoned an air charter company to book a flight.

"I've already got a booking for Lizard tomorrow from an American couple," Greg the pilot said. "But it's a six-seater plane, so I'll give them a call to see if they're willing to share — as long as that's all right with you?"

"That'll be fine," I replied.

"It'll be cheaper for you too," Greg added.

Within ten minutes it was arranged that Greg's wife Judy would pick us up early next morning.

Right on time, Judy arrived in a transit van at the front of the yacht club.

"I hope you don't mind a bit of a drive, but I've got to go back into town, past the airport, to pick up the couple who are going with you."

"That's OK, it will be good to see the sights," I replied.

Fifteen minutes later Judy pulled into the driveway of a luxurious hotel. The concierge almost ran towards the transit van, slid open the door, bade us good morning, looked in, picked up my small backpack, and said with some surprise:

"Is this all your luggage, sir?"

"It is, but we're not staying. We're just picking someone up."

"Oh, sorry sir," he said, just as a man and woman, closely followed by a bellboy carrying two huge beach bags, walked down the steps from the foyer towards the van.

"Are you the guys goin' to Lizard," the woman said in a shrill American accent.

"That's right," Judy replied. "You must be Randy and Lisa."

Judy went on to introduce us.

Lisa was a flashy, but very attractive blonde in her late twenties, at least ten years younger than Randy, who was balding and a little overweight.

"It's probably best if Lisa sits in the front with me," Judy said. "There's more room in the front. Randy can sit in the back with Shirley and Stuart."

Lisa intervened:

"I'll sit in the back with Shirley and Stooort, I've got a smaller ass than Randy's."

Perhaps she did have a smaller "ass" than Randy's — but I hadn't noticed, because I had been too busy noticing her breasts. They were astonishing. It wasn't so much their size, as their ramrod horizontal projection. If they were natural, Sir Isaac Newton's law of gravitation had just been shot to pieces.

"Which part of America are you from, Randy?" I asked when we were underway.

Randy started to speak, but Lisa broke in:

"Miami Keys, Florida. Are you guys tourin' Australia too?"

"Not really, we're sailing up the coast on a yacht," I replied.

"Oh, that's swell. We've got four boats back home," Lisa said. "We keep them all at the bottom of our waterfront villa."

She then went on to describe the boats, the house and the décor of almost every room in it, including all the "real nice pictures on the walls".

Randy didn't appear to be a great conversationalist, in fact he didn't say a word during the whole journey.

As soon as we arrived at the airport and met Greg the pilot, Lisa got out a video camera and began prattling into the microphone as she filmed everything in sight:

"This is the airport . . . and this is the little plane we're goin' in . . . and this is Greg the pilot . . . and this is Stooort and Shirley who are goin' with us in the little plane . . . and . . . "

"OK," Greg interrupted, "we're ready to go. The weather forecast looks pretty good. There might be just the odd shower or two, but other than that it looks as though it will be another perfect day in paradise."

Greg gave us a safety briefing before we climbed into the plane; then he demonstrated how to use the headphones so we could communicate with each other over the noise of the engine. The Cessna slowly taxied to the airstrip, turned and roared down the runway before lifting effortlessly into the sky.

"Are we going anywhere near Endeavour Reef?" I asked Greg.

"Yep, it'll be on our starboard side."

Greg went on to explain the significance of the reef to Randy and Lisa. Randy didn't appear particularly interested, but I faintly heard Lisa in the background trying to say something. I turned round. Her mouth looked as though it was shouting something, but hardly any sound was coming out over the noise of the engine.

"I don't think Lisa's headphones are working," I said to Greg.

"Are you switching on when you want to speak, Lisa?" Greg shouted at the top of his voice.

I turned round to see Lisa vigorously nodding her head.

"Yes, she is," I said.

"Her headphones mustn't be working then," Greg replied.

It wasn't a problem that worried me all that much.

It was an incredible sight to see the reef from the air. The Outer Barrier was plainly visible, its reefs end to end, almost in a straight line disappearing over the horizon. Then the hundreds of reefs scattered willy-nilly between it and the mainland. I sat in awe wondering how I had safely navigated tiny *Pluto* through this huge maze, and not for the first time paid mental homage to the early seafarers who sailed our coastline. No detailed charts and GPS for them — just seat of the pants sailing.

Before long we were circling Lizard Island and coming in to land. I looked at my watch. It had taken just sixty-five minutes to get here from Cairns.

As we were disembarking from the Cessna, a shower of rain came in.

"I think this is a good opportunity to have some morning tea," Greg said.

As we sheltered under the plane's wing, Greg brought out a large brown paper bag and offered it around.

"Here, have a croissant, they're beautiful — the best in Cairns," Greg assured us.

They may have been beautiful if they were warm and filled with jam and cream. But cold and unfilled they were chewy, tasteless and greasy.

"Beautiful, aren't they?" Greg said as he wolfed his down.

Lisa looked at hers, turned it over a couple of times and took a small nibble. I managed to eat half of mine; I didn't see what Shirley did with hers.

The shower cleared and the sun came out.

"Right," Greg said, "what we usually do is walk to the end of the runway and follow the track to Blue Lagoon, where we have a swim; then we go to Watson's Bay for a picnic lunch on the beach; that will give us a couple of hours to snorkel over the reef in the bay or walk along the beach. Is everyone happy with that plan?"

Everyone agreed.

When we arrived at Blue Lagoon, Greg, Shirley and I changed for a swim.

"Are you going for a swim?" Greg said to Randy and Lisa.

"Nah, we'll just go for a walk along the beach," Lisa replied.

Greg, Shirley and I swam around the reef for quite a while. When we returned to shore there was no sign of Randy or Lisa.

"I wonder where Randy and Lisa have got to?" Greg said.

The couple still hadn't returned thirty minutes later, and I could see that Greg was becoming concerned.

"I'd better go and look for Randy and Lisa," Greg said. "They might have injured themselves."

"We'll give you a hand," I replied.

"OK, thanks," Greg said. "I'll cut across inland, if you follow the beach. We'll meet back here in half-an-hour."

"All right."

"Be careful though," Greg advised as we were setting off, "just in case they're at it. These Yanks will sue you for anything."

Shirley and I walked along the beach and started to climb a small headland, just as Randy and Lisa came into view, walking nonchalantly down the slope.

"Ah, there you are," I said, when we met. "Greg was worried that you might have had an accident."

"Nah, we've just been walkin'," Lisa replied.

Lisa had changed her clothes. She was now wearing a skimpy leopard-skin patterned bikini, the sight of which even made Shirley gape.

As we walked back to meet Greg, Lisa chatted non-stop about what shells she had seen on the beach, and about the much better shells she and Randy had seen in The Bahamas.

Greg appeared very relieved to see the four of us again.

"OK," he said, "we'll head over to Watson's Bay."

"Jeez," Greg whispered to me, as we started out along the track, "have you seen Lisa's tits?"

"They're hard not to see," I replied.

We walked back along the runway, all the while listening to Lisa talk loudly about everything and anything. When we arrived back at the plane, Greg unloaded a couple of eskies and some large thermos flasks.

"That's our lunch," he said with a wink.

We set off for Watson's Bay, Randy and I each carrying an esky, while Greg carried the flasks. Greg led us to the shade of some trees that overhung the beach, where he began to unpack the food. I was looking forward to lunch, but after the dry croissants for morning tea, I wasn't expecting five star silver service. But I was pleasantly surprised — the cold tropical salad, large tasty fresh prawns, crab, ham and chicken were excellent. Lisa filmed everything around her, then handed the camera to Randy.

"Take my picture eatin' a shrimp, Randy . . . Take my picture holdin' this crab Randy . . . Take my picture in the shade of the trees, Randy . . . Take my picture goin' for a swim, Randy . . . "

When Randy wasn't taking Lisa's picture, she was talking continuously into her video.

Then, at long last, Randy spoke:

"I'm goin' for a snorkel," he said, removing his watch from his wrist. "Here, look after my gold Rolex, Lisa."

"I don't want to ask how much your watch cost," Greg said, "but how much does a watch like that cost?"

"About $17,500 US," Randy replied, and then launched into his longest speech of the day:

"I bought one for Lisa the other day. It's got a lot of jewels on it — pretty gaudy — but Lisa loves it. It cost $36,000."

Randy then opened his beach bag and took out a pair of flippers nearly a metre long.

"Jeez, Randy," Greg said in surprise, "I've seen a few flippers in my time, but I've never seen a pair that big."

"They're special deep free-divin' flippers," Lisa said. "Randy can free-dive to 72 feet."

Lisa accompanied Randy down to the water's edge.

"Randy doesn't say much," Greg said.

"Lisa doesn't give him much of a chance," I replied.

"It's funny how there're so many American blokes called Randy," Greg said. "I get a lot of them on these trips. I told one of them once what 'randy' meant in Australia, but he didn't seem to find it very funny."

Leaving Greg to clear up after lunch, Shirley and I walked along the beach towards the start of the track that led to Cook's Look. There were six yachts anchored in the bay, but I recognised only two of them. It seemed as though I had never left the island, and it felt strange not to see *Pluto*'s familiar shape amongst the other yachts, nor see the little red rubber duckie pulled up above the high-water mark. We passed a couple of yachties on the

beach; they nodded and said hello, but kept on walking. We were tourists now, not yachties — we belonged to another world. We didn't have enough time to walk to the summit, but even from a third of the way up the track the view was great.

"Well, what do you think of Lizard?" I asked Shirley.

"It's a really beautiful island," Shirley replied. "I can see why you couldn't stop talking about it. I'd love to come back and stay at the lodge some day."

When we returned from our walk, Lisa was still filming and yackety-yakking into her video.

"OK, folks," Greg said, "it's time to head for the plane."

Lisa's headphones again didn't work on the flight back to Cairns. We were blessed with sixty-five minutes of beautiful silence.

When we landed at the airport, Randy walked up to Greg and said:

"Hey, Greg, where do you buy those headphones that don't work? I want to get a set for Lisa."

Everyone but Lisa doubled up in laughter.

I didn't think Randy had it in him.

Chapter 19

A QUIET LITTLE PLACE

It was nearly the end of September; approaching that time of year when, from Cairns south, the persistent south-east trade winds are normally replaced by northerlies, the winds that I hoped would provide me with an armchair ride south. Well, that was the theory. Two days after Shirley flew back to Brisbane, I sailed over to Fitzroy Island to await the predicted easterly, which would give *Pluto* a close-hauled run 43 miles down the coast to Mourilyan Harbour.

The weather bureau was right. I left Fitzroy Island early next morning heading into a 15 knot easterly. But during the morning the wind increased to 20 knots, turning a reasonably comfortable sail into an extremely bumpy one.

Hour by hour the prospect of a calm anchorage became more appealing. Around 3.30 p.m. I dropped sail and motored *Pluto* between the two steep, heavily rainforested headlands that form the narrow, natural entrance to the harbour. Once inside though, the entrance opened out into a wide basin edged with rock and mangroves. Immediately to starboard there was a sugar terminal and wharf, built for the occasional large ship that berthed there to load raw sugar and molasses. A short distance further on I could see a couple of jetties and a boat ramp. Apart from a large trawler at the public jetty and a few unattended vessels tied to piles further upstream, only one other yacht lay at anchor. I recognised her as the 13 metre sloop *Serendipity*, owned by Don and Fran who I had met a few weeks ago in Cairns.

As I sat on the foredeck paying out the anchor chain, I felt the harbour had a pleasant tranquility about it. It seems a quiet little place, I thought, I might spend a couple of days here.

About ten minutes later, I received a radio call from Don.

"G'day, mate," he said. "We've got a bit of a problem here. A valve fitting on the fresh water tank has broken and all our water has drained into the bilge. I was wondering if you have any jerry cans on board that I could borrow to transfer some water from the public jetty."

"Yes, Don, I've got three 20 litre jerry cans. Do you want me to bring them over now?"

"No, thanks all the same, we've got enough water for tonight." Don replied, "and it's getting a bit late in the afternoon. Would tomorrow be all right? — unless you're planning on leaving tomorrow."

"No, I'm staying a couple of days. How about I meet you at *Serendipity* at 0900 hours and give you a hand to transfer the water?"

"That'll be great, thanks mate."

Later in the afternoon another yacht came into the harbour and anchored. Through the binoculars I could see the yacht was *Witch-Away*, owned by Brian and Margaret. I had met the couple on a number of occasions along the coast.

Next morning I launched the tender and motored over to *Serendipity*.

"G'day, mate," Don said as I pulled alongside. "Leave the rubber duckie here and we'll go across in our tender. I might sink yours if I get into it."

I laughed. Don was a big man, tall and heavily built, and although I didn't think he would sink *Pluto*'s tender, I knew that with the two of us and three filled jerry cans it would certainly be a tight squeeze.

When we arrived at the public jetty and climbed the concrete steps to wharf level, we saw that the steel trawler berthed there was taking on water with a hose connected to a nearby tap.

"It looks as though that's the only tap," Don said.

"I can see another one up near the roadway," I replied. "It won't be too far to carry the jerry cans."

The three young crew from the trawler looked a tough, sullen lot. Wearing only shorts, their muscular bodies, arms and legs were covered with tattoos; their heads were shaven except for a few long tufts that hung well down their backs.

"I wouldn't like to see those three walking towards me late at night in a quiet street," Don said, not too quietly.

"I'd be running like hell in the opposite direction, that's for sure," I replied.

As we started walking with the jerry cans towards the tap, one of the trawler blokes shouted:

"Hey!"

Don and I froze. I don't know what Don was thinking, but I was considering dropping the jerry cans and running. I thought they must have overheard us talking about them.

"Yeah?" I answered, trying to sound tough, but thinking my reply came out more like a plaintive squeak.

"Are you blokes after water?" the trawlerman asked.

"That's right," Don replied.

"Well you can use our hose, mate, it'll save you a walk."

"Oh, thanks very much," I said, relieved that I wasn't going to be beaten to a pulp and left to die on the public jetty at Mourilyan Harbour.

Don was a hearty, hail-fellow-well-met sort of bloke, and soon he and the three crew were talking away as though they had been mates for years. We were invited on board for a tour of the prawn trawler. The vessel was well set up with all the latest sophisticated navigational equipment. Nevertheless, it was quite disconcerting listening to this tough-looking crew fluently rattle off terms such as satellite derived positions, waypoints and course deviation indicators.

We were shown the huge freezers that snap-freeze the boxes of freshly caught green prawns.

"It takes three minutes to freeze a box of prawns," one crew member said.

As we were leaving I asked if we could buy some prawns.

"We can't sell you any," one of the men said, "but we can swap you some for beer."

"OK, fair enough," I replied, as Don nodded in agreement, "we'll see what we can rustle up."

I didn't have much beer on board, and neither did Don and Fran; between us, we managed to come up with nine cans of Fourex.

"Perhaps Brian and Margaret from *Witch-Away* have got some beer on board," I said to Don. "I'll nip over and see them."

"I wouldn't mind swapping some beer for prawns," Brian said, after I explained the situation to him. "But we've only got home-brew. It's a good brew though."

"With all due respect to you home-brewers," I replied with a laugh, "I've never tasted a really good home-brew yet. I don't know whether the trawler blokes will be interested in that, but I'll take some and try."

Brian went below and returned with one bottle of beer.

"One bottle!" Margaret exclaimed. "Don't be so mean, Brian. It only costs you a few cents a bottle to make."

Brian reluctantly went below to get another bottle.

"How many prawns are we going to get for this?" he asked, as he stood there almost unwilling to relinquish possession of the second bottle.

"I wouldn't have a clue." I replied.

"For goodness sake, Brian!" Margaret said in exasperation.

Brian handed over the bottle as if it was his last dollar.

Don and I returned to the trawler.

For the nine cans of Fourex we were given well over 3 kilograms of top quality export prawns and two dozen Moreton Bay Bugs.

"I've got some home-brew here from the couple on *Witch-Away*. Are you interested in swapping some prawns for that?" I asked the crewman, as I showed him the two bottles.

"Mmm, I suppose so," he said, picking up a plastic bag with at least 2 kilograms of prawns.

"Give 'em that," he almost snorted in contempt, "they're not as good as the others."

Perhaps they weren't, but they were as good as any you'd see in a top class seafood outlet.

When we returned to *Serendipity* I asked Fran for a tiny plastic bag, into which I put two prawns from Brian and Margaret's bag; then I motored over to *Witch-Away*.

"How did you go?" Brian asked.

"Not too well, I'm afraid. The crew don't particularly like home-brew. But they took it and gave you what they thought it was worth in return," I said, holding up the bag with two prawns in it.

Margaret, who was standing behind Brian, exploded with laughter. But Brian just stood there open-mouthed with a horrified look on his face. I couldn't continue the torture any longer; I picked up the 2 kilogram bag that I had hidden in a bucket and handed it over.

It was arranged that later in the afternoon we would all meet on *Serendipity* for a seafood barbecue dinner.

During the afternoon a commercial fishing boat towing six aluminium dinghies came into the harbour. No sooner had it anchored than a crew member untied one of the dinghies and sped across towards *Serendipity*. And sped was the word. It was quite a sight — the crewman standing full height, steering with an extended tiller attached to the powerful outboard, his long, black ponytail streaming out behind him, as the craft rocketed across the harbour at a speed of at least 30 knots. He banked the vessel in a sharp turn and pulled expertly alongside the yacht. But after a few seconds he took off and headed towards *Witch-Away*. I saw Brian hand him something, then with a wave the crewman accelerated and sped back to the fishing boat.

At about 5.00 p.m. I motored over to *Serendipity*; Brian and Margaret were already on board.

"It looks as though I've seen the last of that hose fitting," Brian said despondently when we were all sitting in the cockpit.

"What hose fitting is that?" I asked.

"A few hours ago a fellow from that fishing boat over there borrowed a $1^1/_2$" connector hose fitting from me," Brian replied. "He said he'd have it back to me within fifteen minutes, but it's been nearly three hours now."

About ten minutes later, a dinghy with 'Ponytail' standing in it screamed towards *Serendipity*, swung around and pulled up alongside.

"I saw your dinghy here," 'Ponytail' said to Brian. "I've brought your hose fitting back. Sorry I'm late, but we got on the booze with the blokes from the trawler."

He certainly had; he was slurring and finding it difficult to keep his balance in the wobbling dinghy, which kept banging against the side of *Serendipity*.

"Have you been line fishing out at the reef?" Don asked, using his foot to fend off the dinghy from the side of the yacht.

"Yeah, mate, we send the fish live over to Japan.

"Do you have tanks on board to keep them alive?" I asked.

"Yeah — we'll still be here tomorrow if you want to come over and have a look at the boat. Anyhow, I've got to get back. Oh, I nearly forgot, I've got a few trays of coral trout fillets for you — thanks for lending us that fitting, mate," he said, handing Brian a few plastic packets of thick white fillets, at the same time as he twisted the throttle and zoomed back towards the fishing boat.

"That's the last I've seen of that hose fitting," Margaret said in a deep voice, trying to mimic Brian. "God you're a pessimist."

We all burst out laughing.

It was a fantastic night. Margaret had made some coleslaw and I had made potato salad and boiled some of the prawns; the remainder of the prawns, together with the Moreton Bay Bugs, we cooked on the charcoal-fired barbecue fitted to *Serendipity*'s taffrail. We were out of Fourex, but we did have some wine and rum and of course Brian's home-brew, whose taste seemed to improve as the night wore on. After dinner, Fran got out her guitar and kept us entertained by strumming a few tunes.

I headed back to *Pluto* about 11 p.m. Brian and Margaret left at the same time. Before leaving *Serendipity*, Brian and I had arranged to call Don on our radios as soon as we had safely boarded our yachts. It was always a good precaution to take, just in case a dinghy should overturn or get into difficulties. We knew that if Don didn't hear our radio call within five minutes he would come looking for us. Don and Fran had told us that late one afternoon a few months previously, when *Serendipity* was the only boat anchored at Breakfast Bay in the Gloucester Passage east of Bowen, they were surprised to see thirty-five boats enter the bay and anchor nearby. It turned out that the boats were on an outing from the North Queensland Cruising Yacht Club based in Bowen. The club members began setting up a barbecue on the beach. Don and Fran were invited too. The barbecue was a very noisy affair, with loud music, bright lights and many of the members drinking heavily. At about 11.30 p.m. Don and Fran left the party and rowed their small dinghy back to *Serendipity*. Because there was no moon it was a very dark night. As they were climbing aboard they heard what sounded like cries for help in the distance.

"Did you hear that?" Don asked Fran.

"Yes," Fran answered, "it seemed to be coming from further down the passage."

Fran remained on board *Serendipity*, while Don rowed the dinghy to the area where he thought the cries had come from. But when he got there and shone his torch around he couldn't see or hear a thing. Don called out over and over again, but received no response. Thinking that the cries must have come from some idiot ashore at the party, he was just about to row back to *Serendipity* when, in the beam of his torch, he spotted a man's head beside an upturned dinghy. When Don reached the man, he recognised him as Larry, one of the yachties from the barbecue; he was alive but hopelessly drunk. As Don's dinghy was too unstable to try to lift Larry into it, he began towing him and the upturned boat towards the beach. Don was now rowing against the tide and making little headway. In the meantime, Fran had managed to attract the attention of a couple with a 4 metre runabout and outboard, who immediately motored down to help Don. But as they were trying to pull Larry out of the water into their more stable dinghy, it overturned too. Now there were three people in the water with two overturned boats.

"Shit!" Don exclaimed, as he flashed an SOS with his torch towards Fran.

Fran, realising that something had gone seriously wrong with the rescue attempt, began shouting at the top of her voice for help.

"Shut up! Go to bed!" some of the drunken revellers shouted back at her.

About an hour later, when Fran was nearly at her wits' end and hoarse from shouting, she caught the attention of a couple in a trailer-sailer who managed to get a 5 metre runabout and go to the rescue. Eventually, about 4.00 a.m., everyone was safely back on their boats. It was a sobering incident, proving that excessive drinking and boating don't mix.

Within ten minutes of Brian and I calling Don on the radio to say we were safely back, a storm came in, lashing us with pounding rain and 45 knot wind gusts. It lasted for about an hour, before disappearing as quickly as it came.

Next morning Don and I went over to the fishing boat. 'Ponytail' invited us on board.

"Did you hear what happened to the trawler last night during that storm we had?" 'Ponytail' asked.

"No," Don replied.

"It dragged anchor while the crew were asleep and hit the Coast Guard boat — it crushed its boarding ladder and put a ding in the stern."

"I see the trawler's gone," I said.

"Yeah," 'Ponytail' replied, "they pissed off at first light this morning. The Coast Guard's been trying to call them but they're not answering their radio. But ah, the cops will pick 'em up somewhere down the track."

'Ponytail' showed us around the boat. He explained how each of the crew had his own dinghy and live fish tank, and were paid a commission on the weight of fish each crew member caught.

"How long do you stay out at sea?" I asked.

"About a week," 'Ponytail' replied. "Any longer than that and the fish start to get blotches on their skin. We've got to airfreight them to Japan while they're in top condition. Over there in the restaurants the Nips pay $250 for an average size coral trout. They're a weird mob the Nips — the chef brings out a live coral trout to the table, skewers the fish onto a silver platter then cuts raw slices out of it while it's still alive."

"It sounds revolting," I said.

'Ponytail' showed us where he and the crew slept. It was in a sort of covered enclosure built on top of the roof of the main cabin. It had a head height of little more than a metre and had only enough room for the six single foam mattresses that were placed directly on the floor. A few nude female centrefolds adorned the walls.

"It looks pretty cosy in there, mate," Don commented.

"Do you make good money?" Don continued.

"It's reasonable," 'Ponytail' replied. "But it's not so much the money as the life. I love everything about it. It's a real adventure out at the reef. I feel as though I'm my own boss and the skipper doesn't treat me like a piece of shit. Eighteen months ago I was a real no-hoper — going from one crappy job to another, always up the pub and getting into trouble with the cops. Then a bloke offered me this job to try and get me on the straight and narrow. I've never looked back."

"Good on you," Don said. "If you're happy in your work, you've got it made."

I saw that 'Ponytail''s attention had suddenly been attracted elsewhere.

"That looks like the bow of a dinghy sticking out of the water over near the rocks," he said, pointing towards the harbour entrance.

'Ponytail' got a pair of binoculars from the cabin and looked through them.

"Yeah," he said, "it looks as though there's a bloke in the water beside it. We'll go over in the dory and help him."

Within a minute the three of us were zooming across the harbour, 'Ponytail' in his usual stance at the helm. When we arrived at the scene we found a man in his seventies trying to clamber onto some oyster covered rocks. Blood was streaming down his arms. Don and I helped him into the dory, only to see that his legs were bleeding badly too. Fortunately he was wearing boots.

"Are you OK, mate?" Don said.

The old bloke didn't answer. He seemed to be in a state of shock. I washed the blood from his arms and legs and found that the wounds were not serious.

"You'll be right, mate," I said. "You've got a few cuts — the salt water has just spread the blood around a bit, making it look worse."

The old bloke was wearing a dark green shirt and shorts, the 'uniform' of a cane-cockie.

"We'll bale out the dinghy," 'Ponytail' said, "and tow it to the boat ramp."

Baling out the submerged dinghy was easier said than done, but by the time it was afloat the old bloke was regaining his senses.

"What happened?" I asked.

"I was trying to pull up the anchor, but it was caught on the bottom. I stood up and gave the line a good heave, and it overturned the boat. I've lost all my fishing gear."

"You'll have to get your outboard stripped as soon as possible or it'll be stuffed," 'Ponytail' advised.

We towed the dinghy back to the ramp and helped the old bloke load it onto the trailer.

"Thanks very much for helping me," he said.

"All in a day's work, mate," replied 'Ponytail'.

During the afternoon I went ashore to walk a few hundred metres up the road to a small kiosk and boat hiring business, where 'Ponytail' had told me I could get a hot shower. Apart from the sugar terminal and the kiosk, there was little else at Mourilyan Harbour.

"Are you off a yacht in the harbour?" the young proprietor of the kiosk asked.

"Yes," I replied.

"Were you there the night of the shooting?" the young man asked with some excitement.

"Shooting?" I queried. "What shooting?"

The young man could hardly contain himself as he told me that a few days ago the crew from an anchored trawler went into Innisfail for a night on the town. The skipper's wife, who was with them, slipped back to the harbour with a crew member from another trawler, obviously with more than fishing on their minds. Her husband, on discovering this, followed them back, got his rifle and began shooting at everything in sight. The police came, disarmed the man and took him away.

Yes, I thought, as I walked back along the road, Mourilyan Harbour has certainly turned out to be a tranquil, quiet little place.

That evening, Don, Fran and I were invited over to *Witch-Away* to finish off the rest of the seafood. The night developed into a musical soiree with Margaret playing her violin, Brian plunking away at his banjo and Fran on her guitar.

"Are you leaving tomorrow?" Don asked me.

"Yes," I replied, "the met bureau reckon there's a large high heading for the Bight, which will probably send a strong south-easterly up the coast in about three days, so I'll try to get into Townsville before then. But I think it's going to be a close-hauled run most of the way — the wind doesn't seem to want to blow from anywhere else but the east. What about you — when are you leaving?"

"Where are the northerlies, mate?" Don said. "Where are the northerlies? But yes, we'll be leaving tomorrow too."

"When are you going, Brian?" Don asked.

"Tomorrow, if the weather stays reasonable," Brian replied.

At first light I up-anchored and made my way out of the harbour. *Serendipity* was right behind me, but she soon overtook *Pluto* and headed off into the distance. *Witch-Away* was well behind me. The wind was blowing about 12 knots from the east-south-east, just 20° off *Pluto*'s port bow, forcing me to motor with only the mainsail up for the first 7 miles, until I rounded the North Barnard Islands and turned south. Abeam of Kent Island I hoisted the genoa and stopped the motor. It was a slow, close-hauled run and not a very comfortable one. I had plotted the course to take me about 3 miles out from the eastern side of Dunk Island, but the leeway and flood tide pushed me inshore, so that by midday I had to make a long tack out to sea to clear the island. The breeze increased during the early after-noon to about 17 knots, but because of the sea direction the ride became more lumpy and uncomfortable. Both *Serendipity* and *Witch-Away* had disappeared from sight.

Pluto forged slowly on down past the Family Islands. It should have been a good sail, but the seas were short and steep. Every time *Pluto* picked up a bit of speed, a couple of steep waves would knock him almost to a standstill. It was just on dark by the time I anchored behind Cape Richards at the northern end of Hinchinbrook Island. Twelve hours to cover 42 miles — wow! *Serendipity* was anchored a few hundred metres away. Don called me on the radio to say that *Witch-Away* had anchored behind Goold Island a few miles to the north-west.

At first light next morning it was on again. Motor and mainsail as I rounded Cape Richards and headed for Cape Sandwich. As I rounded the latter and made my way down the eastern side of Hinchinbrook Island, the wind turned to the south-east, meaning that if I went under sail alone I would have to tack for the next 30 miles. To hell with that, I thought, I'll keep on going under motor and main. But three hours later, the wind turned more to the east and I was able to sail close-hauled the remainder of the way. It was quite a comfortable ride, probably because the bulk of the Palm Isles to port reduced the wave height. I anchored *Pluto* in Casement Bay off Great Palm Island shortly after 3 p.m. *Serendipity* was the only other vessel there.

Next morning I awoke to find the wind had swung to the east-north-east, enabling me to sail *Pluto* on a shy reach for most of the trip to Townsville. But under the lee of Magnetic Island, with 5 miles of the leg remaining, the wind dropped right out and I had to motor for the rest of the way to the marina.

"The last three days haven't been the best sailing we've ever experienced," Don commented dryly, when I met him later that afternoon at the marina. "But at least we got here. *Witch-Away* is still up at Hinchinbrook — if that south-easter comes in, they could be stuck there for quite a while."

Later that evening, I was awakened by the sound of wind screaming past the rigging; the predicted south-easterly had arrived with a vengeance.

Chapter 20

BETTER THAN SEX

It blew and blew and blew. For almost a week the 25 to 30 knot south-easterly wind had blasted the coast. While sailing north, the south-east trade wind had been my friend, now it was my enemy. To fill in the time I did a few odd jobs on *Pluto*, revisited some of the sights of Townsville and went to the pictures, something I hadn't done for years.

The yacht berthed next to me belonged to a Townsville resident called John who lived on board with his girlfriend Elizabeth. One afternoon he invited me to join them later for a few drinks and dinner.

"It'll be nothing flash," John said. "Some of our friends are coming. What we usually do is have a few drinks until everyone gets here, then a couple of us go up the road to buy some fish and chips."

"Thanks," I replied, "I'd like to come."

When I arrived at the appointed time, John was the only one on the yacht.

"Come on board," he said. "No-one has arrived yet. Not even Elizabeth is here. But we might as well have a drink while we're waiting."

Almost an hour passed and still no-one had arrived. My stomach began to rumble from too much beer and no food.

"I wonder where everyone is?" John said. "They should be here by now."

Just as the hunger pangs were becoming unbearable, Elizabeth arrived.

"Ah, there you are," John said. "The others haven't turned up yet."

"What others?" Elizabeth asked.

John rattled off a few names.

"It's tomorrow night they're coming," Elizabeth said.

"Are you sure?" John queried.

"Positive."

"I'm sure it was tonight," John persevered.

"Well, no-one's here, are they?" Elizabeth answered.

"I suppose we'd better go and get some fish and chips then," John said. "What do you want Liz?"

"Nothing, I had something to eat with Jan before I came home."

It was almost nine o'clock by the time John and I sat down to some half-cold fish and chips, as Elizabeth, in the tight confines of the yacht, made it obvious she was preparing to go to bed.

Next day I saw John removing his yacht's sail covers.

"Are you going out sailing?" I asked in surprise.

"Yes, I'm taking Liz out for a sail on the bay."

"It still looks very blowy out there," I said.

"I think it should be reasonably sheltered in the bay," John replied. "But if it isn't, we won't be out for long."

Within thirty minutes I saw the yacht coming back into the marina. I stepped off *Pluto* onto the pontoon waiting to give John a hand to tie up. But as the steel sloop headed in towards the berth, John called out:

"We'll be right, thanks, we don't need help — we've got a system."

I waved and stepped back onto *Pluto*, noticing that John's yacht didn't have any fenders out. It must be part of the "system", I thought.

As the yacht came in to berth, the wind blew her hard against the pontoon. All I could hear was a teeth-clenching squeal that could only be made by metal to metal contact. I jumped back onto the pontoon and helped John tie up. John quickly joined me to inspect the damage. Along half the length of the hull there was a scrape that had cut through the paintwork and well into the steel. John spoke the words that I had just been thinking.

"Some fucking system," he said.

We found a bolt sticking out from the pontoon that had caused the damage.

Two days later, on Sunday afternoon, I decided to go out for dinner. It had crossed my mind that John was a bit of a jinx, but as I didn't believe in that sort of thing, I asked him if he knew a decent restaurant.

"The Sea View Hotel just along The Strand has really good meals," he said.

"Is it open on Sunday?" I asked.

"Yes, it's open every night of the week."

Even before I got within 100 metres of the hotel, I knew it was a bad choice. Disco music blasted from the premises. A few dozen unsavoury types stood loitering on the footpath outside the hotel's fenced beer garden, under the watchful eye of four uniformed police officers. When I reached the hotel, I saw the beer garden was packed with people.

"John *is* a jinx," I said under my breath. "There's no way I'm going in there."

I walked round the corner to a small shopping centre, bought some fish and chips, then went into the bottle department of the Sea View for a can of beer. I crossed The Strand opposite the hotel and found a comfortable rock at the top of the stone retaining wall that dropped down to the beach. Although the night was dark, the streetlights from The Strand provided enough light to see what fare I was tucking into. Before long, a black cat appeared beside me and mewed. I threw a piece of fish onto the rock beside me; the cat went over and ate it with relish. I then tossed a couple of chips onto the rock; the cat sniffed them and walked disdainfully away.

"You're not that hungry then, puss," I said to it.

John the jinx and now a black cat, I thought — I'd better watch my step.

A few minutes later I saw a shadow move on the rocks beside me. I quickly turned round, thinking it might be a couple of the patrons from the Sea View Hotel up to no good. But instead, it was a woman dressed in jeans and a tight white top.

"Do you want to be alone," she said, "or do you mind if I sit here too?"

"No," I replied, "you can sit here."

Before I had finished speaking, she plonked down right on top of the two chips the cat had rejected. The woman looked to be in her late thirties; she had teased blonde hair and a well-proportioned figure. In her earlier years she would have been exceptionally good looking; she was still quite attractive, although a little rough around the edges. I imagined her looking very much at home behind the bar of some hotel.

"Do you live here, or are you travelling?" she asked, before taking a sip from the can of beer she had with her.

"Travelling," I replied.

"So am I," she said. "I'm on a working holiday — travelling around Australia. I'm working at a hotel in Charters Towers at the moment. I got the weekend off, so I thought I'd come into Townsville for a bit of action. I'm staying at a motel just up the road, and riding back tomorrow morning."

"Riding back?" I queried.

"Yeah, I ride a Harley-Davidson," she answered.

"Is that what you're travelling around Australia on?"

"Yeah, it's been a dream of mine for years," she continued. "Six months ago I was up in Darwin, stuck in a dead-end marriage with a dickhead husband and two teenage kids who I didn't like very much. I was going to stay until the kids were off our hands. But things just kept closing in on me. I couldn't wait any longer — I bought the Harley and kept it at a girlfriend's place until I was ready to leave. I left a note for my old man telling him I wouldn't be back — and here I am."

I wasn't quite sure what to say, so I didn't say anything.

"Do you mind if I smoke?" she asked.

"No, go ahead," I replied.

She took a cigarette out of her bag and lit it.

"I'm smoking shit," she said, "is that all right?"

Again, I wasn't sure what to say. Until now I hadn't been in the company of anyone while they smoked marijuana.

"Do you want a drag?" she asked. "I've got plenty here."

I declined her offer. To make matters worse, she didn't smoke the way normal people smoke a normal cigarette. She held it between her thumb and forefinger, tilted her head well back and sucked on the joint with all her might, before inhaling deeply with a loud hiss and then blowing out a thick cloud of smoke. If the four policemen standing just across the road spotted her, there would be no doubt what she was smoking.

I've got to get away from here, I thought. I could just imagine Shirley's reaction if the Townsville police telephoned her at nine o'clock on a Sunday night to say that her husband is requesting bail money after being charged with drinking alcohol in a public place in the company of a pot-smoking, Harley-Davidson-riding blonde.

"I'd better be going," I said, standing up.

"Going?" the blonde replied with surprise. "I thought we could make a night of it, and go back to the motel later on."

I was beginning to suspect what sort of working holiday she was on.

"Look, thanks all the same, but I've got a very early start tomorrow morning," I lied.

Leaving her sitting there on the cat's two greasy chips, I climbed over the rocks onto the footpath and walked hurriedly along The Strand towards the marina.

That's the last time I ask John anything, I promised myself.

Although I had refused the blonde's offer to "make a night of it", I didn't refuse the offer made by Fran from *Serendipity* a day later. However, unlike the blonde, Fran's offer didn't include a night of unbridled passion — it was better than that; she invited me on board for a roast lamb dinner.

"I know you don't like garlic," Fran said, "but would a roast onion be OK?"

"Yes, yes, yes please," I drooled.

It was almost unbearable — sitting in *Serendipity* having a pre-dinner drink as the smell of roast lamb permeated the cabin.

At last, a plate of roast vegetables, fresh bright green peas and slices of tender-looking roast lamb was placed in front of me, followed closely by a cruet of steaming gravy and another of mint sauce. I ate slowly, relishing every mouthful. It was the best meal I had tasted since leaving Brisbane.

"Fran," I said, shaking my head slowly, "this is fantastic. I'll be indebted to you for the rest of my life."

"While we're talking bullshit, mate," Don interrupted, "did you hear the latest weather report?"

"Yes," I replied, with a laugh, "it looks as though it's going to improve."

"I reckon it is too," Don continued. "I think we'll leave tomorrow or the next day and anchor over in Horseshoe Bay at Magnetic Island, and then when the weather's right we'll just head south as fast as we can. We've seen enough of Townsville for a while. In fact we're looking forward to getting home. What about you?"

"I'm going to reprovision tomorrow," I answered. "Hopefully, the weather will be right the next day."

Two days later I left Townsville and motor-sailed across Cleveland Bay with a 15 knot easterly 20° off *Pluto*'s starboard bow. I rounded Cape Cleveland, turned off the motor and sailed close-hauled on a port tack down into Bowling Green Bay. I knew that once I rounded Cape Bowling Green, I would have a close-hauled run down to Bowen, but getting round Cape Bowling Green was going to be the problem. The easterly was taking me further and further into the bight of the bay. To sail out of it, I had to steer *Pluto* north-east on a starboard tack; it felt as though I was sailing back to Lizard Island. Just on dusk that evening *Pluto* was abeam of Cape Bowling Green; I had sailed 60 miles to cover a distance of 37 miles.

The worst of it is over now, I thought, only 35 miles to Cape Upstart on a straight close-hauled run. During the afternoon the easterly had increased slightly, but it was still a fairly comfortable motion with *Pluto* averaging 6 knots. I connected the autopilot and went below to switch on the navigation lights. On returning to the cockpit, I found *Pluto* was well off course. I tried to reset the autopilot but discovered it was as dead as a dodo. Power was getting into the unit all right, but nothing was coming out.

I tied a temporary line from the tiller to a cleat, and began to set up the wind vane, only to find that some of its moving parts had frozen from long exposure to sea-spray. Holding a torch in my mouth, I lent through the taffrail and began to unscrew some fittings so I could clean them, but the bumpy movement of the yacht made it a difficult task. Certain that I was going to drop a vital part into the water, I decided to leave it until I reached the shelter of Cape Upstart. I wasn't looking forward to steering for the next six hours without a break, but when I looked at the compass I discovered that *Pluto* was steering a fairly true course just with the tiller lashed. I adjusted the sails slightly and found that the yacht continually sailed within 10° of the course. I felt very relieved.

I anchored behind Cape Upstart about one o'clock in the morning, had a quick rum and crashed into my bunk. At first light I dismantled the wind vane, cleaned and greased the parts and reassembled them. By 8.30 a.m. *Pluto* was underway again. The wind was still blowing 17 knots from the east, which forced me to sail 15 miles out to sea on a starboard tack, so that I could turn and sail close-hauled towards Bowen. It seemed ridiculous to reach that turning point after nearly four hours of sailing and be 5 miles north of where I started that morning. But that's just a part of sailing. Just on dark I rounded Cape Edgecumbe, 5 miles from Bowen, sailed through the narrow but well lit passage between North Head and Stone Island, and turned towards Bowen Boat Harbour. All I could see ahead was a maze of lights. The red and green lateral marks leading into the harbour were lost in a confusion of almost blinding white lights from the fleet of trawlers berthed at the Bowen Seafood Wharf. Except for the fact that I knew the layout of the harbour from my northbound visit, there was no way I would have attempted entering this place at night. As I approached the entrance, I picked out what I thought was the first set of red and green lights. There were no lead lights to the entrance, so it was just a matter of moving ahead cautiously. But the closer I got, the more obvious everything became, and soon *Pluto* was motoring along the narrow channel that led into the harbour. I hoped to tie up at the yacht club, but as I motored past I saw there were no vacant berths, so I turned *Pluto* around and headed into the darkness of the duckpond. Away from the bright lights of the trawlers, my eyes soon regained their night vision and I found a space between two drum moorings; but each time I approached to pick up the line strung between the drums, by the time I had run to the bow, the easterly wind had blown *Pluto* out of reach. After my fourth attempt, I saw a man climb into a dinghy from a nearby yacht and row over to the drum line.

"Throw me a line," he shouted.

With his help, *Pluto* was soon securely moored.

"Thank you very much," I said. "Would you like to come aboard for a drink?"

"Thanks," he replied.

"What would you like?" I asked. "A warm beer or a rum?"

"A beer will do."

The young man was a nice bloke and I was extremely grateful for his help. But after the pleasantries, he settled down for what I suspected was going to be a long chat. Tonight, all I wanted was to make something hot to eat and go to bed. With only four hours sleep in the past forty-eight and two long days of fairly rigorous sailing I was dead on my feet. Tomorrow, I would have enjoyed talking to the young bloke for hours — but not tonight.

"Would you like another beer?" I asked, hoping he would say "No, look, I've been here long enough. I'll leave you to it".

But instead, he said:

"Yes, please."

On and on it went. I yawned numerous times and made many strong hints, but they all went unheeded. I considered just falling sideways on my bunk pretending to have gone to sleep; perhaps he would leave me to it. Eventually, I had to say it:

"Look, mate, I'm stuffed. I'll just have to get some sleep. Thanks for your help and I'll have a chat with you tomorrow."

After he left, I didn't even bother making a meal; I just collapsed into my bunk.

Next day, although it was Saturday, I decided to walk uptown to see if the autopilot repairer's shop was open. Fortunately it was; the repairer said he'd have a look at it over the weekend and that I should call back on Monday. It seemed as though I was going to have another riveting few days of looking at murals and real estate office windows. However, while walking through town I had noticed posters advising that a parade was going to be held in the main street at one o'clock that day as part of Bowen's annual festival; the crew from the Australian Navy's patrol boat *Gladstone* was going to take part in it.

At a quarter to one I arrived in the main street. It was all but empty. I walked into a pub and ordered a beer.

"I thought the street parade was supposed to be on at one o'clock today," I said to the barman.

"Yeah, mate, that's right," he replied.

I walked to the door and looked outside; nothing much had changed, the street was still deserted. I looked at my watch — it showed ten to one. Then, within five minutes, at least a thousand people appeared from side streets and took up their positions on each side of the main road. A few minutes later there was the sound of a marching band and the parade appeared. The crew of the patrol boat *Gladstone* led the way, each crew member dressed immaculately in white uniform. They were followed by a marching band, marching girls and a number of floats, some of which were carrying Miss Bowen beauty contest finalists. The parade was short, but to make up for it, it went up and down the main road three times, each time being cheered wildly by the spectators. At the end of the third circuit, the parade quickly dispersed; and so did the crowd. Within five minutes the main road was deserted again. I walked back into the pub to put my empty glass on the bar.

"Did you see the parade, mate?" the barman asked.

"Yep, sure did," I replied, as I wandered off to look at the murals and real estate office windows.

The North Queensland Cruising Yacht Club built beside the harbour was a pleasant haven with a friendly atmosphere. The woman behind the bar gave me a key to the club's amenities block, so each evening I motored across to the club for a shower and dinner.

To my delight, when I returned to the autopilot repairer's place on Monday afternoon, the unit was repaired.

"A couple of capacitors had burnt out, that's all," Peter said. "There was no need for me to order parts from down south.

I bought some fresh meat and vegetables, topped up the icebox with ice and next morning slipped the mooring lines. There was only a slight breeze from the east, so I motor-sailed across Edgecumbe Bay. But as I approached the narrow Gloucester Pass the wind increased to 15 knots right on the nose. The wind, together with the ebbing tide, slowed *Pluto* down to the extent that he was hardly moving. The only way I could make headway was by making a series of short tacks from one side of the passage to the other; even then, progress was dreadfully slow.

Eventually, after clearing the passage, I made a 5 mile tack to the north-east before going about and running down the coast close-hauled to the south-east. The wind had been increasing all morning and was now blowing 20 to 25 knots. I put a reef in the main and returned to the cockpit, only to notice a slight tear along a line of stitching near the clew of the genoa. As I made my way across the deck to have a closer look at it, there was a sudden rrrrrip as the sail opened up along the full length of the split. I quickly went to the mast, released the genoa halyard and climbed out onto the bowsprit to gather in the sail and lash it to the safety lines. With only the main up, *Pluto* had slowed to about 3 knots, causing the bow to rise high in the air over the wave crests before crashing down into the troughs. The bowsprit often plunged below water-level, taking me with it. Dripping wet I went below and pulled out a small headsail from the sail locker and returned to the bow; then with one arm wrapped around the pulpit railing, hanked the sail onto the forestay. By the time I changed over the sheets and hoisted the sail, my arms felt as though they were pulled out of their sockets. I was aware that I could have made it easier on myself while changing the headsail by going about and running with the wind, but that would have meant losing ground that I had so painstakingly gained. At least this way I was getting closer to my destination.

I had planned on anchoring overnight in Woodwark Bay, 5 miles north of Airlie Beach; then the following day continuing on down through the Whitsundays. But now, I decided to sail on to Airlie Beach, where I knew I could get the damaged genoa professionally mended.

Two days later, with the sail repaired, I set off again. That morning the weather bureau had predicted north-east to south-east winds of 15 to 20 knots. It was presently blowing a 15 knot easterly, which gave me a close-hauled run down the Molle Channel. If the wind swung to the north-east it would give me a good run down the coast; but if it swung to the south-east it would be right on the nose. By 11 a.m., when *Pluto* was at the southern end of South Molle Island, it was blowing 20 knots from the south-east.

"To hell with this," I said out loud.

I put *Pluto* about, ran along the eastern side of Daydream Island, sailed through Unsafe Pass and anchored in Bauer Bay under the shadow of South Molle Island's Spion Kop. By midafternoon the south-easterly was blowing a consistent 25 to 30 knots, with the occasional bullet of 40 knots that screamed down the mountain and accelerated across the bay, causing *Pluto* to snatch at his anchor chain and heel well over. But there was little swell and I had reasonable faith in the holding ground.

I decided to stay here until the wind was actually blowing from the north, not just a prediction that it might be. From where I was anchored it was 167 miles to Island Head Creek, a distance that I wanted to cover in one overnight leg. I could only achieve that with a brisk northerly. I had noticed that since leaving Townsville my return trip had become almost a mission; every opportunity to be driven south was taken. And it wasn't just me that felt this way, almost every other yachtie I had spoken to was sweating on the wind from the north.

For three days and nights the wind howled in from the south-east. A day didn't pass that at least a couple of bareboat yachts dragged anchor and headed off towards North Molle Island. And I was told that the same thing happened at night when the crews were ashore enjoying themselves. Resort staff would alert the yachties over the public address system, and there would be a wild dash of inebriated charterers heading for their dinghies so they could chase after their yachts. Although *Pluto*'s anchor hadn't budged since my first day here, I was reluctant about going ashore and leaving the yacht unattended, as some of the bullets that swept across the bay were extremely vicious. But even so, each day I went ashore for a quick walk up to Spion Kop to look down the Whitsunday Passage, only to see an ocean of white foaming breakers that disappeared into the hazy horizon.

On the fourth afternoon the south-easter began to ease. By nightfall there was hardly a breeze with a prediction from the weather bureau of a north-easterly change. Shortly before dawn I was awakened by a different motion in *Pluto*. Even before going on deck I knew that the north-easterly had arrived. I up-anchored and set off.

During the morning the wind steadied at about 15 knots, which gave *Pluto* a comfortable reach through the Whitsunday Passage and into the Cumberland Channel, past the many islands I had explored on the way north. By dusk I was clear of the main bulk of islands and was abeam of St Bees Island. The north-easterly had increased to between 17 and 20 knots, which pushed *Pluto* along under full sail at a constant 7 knots. This was magnificent sailing.

My only worry was the unlit Double Island, which lay 35 miles ahead. Although my course took *Pluto* 3 miles off the eastern side of the island, I was concerned that the flood tide, which ran at 2 knots from the north-east, would push the yacht dangerously close to the island. But allowing for the drift and checking my course with 'Shirley's GPS' I didn't have a problem. The night was almost pitch black with about eighty per cent cloud cover, but the few stars that I could see, provided enough light to faintly make out the black mass of Double Island as I approached it.

Around three o'clock in the morning the wind began to ease, slowing *Pluto* to a relaxed 4 knots. Just before the chill of dawn I connected the autopilot and went below to make some coffee. By the time I returned to the cockpit and took the first welcome sip of steaming liquid, it was almost daylight. *Pluto* was 3 miles abeam of the passage that separated Middle Percy and South Percy Islands. Through the passage I could see the outline of North East Island, also known as 'the sleeping giant' because its silhouette clearly resembles a large man lying on his back. There was still a fair covering of cloud, consisting mainly of overlapping layers of massive, woolly cumulous balls that appeared to have bubbled up from behind the islands spread out along the eastern horizon. Although the sun was hidden by cloud, I could see the increasing brightness as it rose higher and higher. Then, slowly, narrow delicate beams of silver and golden light began to radiate from behind each layer of cloud, spearing their way like spotlights across the sky. As the beams increased in strength, the two colours merged, filling the surrounding atmosphere with a bright, supernatural glow. When it seemed that the sight around me could only fade, the edge of each cloud progressively lit up with a line of deep, silvery gold, so bright, so intense, it appeared that some invisible hand was following the outline, setting it alight with a finger of burning molten metal, brighter than the sun itself; and as if to complement the burning clouds, the narrow beams of light intensified in depth and colour to the point that I thought the whole atmosphere must explode. But unlike a sunset, which holds its zenith of brilliance for only seconds, this amazing sunrise held its climax for minutes. No longer did I feel like a distant observer watching a magnificent natural phenomenon from the deck of a yacht, but instead felt enveloped and absorbed by it. Then as it faded, I gradually became aware of my immediate surrounds, as though the advance of daylight was drawing me back to reality. As a lighthouse keeper I had seen hundreds of glorious sunrises along the Queensland coast. Never had I been privileged to witness anything like this.

Some time later I went below to cook breakfast. The wind had eased even further, reducing *Pluto*'s speed to 2 knots. While at the galley, something through the porthole caught my eye. In the water, close to the yacht, I saw a calm patch, almost like an oil slick. It disappeared behind the yacht, so I kept on cooking breakfast. A minute or so later I noticed another calm patch close to the yacht. This time I went on deck to see what was going on. I didn't see much — just the calm patch disappearing slowly behind me.

"Some bastard must have dumped oil in the water," I said out loud.

As I turned to go below, a whale surfaced right beside the yacht, so close I could have stepped off the deck onto its back. Bloody hell, I said to myself, scared to say the words out loud. After a few seconds the whale dropped below the water, leaving a calm, oily-looking slick on the surface. As I stood there frozen, it surfaced again. The monster had to be over 12 metres long. I had read that running the boat's motor was thought to keep whales away, but I didn't want to start the motor now, in case the whale got the fright of his life, gave his massive tail a flick — and goodbye *Pluto*. This area lay only

15 miles away from where I had my encounter with the whale or whales when I was northbound. This bloody place must be lousy with whales, I thought. God only knows what had been going on around me during the night. The monster kept pace with *Pluto*, surfacing every now and then. It didn't blow or make any noise — just appeared and disappeared. I must admit, that on this occasion I didn't feel as threatened as before; at least this bloke was swimming with me and not against me. Still, I was relieved when after about ten minutes of accompanying *Pluto* it disappeared.

An hour or so later the north-easterly breeze picked up and *Pluto* once more moved along at a lively pace. I was abeam of Island Head Creek at 2.45 p.m., earlier than expected, so I decided to continue on a further 15 miles to Port Clinton. The more miles covered today, the less tomorrow. As the evening approached, the wind eased, so I started the engine and motor-sailed the last 4 miles. I was very happy with my progress. *Pluto* had covered 182 miles in thirty-five hours, which left me only 44 miles to reach Rosslyn Bay tomorrow; and if the weather bureau was right, the 15 to 20 knot north-easterly would have me there in no time.

I anchored *Pluto* almost in the same spot as on my way north. There was only one other yacht in Port Clinton; it was a catamaran anchored about a mile further up the inlet. The wind had dropped right off and there wasn't the slightest breath of breeze. Even after thirty-six hours without sleep I felt wide-awake, so I began to cook some dinner. But as darkness fell, hundreds of tiny black bugs, attracted by the light, flew into the cabin. I fitted the insect screens over the hatches, but the bugs were so small, many of them crawled right through the mesh. By the time I had finished dinner and washed up, I was running with perspiration as bugs crawled into my ears and around my eyes; the cockpit was carpeted with millions of the pests.

"The start of summer is definitely with us," I said out loud, as I got into my bunk. "I'll be glad to get out of here tomorrow."

I was awakened in the early hours of the morning by the sound of wind screaming past the rigging. I climbed out into the cockpit only to have my fear confirmed — the wind was coming from the south-east.

I arose at first light; the sky was heavily overcast and the south-easter was blowing 25 to 30 knots. I listened to the weather bureau's early morning forecast only to hear their prediction of 15 to 20 knots from the north-east. However, the Keppel Sands Coast Guard advised that Rosslyn Bay was experiencing similar conditions to Port Clinton. As morning turned to afternoon, the wind increased to 30 to 35 knots, still from the south-east. I wasn't looking forward to another evening of black bugs, but as darkness approached there wasn't a one; it seemed that the strong wind was keeping them away.

Next day the south-easter rarely dropped below 40 knots. The wind shrieked past the rigging; at some stages of the tide, when *Pluto* was pushed sideways to the wind, the yacht was almost constantly heeled over at 15°. Each weather report from the bureau read 15 to 20 knot winds from the north-east; each report from the Coast Guard confirmed what I was experiencing here.

Conditions deteriorated even more on the third day. The wind roared in at 45 knots, accompanied by heavy rain squalls. Visibility dropped to 500 metres. Despite the atrocious weather, I was very comfortable on board *Pluto*; the temperature had dropped, and although I had run out of fresh meat, there was still an adequate supply of potatoes and eggs. I spent most of the day writing, stopping only to make fresh scones or pancakes for lunch; after dinner I'd settle down in my bunk to read. It was pure pleasure lying there with a good book, feeling dry and warm while the wind and rain lashed and buffeted the yacht.

During early afternoon on the following day, I saw a large motor vessel approaching through the haze from seaward. As she came closer I recognised her as the 18 metre Australian Customs' launch *Sir William Lyne*. She anchored further up the inlet between *Pluto* and the catamaran. A short while later I called her on the radio.

"Customs' launch *Sir William Lyne*, this is the yacht *Pluto*. Do you receive? — over."

"Yacht *Pluto* calling Australian Customs' launch *Sir William Lyne*. Go ahead."

"Just enquiring about what wind speed and direction you were getting out at sea — over."

"A consistent 50 knots from the south-east — over."

"Thanks *Sir William Lyne*, I might stay here for a while then — over."

"I think that's a good idea, *Pluto*."

Two days later the wind eased to 25 knots. *Sir William Lyne* departed during the morning, followed shortly afterwards by the catamaran. But two hours later the catamaran returned; obviously the sea conditions had been too rough.

When I awoke on the seventh day, the wind had dropped to 20 knots and was blowing from the east-south-east. I up-anchored, cleared Port Clinton and made a long tack out to sea before going about and heading for Cape Manifold 10 miles away. I rounded the cape about midday, my new course putting me on a shy reach all the way to Rosslyn Bay. Despite the strong winds of the past week, the sea had dropped off quicker than I expected, making it quite a comfortable run down the coast. As the afternoon wore on, the wind swung more to the east, giving me an even better run.

Although I had enjoyed the first few days in Port Clinton, I had become more eager to leave as the week wore on. With Rosslyn Bay now only an hour away, I began to look forward to visiting the Capricorn Coast Yacht Club that evening. I knew they sold barbecue packs to cook on the club's barbecue. It was Friday, so I imagined the club would have a good attendance. The closer I got to the harbour the more I thought about the delights of a hot shower followed by a juicy steak and a few cold beers. But most of all I was looking forward to a talk with some fellow yachties; I hadn't had a proper conversation with anyone for nearly a fortnight.

I anchored in Rosslyn Bay Boat Harbour just on dusk, threw some clean clothes into my backpack and motored ashore. As I headed for the back entrance to the showers, I noticed a few people laughing and drinking in the bar. You beauty, I said to myself, within fifteen minutes I'll be joining them. I shaved and had a steaming hot shower, the sensualism of which could only be appreciated by those who haven't had a shower for a fortnight. I tossed my dirty clothes into my backpack and walked out ready for a night of revelry. When I got to the door of the yacht club, I couldn't believe my eyes — the place was locked up as tight as a drum and not a bloody soul in sight.

Thoroughly disappointed, I returned to *Pluto* for another solitary meal of more damn eggs and potatoes.

Chapter 21

"IT'S ALL GOOD FUN"

I suppose the Bureau of Meteorology had to get it right eventually. After spending seven days in Port Clinton and two days in Rosslyn Bay listening to them tell lies about the predicted north-easterly, it finally arrived. On a broad reach I sailed *Pluto* across Keppel Bay and into The Narrows. The high tide that would take me through the shallowest section of this waterway wasn't until six-thirty the following morning. So, to be within striking distance, I anchored for the night in Badger Creek, a narrow but deep mangrove-lined inlet that snakes its way into the western side of Curtis Island.

During the night the fresh breeze kept the sandflies and mosquitoes away. But at first light, I awoke to a dead calm broken only by the loud buzzing of millions of these insects trying to find their way through the screens. Armed with a can of Aerogard I ripped back the companionway hatch screen and dived into the cockpit, at the same time spraying myself with insect repellent. But it had little effect. As I winched in the mud-covered anchor chain, the sandflies ferociously attacked my legs, arms and face. They crawled into my ears and nose, and found their way under my hat and into my hair. While trying to brush them away with my muddy hands, thick dollops of sticky black slime splattered over the deck, genoa and me. Even when I was clear of Badger Creek, *Pluto* remained enveloped in a cloud of sandflies.

High tide had just passed by the time *Pluto* was abeam of the entrance to Monte Christo Creek, the shallowest part of The Narrows. A little further on, round a bend near the mouth of Boat Creek, I saw a yacht about 11 metres long that looked aground on the wrong side of the green lateral mark. The tide was now running out at about 2 knots, so, keeping an eye on the depth sounder, I passed the yacht, turned *Pluto* around in the narrow channel and motored abeam of the grounded vessel, holding *Pluto* stationary against the tidal run.

"What happened?" I shouted to the two middle-aged men who were on deck.

190

"We took the wrong side of the green," one of them shouted back.

I was well aware of how it could have happened. Normally on entering a harbour the red marks are kept to port and the greens to starboard. But in this case, because Rockhampton at the northern end of The Narrows is regarded as the harbour and not Gladstone to the south, the marks are passed red to starboard and green to port. Obviously the man who had been at the helm of the grounded yacht had lost concentration and mistakenly kept the green to starboard.

"Can you tow us off?" the man shouted to me, just as a fisherman in a powerful runabout zoomed up the channel and pulled up near us.

"I'll give it a go," I replied.

The fisherman ferried a long line from the grounded yacht to *Pluto*. I cleated the line onto the stern and manoeuvred *Pluto* into the best position for the tow. The strong tidal flow in the confines of the narrow channel made the exercise quite awkward. As well, I was keeping an eagle eye on the depth sounder; the last thing I wanted was to go aground on the falling tide. Eventually I got into position and gave *Pluto* full revs forward at the same time as the grounded yacht gave full revs in reverse, but the vessel didn't budge.

"What size motor do you have?" one of the men on the yacht asked.

"15 horsepower," I answered.

The man snorted and shook his head in derision.

"That's not much use," he said.

"That's gratitude for you," I mumbled under my breath.

The fisherman tied a second line from the yacht onto his boat, but even with this additional power the vessel didn't move. The tide was really beginning to rush out now, and a fresh north-easterly breeze had set in. Because it was a neap tide, there hadn't been all that much water under *Pluto*'s keel to begin with, and the depth sounder was showing less and less as the time went on.

"How about you run your anchor out to the channel and try to winch the yacht off," I suggested. "And if you hoist the main, that breeze might just heel you over enough to free the keel. It's coming from the right direction to blow you back into deep water. Even a halyard from the top of the mast to the runabout would help heel her."

"Those theories might sound all right in books, pal, but they don't work in the real world," the other man on the yacht replied sarcastically.

"You've just lost my help — 'pal'," I said under my breath.

"I'm afraid I'll have to leave you to it, gentlemen," I said in a loud voice, untying the line from *Pluto*'s cleat and letting it drop unceremoniously into the water. "The tide's dropping quickly and I don't want to get caught here too."

It wasn't as if the men's lives were in danger; at low tide they could walk ashore, even if it meant sinking over their knees in mud. According to the tide book, there was very little difference between the morning and evening high tide heights and the heights were reducing each day. If the yacht didn't get off tonight, it certainly wouldn't get off for three days until the tide heights began to increase again. I must admit, the thought of the two men sharing the next three nights with a few billion sandflies and mosquitoes didn't worry me a bit.

The brisk north-easterly, combined with the outgoing tide and smooth water provided a marvellous sail into Gladstone. Well before lunch I berthed *Pluto* in the Gladstone Marina.

Two days later, Shirley flew up from Brisbane to accompany me to Bustard Head, where we were going to spend a week anchored in Pancake Creek. A couple of days before we planned to leave Gladstone, Shirley and I were walking along the main street back to the marina, when I heard a car pull up beside us.

"Hello, you two," a refined English voice said. "Have any trawlers run into *Pluto* lately?"

I looked round to see the driver was Paul Chapman, the Gladstone harbour pilot who Shirley and I had met in Pacific Creek while on the way north.

"Ah, it's Paul the pilot from the good ship *Equinox*," I replied with a laugh. "How are you, Paul?"

"Good, good. Are you going back to the marina? I'll give you a lift if you like."

"All right, thanks," I answered. "How about having a cup of coffee with us on *Pluto* when we get there?"

"I'd like to," Paul said, "but I'm due at the airport shortly to catch a helicopter out to a ship. What say I call in later this afternoon — say about 1600 hours?"

"Fine, we'll look forward to it."

"Are you working on another book, Stuart?" Paul asked on the way to the marina.

"I am, as a matter of fact."

"What's it about?"

"Bustard Head lighthouse," I replied. "Its history is full of tragic events — shipwreck, drownings, murder, abduction, suicide. I want to record it because it's such an important part of our maritime history."

"When will it be out?" Paul asked.

"Not for a while, Paul. Both Shirley and I are working on the research. There's still a lot to be done. As a matter of fact, only about an hour ago, we were interviewing a Mrs Anderson from Gladstone — she's related to a Bustard Head lightkeeper whose daughter was abducted and murdered."

"Not Audrey Anderson?" Paul queried.

"Yes, do you know her?" I replied in surprise.

"Audrey is our next-door neighbour," Paul laughed.

Later in the afternoon, while Paul was having coffee with us on board *Pluto* he said:

"How would you both like to accompany a pilot while he brings a ship into the harbour?"

"You mean fly by chopper out to a ship?" I answered in amazement.

"Yes," Paul replied, "it's not something that many are permitted to do, but you're both maritime historians. If you want to go, I'll check and see what I can do."

"Want to go? I'd love to. Wouldn't you, Shirl?" I asked.

"Of course — I love helicopter flying."

Paul made a few calls on his mobile.

"OK," he said, "it's all arranged. Captain Peter Domigan — he's our senior pilot — will pick you up in front of the marina at one o'clock tomorrow afternoon. I'm sure you'll enjoy it, and Peter is a really nice bloke."

Next day on the way to the airport, Peter explained that the ship we were going out to meet was a 'panamax', which meant it was about 230 metres long, 32 metres in beam, could carry 65,000 tonnes of cargo — in this case coal — and had seven hatches on deck. The ship was Panamanian registered with a Chinese crew.

"We'll be taking her right up the harbour to the Clinton Coal Wharf," Peter said.

When we arrived at the airport, Peter introduced us to the helicopter pilot.

"We're going out on the Hughes 500," Peter said, as we walked across the tarmac towards the five-bladed helicopter with the word PILOT painted on it. "It's a good little machine."

Peter helped us put on self-inflating lifejackets and went to great lengths explaining what to do in an emergency.

"If the helicopter *does* go down in the sea, wait for the blades to stop turning before you attempt to leave the cabin; and get out of the machine *before* you inflate your lifejackets," Peter said.

Peter made us sit in the helicopter and unlatch the doors the way he had shown us.

"Remember," Peter instructed, "when you're getting into the helicopter, it's head first. When you're getting out of the helicopter it's bum first. We'll be landing on one of the cargo hatches, so when we get there, climb out of the chopper, undo your lifejackets and put them back on the seat and shut the door. Walk around the front of the chopper, not the back of it, and then keeping close together, follow me off the hatch."

At the pilot's command we all climbed into the machine, strapped ourselves in and fitted our headphones. I sat in the front with the helicopter pilot, while Shirley sat in the back with Peter.

"Remember which pedal to press if you want to talk," Peter said. "If you press the wrong pedal, Harbour Control and the ships will hear what you're saying. And that's happened before. Just recently, when one of our pilots was coming in to land on a ship, he pressed the wrong pedal, and thinking he was talking only to the chopper pilot said: 'Look at that heap of shit we're going to land on. How come I get all the bloody rust buckets?'."

The helicopter slowly whined into life, as the pilot pulled out levers, pushed in levers, turned things and switched on things. The whine increased to a powerful, throbbing crescendo as the machine quivered and the pilot requested clearance for take off. We lifted off the tarmac and made our way towards the runway, where we turned and followed it for a short distance before lifting high into the air. As we thundered along, Peter called the ship we were heading for, gave the captain our estimated time of arrival and requested the hatch number we were to land on.

"Nummer five hatch, nummer five hatch," the Chinese skipper replied.

"Number five hatch," Peter rogered. "Is the firefighting team standing by beside number five hatch, Captain?"

"Standing by."

As the helicopter thundered along, Peter described the various points of interest below us. We crossed over the Gatcombe Channel, skirted the southern end of Facing Island and headed out towards the Fairway Buoy, which marked the entrance of the 16 mile-long channel leading into Gladstone. There were three ships at anchor in the vicinity of the Fairway, while the one we were going to land on was steaming towards the entrance.

"We might do a circuit first," Peter said to the pilot, "just to confirm that the firefighting equipment is in place. Firefighting equipment to some of these people, Stuart, means one man and a bucket of water."

The pilot completed his circuit.

"Yes, I can see some men with a fire hose down there," Peter remarked. "OK, we'll go in."

As the machine descended, the ship below us looked miniscule. It seemed impossible that the helicopter could land on the ship, never mind on one of its hatches. Not only that, the ship was moving at a fair clip and the helicopter was approaching on a 90° course to the vessel's starboard side, straight into a 20 knot south-easter. But the lower we got, the more I realised that the helicopter would fit comfortably on the hatch. The pilot brought the machine down without the slightest bump. We unbuckled our seat belts, opened the doors and climbed out of the cabin to the sound of the screaming jet engine and the swish of the blades above our heads. Shirley and I carried out the instructions Peter had given to us in Gladstone, followed him across the hatch and climbed down onto the deck. The scream of the helicopter intensified as it lifted, banked into the air and headed back towards the airport.

A crewman led us along the deck and through a bulkhead door.

"Ah," Peter said, "that's good, the ship has a lift. That saves us a long climb."

We got out of the lift and climbed a flight of narrow steps that opened out onto the bridge. After the noise of the helicopter, the bridge, even with the slight rumble of the engines, seemed serene.

"Good afternoon, Captain," Peter said. "I have two observers with me today."

"Good afternoon," the Chinese captain replied, as he bowed and shook hands with the three of us. Peter looked through the window of the bridge and gave the helmsman a course to steer. The view from the bridge was unbelievable. The vessel's bow stretched 200 metres into the distance. The ship was monstrous.

"Starboard 10," Peter said in a precise, authoritative voice.

"Sta-board 10," repeated the helmsman.

The captain and the helmsman appeared to be the only two who could speak English, and the captain certainly didn't look like a captain. He was dressed in baggy, fawn sports trousers, a light grey nylon shirt with a tie that went out of fashion in the 1950s. It looked as though he had picked up his wardrobe for $2 at an op-shop.

We passed the Fairway and headed along the Wild Cattle Cutting, marked by port and starboard piles. From the height of the bridge the piles looked the size of matchsticks; from the deck of *Pluto* I remembered them as telegraph poles.

The log above the helmsman showed the ship was doing 10 knots.

"Is this your fastest speed, Captain?" Peter asked.

"No, no," the captain replied, "can go faster, yes?"

"Yes, I think we'll go faster, Captain."

As the revolutions increased, the vessel began to shudder noticeably.

"She's quite an old vessel," Peter said to me. "She hasn't got much speed."

After a while Shirley walked out onto the portside open bridge-deck. Every so often I'd go out to see her. I had noticed that the ship, since increasing speed, was belching flakes of soot out of her stack, which were landing all over the bridge-deck.

The log showed that the ship was now travelling at 12.5 knots.

"Is that top speed, Captain?" Peter asked.

"Yes, top speed."

"By the amount of soot coming out of her engines," Peter said quietly to me, "I don't think she travels at this speed too often."

I went back outside to join Shirley. Before long a Chinese crewman came out onto the deck. Shirley looked at him and smiled. The man gave a low bow. A few minutes later Shirley looked up at the stack that was still throwing out flakes of soot, looked down at the deck where the flakes were landing, before looking back at the man and smiling. The crewman hurried into the bridge-house and returned with a dustpan and straw broom and began sweeping up the flakes. His efforts weren't very successful, because as fast as he swept an area it was again quickly covered with soot. Finally he gave up, went into the bridge-house and didn't come back.

"What did you do to him?" I asked. "Give him the evil eye?"

"No," Shirley replied indignantly, "I didn't want him to sweep up the soot. I just smiled at him about all that stuff coming out of the stack and falling around us."

"Sure, Shirl," I replied. "Which just goes to prove that a woman's look can scare a man from any country — it's universal."

Both of us returned to the bridge-house, while Peter kept us informed about what was happening.

"You see the navigator over there?" Peter said, indicating a young man who was bent over a chart marking positions on it. "He's writing down the exact time we pass each mark. If there's an accident, that information will be required by the ship's owners."

We were now making our way along the Golding Cutting. Ahead in the distance, a red-hulled yacht was sailing along almost in the centre of the channel, heading for Gladstone.

"Is that someone you know?" Peter asked, handing me the binoculars.

"Yes, Bruce and Elizabeth on the yacht *Polly* from South Australia," I replied. "I met them up the coast. They must have come in through the East Channel rather than go through The Narrows."

Polly was 11 metres long, but from the height of the bridge she looked like a dinghy.

"Gee, Peter," I said, "you don't realise how small even a fair-sized yacht looks until you see it from a ship like this."

"I don't think they know we're behind them," Peter said. "We'll have enough room to pass. Still, seeing you know the couple, do you want me to give them a blast and let them worry for a while?"

"Why not," I answered.

While I watched through the binoculars, Peter gave them one, long, loud blast with the ship's horn. Bruce and Elizabeth, who were both in the cockpit, got the fright of their lives. Their heads shot round, and within a fraction of a second *Polly* swung to port and headed for the edge of the channel.

"That got them moving," Peter laughed.

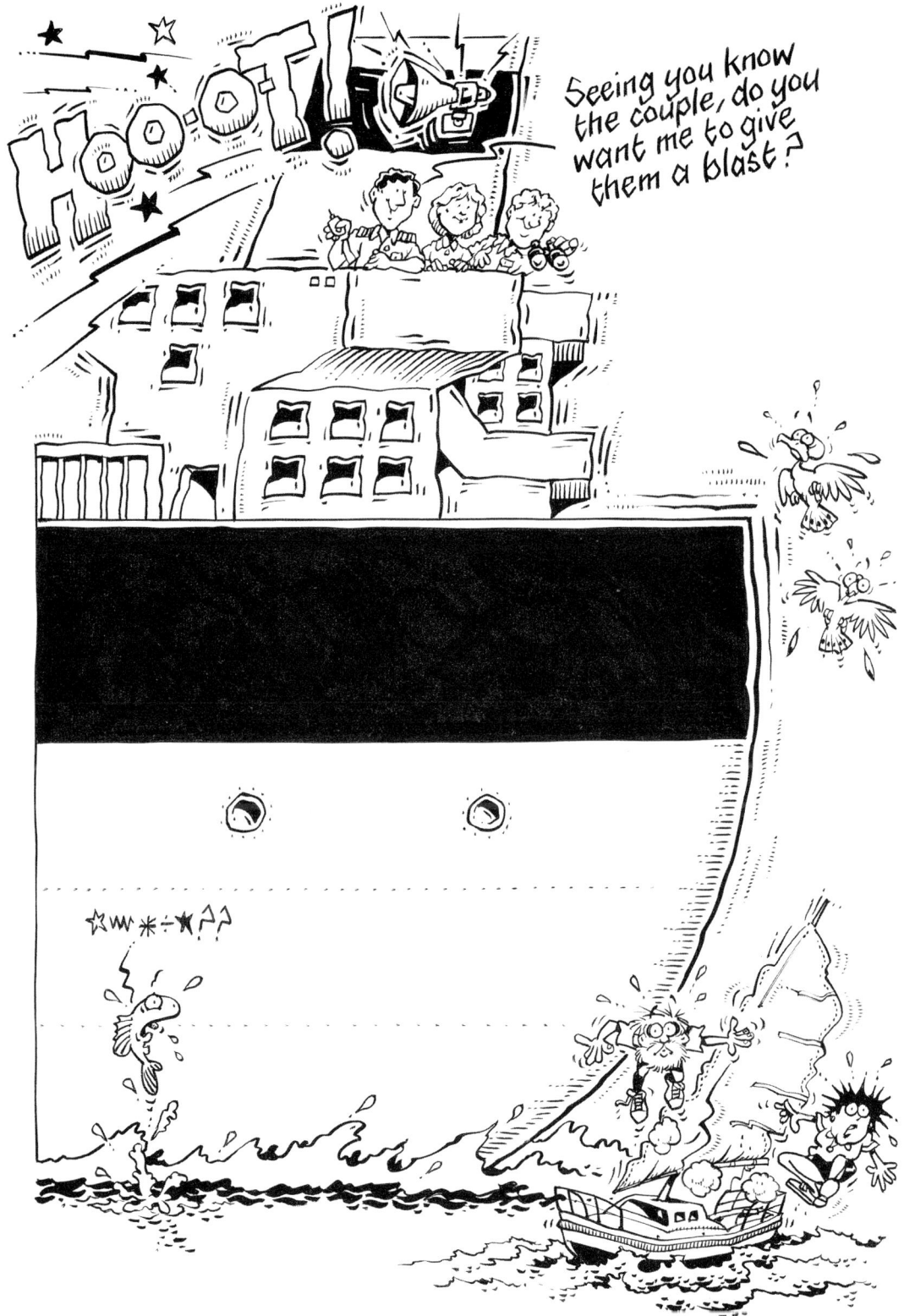

For the slightest moment, I understood the perverted pleasure that my pilot 'mate' in Cairns got from scaring the pants off yachties by not answering their frantic radio calls. I almost felt ashamed.

"*Polly* probably didn't come through The Narrows because of the neap tides," I said to Peter. "I think she draws about 2 metres."

I went on to tell Peter about the grounded yacht I had tried to help a few days ago.

"A couple of months ago," Peter said, "I took a ship into Port Alma and was later picked up by chopper to go back to Gladstone. On the flight back, we followed The Narrows. It was low tide and all I could see in the mud were these strange looking scars — there were hundreds of them, going in all directions. It took me a while to realise they must have been made by boats going aground."

"Are you interested in sailing?" I asked Peter.

"Not in the slightest," Peter replied with a laugh. "Golf is my interest."

Shirley smiled in agreement.

As we approached Barney Point, two large orange-painted tugs named *Tom Tough* and *Wistari* steamed towards us.

"What we're going to do," Peter said, "is turn the ship round in the basin in front of the Coal Wharf. There won't appear to be much room between the wharf and Picnic Island, but there's more than you think. We'll steam in pretty fast and let go the starboard anchor — that will hold the bow while the momentum of the ship, helped by the wind and tide, takes the stern upstream, then we'll quickly lift the anchor and steam in towards the wharf, where the tugs will do their bit."

The ship was doing 4 knots when Peter gave the order:

"Hard to starboard and let go starboard anchor!"

"Haad to sta-board!" repeated the helmsman.

"Let go sta-board anchor!" shouted the captain over his handheld radio to the crew on the bow.

A loud squeal of metal and a cloud of smoke erupted from the bow. The ship shuddered as the anchor dug in and the stern swung upstream.

"Heave up starboard anchor!" Peter ordered.

"Heave up sta-board anchor!" the captain immediately repeated over his radio.

"Half-ahead! Starboard 20!" Peter commanded.

"Half-ahead! Sta-board 20!" repeated the helmsman.

From the bridge, the bow of the ship looked as though it was on the island. Shirley's eyes were like saucers. The Chinese captain was sweating. I was sweating, and it wasn't even my ship. The only person who was cool, calm and collected was Peter, who continued issuing a string of clear commands to the helmsman.

On completion of the turn, the tugs made their approach, coming alongside on the ship's port side. The ship's crew took up the tugs' lines.

Before I knew it, the vessel was 60 metres away from the wharf and parallel to it. Peter issued orders over his handheld radio to the tug masters. The line boats came out to take the lines from the ship to the wharf. Peter stood on the starboard side of the open bridge deck, looking down at the wharf and along it as he continued speaking to the tug masters:

"*Tom Tough*, half-power push — *Wistari* quarter-power push."

"Do you see that red marker on the wharf, Stuart?" Peter said. "We have to line the bridge-deck up with that."

All the time issuing commands to the ship's helmsman and the tugs, Peter watched as the ship approached the wharf centimetre by centimetre. Eventually, 230 metres of ship with a weight of 50,000 tonnes closed against the rubber buffers of the wharf without the slightest bump whatsoever. Bow, stern and spring lines were winched up and the ship's gangway lowered.

"Well," Peter said, "that's another one done. Did you enjoy it?"

"Enjoy it?" I replied. "It's been the highlight of my trip. I just can't believe the size of these ships — they're massive. And it was berthed so gently."

"You'll have to come out with me on a 'cape size' ship sometime," Peter said. "They *are* big — 300 metres long and nine hatches. They carry three times the load of this one."

"How do you get on berthing these things at night when it's blowing 35 knots and raining?"

"It gets a bit hairy sometimes," Peter replied with a smile, "but it's all good fun."

Still on a high from our trip with Peter, we left Gladstone a few days later, taking advantage of the outgoing tide. The south-easterly wind had been blowing strongly for some days but had now dropped off to 10 knots. On leaving the channel, we had to make a series of short tacks all the way to Bustard Head, turning a normal 32 mile trip into a 48 mile one; even so, we were safely anchored in Pancake Creek well before nightfall.

Each day we awoke to delightful weather. The south-easter rarely blew over 15 knots and there wasn't a cloud in the sky. We fished, crabbed, and explored the headland that had been our home for five years. Early one morning, we motored the tender over to Rodd's Peninsula on the northern side of Pancake Creek and spent the day beachcombing for kilometres, stopping every now and then for a swim in the calm, crystal-clear bays formed by the lee of small rocky headlands.

"Bustard is still my favourite place," Shirley said as we walked hand in hand back along the beach towards Pancake Creek. Far in the distance, the

Bustard Head lighthouse stood out brilliantly white, illuminated by the late afternoon sun.

"Although it's fifteen years since we were here as lightkeepers," I said, "it still feels as though we should climb into the old Land Rover and drive up to the station to put the light on."

"I know," Shirley replied. "It seems like yesterday. And you're still dressed the same — battered felt army hat, khaki shirt, swimming togs and plastic sandals."

"Old habits die hard, Shirl."

After six days in Pancake Creek, the weather bureau predicted that a strong north-easterly was on its way.

"I've got a feeling they're going to be right this time," I said to Shirley.

"It will be well-timed if it does come in," Shirley answered. "We've had a great week, and Des is bringing the LARC up to Bustard tomorrow with a group of tourists — so I'll go back with them to Seventeen Seventy and make my way to Brisbane from there. And you and *Pluto* can let the north-easterly take you down the coast."

Shirley had joined forces with Des in a campaign to restore the vandalised Bustard Head lightstation. They were going to prepare a submission to government, while Shirley was at Seventeen Seventy. It was a campaign I was going to become involved in on my return to Brisbane.

That evening I called Des on the radio and arranged to meet him next afternoon at their picnic spot in Jenny Lind Creek.

"Come over about noon," Des said, "and have some lunch with us. Is there anything you want me to bring on the LARC?"

"A loaf of bread and a couple of bags of ice would be good."

"Consider it done," Des replied.

"Thanks Des, see you tomorrow."

So next day Shirley and I set off from Pancake Creek across the mangrove flats to Jenny Lind Creek. It seemed strange to be carrying Shirley's overnight bag and seeing Shirley carrying her handbag as we both squelched across the mudflats, skirting mangrove roots and walking through knee-deep water.

"Not exactly the conventional route to take to a bus stop, Shirl," I said.

"Well, it's not exactly a conventional bus."

When the LARC was ready to leave I gave Shirley a hug.

"Bye, honey. The next time I see you will be at home," I said.

"Take care," Shirley replied, "I'm looking forward to having you home again."

The LARC's diesel motor roared into life and the amphibian splashed into the clear water of Jenny Lind Creek, as Shirley and thirty-two tourists waved me goodbye.

By the time I returned to *Pluto*, lifted the outboard and tender on board, removed the sail covers and hanked on the genoa, ready for my early departure the following morning, there was enough daylight left to enjoy a rum with the luxury of ice while sitting in the cockpit. As darkness fell I noticed a bank of black cloud far to the west, well over the mountain ranges.

"Someone's getting it out there, by the look of things," I said.

I went below and cooked some Pancake Creek whiting fillets for dinner. They were delicious. After washing up, I went out to the cockpit to drink a cup of coffee. Most of the sky was clear; the bank of black cloud inland was still there, but hadn't increased.

Around nine o'clock, just after I had set the alarm for 4.30 a.m. and settled down in my bunk with a book, I heard a few drops of rain on the cabin top. I got up and shut the forward hatch and got back into my bunk. How cosy, I thought, a safe anchorage, a meal of whiting fillets, an enjoyable book, the patter of rain on the deck and the prospect of a good night's sleep before an early morning start.

Five minutes later the rain became quite heavy and the wind increased sharply to about 20 knots.

"Mmm, it must be a storm," I said out loud, as I got out of my bunk yet again. The wind was coming from the south-west, and because it was almost dead low tide and there was little tidal flow, *Pluto* had swung head in to the wind. Suddenly, there was a crack of lightning loud enough to wake the dead, the rain became torrential and the wind increased to over 30 knots.

Although the companionway hatch was facing away from the wind and rain, heavy spray gusted into the cabin. I slid in the companionway hatch boards and pulled the hatch shut. Apart from *Pluto* there were five yachts and two large cruisers in the creek, all of which were displaying anchor lights. I checked their positions in case *Pluto*'s anchor should drag. The storm should be over soon, I thought.

Within minutes the wind increased to between 40 and 50 knots. The wind shrieked past the rigging and the rain pounded the yacht. Then to my disbelief and concern the wind increased even more. *Pluto* wasn't equipped with a wind gauge, but after years of living on lightstations that did have them, I felt confident of correctly assessing wind speeds up to 45 knots. But this was out of my realm. I had only experienced conditions similar to these once before, when Cyclone David hammered Bustard Head in 1976 with a top wind speed of 100 knots.

Until this latest bombardment I felt as though I had some control of *Pluto*. Now, I felt wholly at the mercy of the elements. The shriek of the wind rocketing past the rigging had developed into a deafening screech, which was almost overshadowed by a deep reverberating throb that seemed to engulf not only *Pluto* but the night itself. *Pluto* shuddered and shook, pounded by a force that I felt could easily destroy my safe manmade cocoon of fibreglass and aluminium. I looked through the portholes and saw that some of the other boats' anchor lights were no longer in the position I had last seen them. Two of them seemed to be in the same place, but the remaining five had moved much further away from *Pluto*. I slid back the hatch and pulled out the top board from the companionway in an attempt to see what was happening around me. Closer to the elements, the noise of nature's fury doubled. As my night vision was taking effect, a sharp crack of thunder and jagged fingers of lightning ripped the black heavens apart, illuminating the night to expose a macabre scene of devastation. Three yachts lay over on their sides hard aground, their masts tilted drunkenly at 45°. The wind roared and the rain lashed as streaks of lightning continued to crack across the sky, creating a mixture of weird dark shadows and bright shiny reflections from the stranded vessels. And high above this dramatic scene, as if suspended in space, the Bustard Head lighthouse flashed its message out into the night. The power of the wind was frightening. Even from inside the yacht I could feel its destructive force pulling, sucking and buffeting. On and on it went. There was nothing I could do but let each minute pass, watch that *Pluto* wasn't dragging and hope for an end to the storm's wrath. After thirty minutes, and with the rain still bucketing down, there was a sudden reduction of wind, making me believe that the storm was drawing to a close. But within a minute the wind swung to the north-west and intensified to its previous strength. For a further fifteen minutes we were assaulted by thunder, lightning and cyclonic strength winds. Then suddenly the rain eased and the wind dropped to about 20 knots.

I climbed out into the cockpit and shone a spotlight on the stranded yachts, but couldn't see any sign of life. I went below and put out a call on the radio:

"This is the yacht *Pluto* calling any vessel in Pancake Creek. Do you receive? — over."

There was no answer, so I called again. This time I received a reply from the largest cruiser in the creek. The skipper told me that his vessel hadn't dragged and his wind gauge had recorded 70 knots. The skipper from the other cruiser joined the conversation, confirming the 70 knot wind speed and saying that although his vessel had dragged, she wasn't aground; he said he would launch his dinghy and check the two yachts that had gone aground near him.

"OK, I'll check the yacht *Cilla*, which is nearest me," I replied.

I was quite concerned about *Cilla*. I hadn't seen any movement on board since the end of the storm, and although I hadn't met her skipper, I knew he was elderly and sailing single-handed. But when I arrived at *Cilla* I found the skipper in his dinghy on the other side of the yacht.

"Are you right, mate?" I asked. "Any damage to the yacht?"

"No, there doesn't seem to be any water coming in. She seems to be lying on sand," he replied.

"You're lucky you didn't go aground 100 metres further up the creek," I said. "There's a stretch of coral rock up there."

"I know," the old bloke said. "It sounds ridiculous to say it, but I've been very lucky. Because it was low tide, the exposed sandbank in the middle of the creek acted as a barrier. It also means I should be able to refloat *Cilla* quite easily as the tide makes. If it had happened at high tide I don't think I'd ever have got her off."

I gave the skipper a hand to take *Cilla*'s anchor out to deep water and to winch in the anchor chain until it was tight.

"You should be afloat well before high tide," I said. "I'll set the alarm for two o'clock and see how you're going. Anyhow, I'll motor down the creek and see how the other yachts are getting on."

Both yachts appeared undamaged, and like *Cilla* the crews had positioned their anchors ready for the rising tide. It was still raining, and by the time I returned to *Pluto*, strapped the dinghy back on deck, dried off and had a cup of hot coffee laced with rum to celebrate *Pluto*'s survival, it was getting on to midnight. As I settled down in my bunk I thought of *Pluto*'s 16 kilogram Bruce anchor. Until buying *Pluto*, I was unfamiliar with this type of anchor, but tonight it had well and truly proved itself. Also, I never skimped in letting out chain. As one old sea-dog had said to me:

"A pile of chain sitting in your anchor locker isn't going to do you much good when the shit hits the fan."

I was awakened at 1.30 a.m. by the sound of a diesel motor and the rattle of anchor chain. *Cilla* was afloat and had re-anchored a little too close to *Pluto* for comfort, but I didn't have the heart to ask the old bloke to winch in the chain and move further away. I noticed by the position of the other two yachts' riding lights, that they too had refloated successfully. I reset the alarm for 4.30 a.m. So much for the good night's sleep before an early morning start.

"Boy," I said to myself as I got into my bunk for the fourth time that night, "didn't Shirley choose the right time to leave."

Chapter 22

AND THE BAND PLAYED ON

Awakened by the alarm clock shortly before dawn, I climbed out into the cockpit to find Pancake Creek like a tranquil lake. The sky was clear and there was hardly a breath of wind. It was hard to believe what fury had been unleashed here only a few hours earlier. I motored past the other vessels still at anchor, hoisted the main and motor-sailed out of the creek into a light north-easterly, past Clews Point, and on towards the passage between Inner and Inner Middle Rocks. Safely past the rocks I altered course to the south-east and hoisted the genoa. Although *Pluto* was now on a reach, the light breeze could only produce a boat speed of 3 knots. But just as I was considering changing the genoa for the much larger drifter, the breeze began to increase. Within an hour it was blowing 15 knots, and by the time I was abeam of Round Hill Head at the southern end of Bustard Bay it had turned to the north-north-east and steadied out to 20 knots. For the next 48 miles *Pluto* bounded comfortably down the coast, with a speed never dropping below 6 knots.

By five o'clock that afternoon I had anchored *Pluto* in the Burnett River, 2 miles up from its mouth. I made some dinner and was in my bunk sound asleep by eight o'clock. As the sun cleared the horizon next morning, I left the river and turned south-east for the 33 mile run across Hervey Bay to the Fairway Buoy. The wind had swung to the north and increased to between 20 and 25 knots. With *Pluto* now on a broad reach, the ketch bolted along with the log rarely showing less than 7 knots.

For some unknown reason, every few months I'd wake up with a migraine headache; and today was one of those days. From past experience I'd found that the pain eased if I vomited, so I connected the autopilot, stuck my head through the safety lines on the lee side of the yacht and went for my life. As I hung there barking at the sea, with tears streaming down my cheeks, and the occasional wave slapping up in my face, I couldn't control a sudden burst of coughing, spluttering laughter as I thought of the picture I must have made, captioned with the words: "God, yachting is fun."

I rounded the Fairway Buoy at 11 a.m. and followed the channel into Urangan Harbour. By 2.00 p.m. *Pluto* was berthed in the Great Sandy Strait Marina. It was nearing the end of November and the marina was quiet, unlike the months of August to October when thousands of tourists descend on the marina each morning to board the whale watching boats that travel out to Hervey Bay. But the humpback whales, having calved and mated in the warm tropical waters, were now well south, heading back to their Antarctic feeding grounds; only a few stragglers remained.

I had arranged to meet a mate of mine, Lawrie Kavanagh, who I had invited to sail with me from Urangan through the Great Sandy Strait to Tin Can Bay. Lawrie, a feature columnist with *The Courier-Mail* newspaper in Brisbane, was no stranger to the area. For years he had sailed the region single-handed in his 4.2 metre Caper Cat.

A strong wind warning was issued by the weather bureau on the day Lawrie was due to arrive. By midday it was blowing 30 knots from the south-east.

"It looks as though we might have to stay here for a few days," I said to Lawrie, as we sat at the boardwalk café overlooking the marina, trying to prevent the wind from blowing the froth from our cappuccinos. "The prediction for tomorrow is a 15 knot north-easterly, but I can't see it happening."

"It doesn't matter to me, Stu," Lawrie replied. "It's just great to be on a yacht — even if it is tied to a pontoon."

But happen it did, and by midmorning we were sailing around the northern end of Woody Island heading for Kingfisher Bay Resort on Fraser Island. Later on I made one of my favourite lunches — ham off the bone and fresh bread rolls, washed down with a can of Fourex.

"A fair breeze, a tiller in one hand and a beer in the other," Lawrie remarked after lunch, as he gazed contentedly at the islands around him while steering *Pluto* along on a broad reach. "What more could you ask?"

"Only for you to keep *Pluto* on course," I answered.

"Smart arse," Lawrie replied, as he swung the ketch back on the compass bearing I had given him.

We anchored off Kingfisher Bay Resort and went ashore for a walk to the lookout. The summer days were becoming hotter, and we were both pretty sweaty by the time we returned to *Pluto*.

"How about we go ashore later, have a shower and stay for dinner at The Sand Bar?" I said to Lawrie.

"Sounds good to me, skipper."

Halfway through dinner, when I went over to the bar to buy another couple of beers, there was quite a bit of activity in an adjoining section.

"What's going on in there?" I asked the barman.

"They're setting up for a karaoke night," he replied.

"It'll be time to leave soon," I said to Lawrie when I returned to the table. "They're setting up for a karaoke night."

But it began before we left. The voices were atrocious. Then suddenly the noise stopped.

"Is that it?" I said to the same barman as we were leaving.

"No," he replied, "we've got the Austrian Symphony Orchestra holidaying at the resort, and some of its members found the karaoke so bad, they've offered to put on an impromptu concert — they've gone back to their rooms to get their instruments."

"In that case," I said, "we might stay for a while — what do you reckon, Lawrie?"

"Sure — I'll get another couple of beers."

Eight members from the brass section of the orchestra returned, and before long they were belting out foot-stamping, blood stirring music that made the floor shake and the walls vibrate. Dozens of resort guests appeared from nowhere and soon there was standing room only. The audience's thunderous applause at the end of each piece kept the performance going for hours. Lawrie and I were in high spirits by the time we returned to *Pluto* in the early hours of the morning.

We spent the next few days making our way slowly through the Strait. One afternoon we anchored off Dream Island north of Garry's anchorage. After dinner we went out into the cockpit for a rum. It was a beautiful night; there was a slight breeze and the dark sky was alight with thousands of twinkling stars, and not another yacht in sight. As we sat sipping our rum, Lawrie related a few stories about his early days in journalism.

"How did you get into journalism, Lawrie?" I asked after a while.

"Well, I didn't set out to be a journalist," Lawrie replied. "I wanted to be either an electrician or a carpenter. But after leaving school I tried for five months without success to get an apprenticeship. Then one day Mum saw an advertisement in the paper asking for a cadet journalist to work at the *Maryborough Chronicle*. I wasn't very good at spelling and not particularly interested in reading, so I didn't think it was a job that would suit me, but Mum forced me to get on my pushbike and ride down for an interview. When I got there, a bloke named Ray Foster, who was the chief sub-editor, told me to go to the Maryborough Gardens and write a two-page composition about what I saw. Next day I was told I had the job. I immediately respected Ray Foster, because out of all the people who must have applied for the job, he had chosen me. So I really worked hard to make sure I didn't let him down. It wasn't easy, because of my limited literary skills, but with his confidence in me, I persevered through some pretty dark times. After three and a half years at the *Chronicle* I applied for a job at *The Courier-Mail* in Brisbane and got it. On the day of my farewell from the *Chronicle* I was quite emotional about leaving. I went up to Ray Foster, shook his hand firmly and thanked him.

"'I owe you everything, Mr Foster,' I said, 'and I promise I'll try not to let you down.'

"'What do you mean — not let me down?' Ray asked, looking surprised.

"'Well, back when you gave me the job over all the other applicants, you'd obviously seen something in me that I didn't know I had. It was the key that opened my future. Your confidence in me was inspirational.'

"'Lawrie, mate,' Ray answered with a grin, 'you were the only bloody applicant.'

I laughed and went below to make some coffee. When I returned, Lawrie continued:

"I enjoyed it in Brisbane. For the first three years I was police roundsman for the paper and then moved onto sport. I played league with Brothers, but I had to make a decision whether it was going to be football or my job — so I chose my job. But I didn't regret it. The paper took me around the world many times, all free and first-class, as well as the best seats in the house for the Moscow and Los Angeles Olympic Games."

"What about the move from being a sports writer to a columnist — how did that come about?" I asked.

"By accident really," Lawrie replied with a laugh. "I was checking in at the airport in Melbourne one day, when I was told I'd have to be downgraded from first-class to economy. I argued, but it didn't do any good. A few other first-class passengers were downgraded too. We boarded the plane and after a while were told there'd be a thirty minute delay.

"'What's going on?' I asked the hostess.

"'We're waiting for some VIPs,' she replied.

"The so-called VIPs turned out to be one of the airline company's pilots, his wife and three kids, who were going for a holiday on the Gold Coast. They were the bastards who took our first-class seats. I wrote a scathing letter to the editor about it and left it on the sub-editor's desk hoping it would get a run on the Letters' page. But next day it turned up as a column on page three. The editor of the *Courier* at that time asked if I'd like to write a weekly general column. I agreed, and before long I was doing three general news columns a week. I love it. If something or someone irritates you, you can write about it and have a million people know about it too. I can slip it into politicians, bungling bureaucrats, bleeding hearts and all the other powerful minorities who are white-anting away at our society."

"It sure beats the hell out of being a carpenter or electrician," I replied.

Next day we moved on to Tin Can Bay Marina. As we were walking along the pontoon towards the showers I heard a female voice say:

"Hello, Lawrie."

Lawrie and I both turned round.

"G'day, Kim," Lawrie said to a blonde woman who was standing on the deck of a yacht. "What are you doing down here?"

"I run my spanner crab boat out of Tin Can Bay now," Kim replied.

"Stuart," Lawrie said, "I'd like you to meet a mate of mine — Kim McKenzie. Kim, this is Stuart Buchanan — he owns a lovely little ketch called *Pluto*."

We shook hands.

"Would you like to come on board for a cup of coffee?" Kim asked. "And you can have a look at my new yacht *Symi II* at the same time."

"How long have you had her?" Lawrie asked.

"Just a few months now," Kim replied.

While we were drinking our coffee in the spacious saloon, Kim stood up, took a book out of a cupboard and placed it before me. It was *The Lighthouse Keepers.*

"Would you sign that for me please, Stuart?"

"Certainly, Kim, but how do you know I wrote it? You wouldn't recognise me from the photograph in the book — I haven't shaved for a week and look like a dag."

"No," Kim smiled, "but about a year ago Lawrie told me that a lighthouse keeper mate of his named Stuart had written a book. It had to be you."

Kim and Lawrie brought each other up to date on what they had been doing since they last met.

"I've got to go," Kim said eventually. "I've got some work to do on the motor of the spanner crab boat."

"Well," Lawrie said, "how about having dinner with us tonight — if that's all right with you, Stu."

"Fine by me," I replied.

"OK," Kim agreed, "the little restaurant at the marina puts on a good meal."

We arranged to meet at seven o'clock.

As we continued on to the showers, Lawrie told me that Kim, a former Australian women's surfing champion, was born into a professional fishing and shipbuilding family and had been involved with boats all her life. Along with her father Roy she had spent many years trawling and fishing along the Queensland coast; and years ago was the official shark catcher for both the Sunshine and Gold Coasts.

"*The Courier-Mail* photographer Jim Fenwick and I went out with Kim one day on her Sunshine Coast shark run," Lawrie continued. "One of her nets had snared a 4 metre tiger shark. The three of us struggled to pull the monster into Kim's boat. Jim took photographs of the shark with Kim straddling it, as she held its massive jaws wide open. The thing could have swallowed a human whole — no trouble at all. Kim was holding a huge diver's knife and wearing a brief bikini. One photo in particular was magnificent, but Kim was too shy to have it or her story published in Australia. It was at the time when the movie *Jaws* was screening across the world and I thought the photo was just too good not to use, so Kim agreed to let us publish it overseas. It was published around the world, including a huge spread on page one of the *London Daily Mirror*."

In the restaurant that evening I told Kim about my encounter with the whales in the waters near the Percy Islands.

"It doesn't surprise me," Kim replied. "As long as I can remember, that area has been known to fishermen as one of the humpback whales' mating areas. Dad and I often used to see them, but I've never experienced the aggression that they showed to you."

"The trouble is, I don't know whether they *were* being aggressive or just playing. But even if they were playing, I'm not all that keen on *Pluto* cavorting with 48 tonnes of mobile blubber — especially when it's blowing 30 knots. What about you, Kim, have you had any close encounters with whales in this area?" I asked.

"Only at night," Kim answered. "On the way out to the fishing grounds I've hit whales on two occasions — I think both times they must have been sleeping on the surface. I was on top of them before I knew what happened. One of them put a ding in the boat."

"That's probably why one yachtie I know refers to whales as marine speed bumps," I laughed. "The humpbacks along the Queensland coast seem to be breeding like rabbits, though. The experts say their population is doubling every seven years. I think they might eventually become a bit of a worry to boaties."

"Don't worry!" Lawrie said, shaking his fork high in the air in a threatening manner. "When I become dictator, I'll bring back the harpoon! I'll make the seas safe for us yachties!"

Once again it was late when Lawrie and I returned to *Pluto*.

Next day Lawrie left by bus for home. I went to bed quite early to get some much needed sleep in readiness for an early morning start and a 66 mile sail to Mooloolaba.

I motored *Pluto* out of the marina about 4.30 a.m. and motor-sailed close-hauled down Tin Can Inlet into a light north-easterly breeze. By eight o'clock I had safely crossed the Wide Bay Bar and was sailing on a broad reach towards the high headland of Double Island Point. It was a glorious day — cloudless blue sky and no haze. By the time I rounded Double Island Point, the wind had swung to the north and increased to 15 to 20 knots. With the northerly directly astern, I winged out the main to starboard and poled out the genoa to port. *Pluto* charged along. If this keeps up, I thought, I'll be in Mooloolaba shortly before dark.

Early in the afternoon I noticed a low bank of very dark cloud appear from inland and travel slowly south a few miles in from the coast. For almost two hours it kept pace with me, then, when I was a few miles north of Noosa, ever so slowly the bank of cloud grew in height, darkened and began to move seaward. Although *Pluto* was about 6 miles from shore, I had learnt by this time to prepare early for the worst that could possibly happen. I dropped the genoa and lashed it to the safety lines, started the motor and put two reefs in the main; then I closed up the companionway hatch, put on my wet-weather jacket and sat at the tiller to wait.

The ominous black cloud was now about 2 miles ahead, and extended from the coast well past *Pluto* out to sea. Before long I could see the dark, rippled pattern on the surface of the water, indicating that wind and rain were on the way. Above the noise of the diesel motor I heard the sound of heavy rain approaching; then, within seconds the 15 to 20 knot northerly swung to a 30 knot southerly and at the same time pounded me with heavy rain. I turned *Pluto* slightly away from the wind on a starboard tack and motor-sailed at about 3 knots away from land. The wind remained at 30 knots but the rain increased until visibility was reduced to less than 20 metres. I had never experienced rain so heavy. The large drops hit me like bullets, peppering my hands and legs, and ricocheting noisily off my plastic wet-weather jacket. It bucketed down unremittingly. I thought it would never stop. I pulled the end of my jacket over my knees and pulled my right hand into my sleeve, but before long my left hand on the tiller was red and stinging. After twenty minutes the rain was still as heavy as when it first began. I peeked out from under the hood of my jacket and shouted:

"Come on! Let's get it over with!"

And then, challenging fate, I shook my fist at the heavens and added:

"Is that the best you can do!? Come on, you bastard! Give me all you've got and let's get it finished!"

Within seconds I was bombarded with hail the size of golf balls. They crashed onto the deck and strafed the water around me. I took cover under the canvas canopy that partly shaded the cockpit, but my exposed hand on the tiller was hit repeatedly. The hail continued for about ten minutes and then the rain returned.

"OK! OK! You've proved your point!" I shouted.

After a short while the rain eased and the visibility improved quickly as the storm moved far out to sea. The southerly wind dropped too, until there was hardly a breath. Then a breeze came in from the north and the clouds began to clear. Within ten minutes it was blowing 15 to 20 knots from the north, exactly what it had been doing before the storm. However, the breaking seas resulting from the storm were still coming from the south.

I shook out the reefs from the main, hoisted and poled out the genoa then turned off the motor. It seemed crazy to have the wind directly behind me and yet *Pluto* was crashing into breaking, white-crested seas coming from the opposite direction. But over a period of about thirty minutes the seas gradually flattened and then began to break from the north.

The storm had slowed me down, so it was well after 8.00 p.m. by the time I entered Mooloolaba Harbour and motored through the canals towards the waterfront home of my friends Phil and Betty Shanahan. Phil must have seen *Pluto*'s navigation lights from the house, because he was there to meet me when I pulled in alongside the pontoon.

"Hello, Phil," I said.

"G'day, Stu, welcome back," Phil replied. "Did that storm miss you?"

"No, Phil, I think I got the worst of it — torrential rain and hail the size of golf balls. But there was no damage to *Pluto*. How about you — did it come down this far?"

"No, we missed it, but Noosa got clobbered — roofs, cars and caravans written off by hail. Millions of dollars worth of damage."

Struth, I thought, thinking back on my challenge to the heavens. Nah, it couldn't possibly be my fault — could it?

Chapter 23

A CALL YOU CAN'T DENY

"Bye Phil, bye Betty," I called as *Pluto* eased away from the pontoon.

"See you, Stu," Phil replied. "I'll give Shirley a ring and tell her you're on your way. With this north-easterly blowing you should get home very quickly."

I waved in acknowledgment and motored *Pluto* through the canals, raising the main and genoa when I reached the large basin near the Mooloolaba Yacht Club. I left the harbour, rounded Point Cartwright and headed for the North West Fairway off Caloundra. With the ketch on a broad reach the 15 to 20 knot breeze made for comfortable sailing.

" . . . you should get home very quickly." Phil had said. Home, I thought, such a simple word that now sounded so enticing. After six months almost to the day, I was only a half-day's sail from home. I was looking forward to being back with Shirley again, and yet at the same time I felt an inner sadness knowing that a lifestyle I had grown to like so much, was only hours from coming to an end.

Like so much? I laughed out loud as I thought back on some of my recent experiences. What was there to like so much about a 70 knot storm, or being strafed by hail, or battling a 30 knot headwind, or being anchored up a mosquito and sandfly infested creek, or trying to prepare a meal in a swell-affected anchorage, where pots, pans, plates and cutlery are thrown from one side of the yacht to the other? What's so great about having a wash in a bucket that barely has a litre of fresh water in it, or living for days on the quality of food you'd throw in the bin at home? Where's the enjoyment in the nail-biting experience of entering an unfamiliar, rock-strewn anchorage at night, or in an overnight sail when you're cold, wet and tired, or being anchored in 40 knot wind and surf with only a few steel links between survival and destruction, or being ever-careful not to overuse fresh water and electricity, or the concern that the solar panel is pumping enough power into the batteries to keep them charged? It sounds anything but a likeable life-style.

What is it about sailing, I thought, that entices me and thousands of others from the comfort and safety of our homes to suffer at the whim of wind and sea? In his poem *Sea Fever*, John Masefield wrote "I must go down to the seas again." Struth, he should have written "*Must* I go down to the seas again?"

Is it that under our thin veneer of civilisation there still remains an urge to have a close relationship with the elements, to get away from the artificial environment in which we live? Or perhaps it's simpler than that. Perhaps those who go down to the seas are prepared to suffer the discomforts for the sake of the pleasures. And I had to admit, the pleasures are many: sitting at the helm as the wind whistles past the rigging, filling the sails and pushing 5 tonnes of yacht along, spray exploding from the bow, with no other vessel or land in sight; the anticipation of visiting new and beautiful places; the satisfaction of reaching them safely; island after island with their dazzling white beaches, coral reefs and clear, clear water; the magnificent sunsets and sunrises; the magical nights in a calm anchorage, with a full moon in a cloudless sky; the time spent with other yachties discussing places near and far; dolphins riding the bow wave for mile after mile. Even the sight of my old mate the humpback whale breaching, although awesome, was something I'll never forget — but I would have been happier if he had come no closer than a mile from *Pluto*. However, at sea there are few compromises, you have to take it as it comes; and perhaps that's part of its appeal — the uncertainty of what's going to happen tomorrow.

Over the past six months I had lived in a world without what many in the cities spend much of their lives working to achieve — late model cars, designer clothes and unnecessarily large and expensive houses. For the past six months, cars to me had simply been things, no matter how decrepit, capable of taking me from the harbour to the shops and back again; clothes had been only to keep me warm and sometimes dry, or to protect me from the sun; houses, such as Andy Martin's or Jon and Lys Hickling's Spartan dwellings on Middle Percy Island did what all houses are basically built to do — provide shelter.

I gybed *Pluto* round the North West Fairway and soon gybed again around the NW2 Special Mark for the leg along Bribie Island. It felt more like six days rather than six months since I had sailed past here heading north with my self-doubt and apprehension. I had missed Shirley, but her idea of meeting me at places of her choice had worked well for both of us. The delight in seeing her walking across the tarmac to the airport terminal knowing that she would be with me for a week or two, more than made up for the emptiness I felt each time she left.

Under a cloudless blue sky I rounded Skirmish Point with a lot less harassment than on my visibility-blurred northern trip. Soon, *Pluto* and I passed Redcliffe and were making our way across Bramble Bay. The distinctive headland of Shorncliffe lay ahead. My destination was just round the corner.

The hot afternoon summer sun beat down fiercely. The past few days had been very hot, making it quite uncomfortable to be on board. Even at night it was hot and sticky. The fruit and vegetables weren't lasting as long as they had done in the winter and spring. And the thought of a cold beer had become much more appealing than my usual warm one. It was the right time to finish the cruise.

I entered the channel to Cabbage Tree Creek, dropped sail and tied up at the marina. Over the next few days there was going to be a lot of work to do, unloading and cleaning the boat. After that, I had another book to write and Bustard Head lighthouse to save. But for now I poured myself a stiff rum.

"Thank you *Pluto*," I said, raising my glass, "for getting me safely to Lizard Island and back again, and helping me fulfil my twenty-year dream of sailing the Barrier Reef coast. I couldn't have asked for a better or more dependable mate to do it with — cheers."

I climbed out into the cockpit with my glass of rum. The wind whistled past the rigging, bringing with it the tang of salt air and the sound of the sea. I breathed in deeply. The red Australian ensign attached to the backstay, although looking a bit faded and frayed, fluttered strongly in the breeze. The mooring lines creaked as the flood tide made *Pluto* strain restlessly at his berth. Yes, I was going to miss it all, this call that may not be denied. But there's always next year, I thought. Right now though, I was going home to Shirley and perhaps, with a bit of luck, a roast lamb dinner.

EPILOGUE

Five years have passed since 1996 when I made my first solo cruise on *Pluto* along Queensland's Barrier Reef coast. During subsequent cruises I've found many changes. The Grand Hotel in Bundaberg has been refurbished; no longer is it a down-at-heel bikies' hangout, but instead provides good quality meals in a pleasant atmosphere to tourists, business people and local residents. A new marina has been built near the mouth of the Burnett River. Called Bundaberg Port Marina, it has top class facilities including a courtesy bus to Bundaberg. In the same complex overlooking the marina is Baltimores restaurant run by the charismatic Brad. If you dine there and paste a photograph of your boat in the visitors' book, Brad will carve your boat's name on one of his restaurant's chairs or tables. It's a relaxing place to sit, while chatting to fellow yachties over a cup of coffee or a drink.

A new marina has been built in Rosslyn Bay Boat Harbour; no need to worry anymore about a dragging anchor when the wind blows over 20 knots.

Andy Martin, the lessee of Middle Percy Island for thirty-six years, has left his island paradise and transferred the lease to Mick and Sue Cotter. Jonathan and Lys Hickling have also left the island and moved on to new horizons.

A large marina has been established at Mackay Harbour, a logical place to restock the galley before heading north to do battle with the bareboat charterers who frequent the Whitsundays and who, I assure you, haven't improved their standard of seamanship since my first visit.

The resort on Brampton Island no longer welcomes yachties and day visitors.

Dunk Island's Bruce Arthur, renowned for his woollen tapestries, has died. His studio, tucked away in the rainforest, is now owned by jewellery maker Sue Kirk, who resided there with Bruce for many years.

At Low Isles, visitors can now follow a heritage walking trail to inspect the lightstation buildings.

But for Shirley and me, the biggest and most exciting change involves Bustard Head lighthouse. In 1999, shortly after the release of my second book *Lighthouse of Tragedy — The Story of Bustard Head Lighthouse*,

Queensland Parks and Wildlife Service, who now control many of Queensland's lightstation sites, asked for Expressions of Interest from the public in regard to four lightstations. Bustard Head was one of them. Shirley and I, along with Des Mergard, proprietor of 1770 Environmental Tours based at the Town of 1770, formed the Bustard Head Lighthouse Association Inc and submitted a proposal. After two years of further submissions, letters, phone calls and meetings with the State Minister for Environment and his officers, in October 2001 we signed an agreement to lease Bustard Head Conservation Park for a period of twenty years. At the same time we were fortunate to be awarded a substantial Commonwealth Government heritage grant to begin restoration of the vandalised lightstation buildings.

Work will begin on the heritage-listed site early in 2002. The two cottages and service buildings will be restored to the condition they were in at the time the lightstation was demanned in 1986. A caretaker will be housed in one cottage while the other will be available for short-term holiday accommodation. Yachties and day visitors will be welcome to visit the station. It is our aim to eventually open the lighthouse for inspection and to establish an interpretive display inside. Visitors will be able to climb the lighthouse to view the lantern room with its still-operating crystal lens, and experience the magnificent panoramic views from the balcony. The Association intends to perpetuate the historical significance of Queensland's first coast light, and to welcome visitors with the same cordiality with which previous visitors were greeted during the lightstation's 118 years of manned operation.

Yes, most things will continue to change; some for the better and some for the worse. But I hope that one thing never changes — and that is the feeling of unfettered freedom and enjoyment that is experienced while sailing a small boat along Queensland's magnificent Barrier Reef coast.